Nikolai Gogol's Quest for Beauty

Nikolai Gogol's Quest for Beauty

An Exploration into His Works

Jesse Zeldin

THE REGENTS PRESS OF KANSAS
LAWRENCE

© Copyright 1978 by The Regents Press of Kansas
Printed in the United States of America

Library of Congress Cataloging in Publication Data

Zeldin, Jesse, 1923-
Nikolai Gogol's quest for beauty.

Includes bibliographical references and index.
1. Gogol', Nikolaĭ Vasil'evich, 1809–1852—
Criticism and interpretation. I. Title.
PG3335.Z34   891.7'8'309   78-2693
ISBN 0–7006–0173–2

Contents

Preface

The pages that follow are the result of many readings of Nikolai Gogol's work (hence an "exploration"), coupled with a general unease brought on by most secondary sources on the subject. Gogol is a "mysterious" writer who lends himself easily to a variety of interpretations, many at variance with one another. It is not my purpose to argue with any of the interpretations except the "realistic" one; indeed, I will occasionally refer to some of them. As a matter of fact, readers may find similarities between some of my views and some of the views of others (I myself detect a likeness at times between my approach and the approach of the Symbolists). However, since I have attempted an exploration rather than a dissertation, I have on the whole avoided extended discussions of other writers on the subject; the focus throughout is upon Gogol's work itself (an excellent bibliography of works on Gogol, including works in Russian, may be found in Dmitri Čiževskij, *History of Nineteenth-Century Russian Literature*, vol. 1, translated by Richard Noel Porter, edited with a foreword, by Serge A. Zenkovsky [Nashville, Tenn.: Vanderbilt University Press, 1974], pp. 201–6; a fine bibliography of works in English, French, and German is in *Letters of Nikolai Gogol*, selected and edited by Carl R. Proffer [Ann Arbor: University of Michigan Press, 1967], pp. 237–44; a highly selected bibliography of works in English is in *Gogol from the Twentieth Century*, selected, edited, translated, and introduced by Robert A. Maguire [Princeton, N.J.: Princeton University Press, 1974], pp. 405–6; in addition, recently published are: Abram Tertz [A. Sinyavsky], *V teni Gogolya* [London: W. Collins and Overseas Publications Interchange, 1975]; Simon Karlinsky, *The Sexual Labyrinth of Nikolai Gogol* [Cambridge, Mass.: Harvard University Press, 1976]; and William Woodin Rowe, *Through Gogol's Looking Glass: Reverse Vision, False Focus, and Precarious Logic* [New York: New York University Press, 1976]).

Preface

The point of view I finally adopted, after a good deal of thought, seemed to me unavoidable, if I wished, as I did, to empathize with Gogol's aims as I found them revealed in his work. This does not mean that what follows is necessarily a reflection of my own tastes and preferences; indeed, the contrary is more often the case than not (particularly in chapters 8, 9, 10, and 11). Certainly, my hope is that Gogol would have assented (he usually disagreed with the opinions of his contemporaries) to at least the general interpretation. I think he was right in insisting that his work forms a unity from beginning to end, without "crises" that made him change his point of view, and the reader will find that I emphasize this unity, thus disagreeing, on this point, with such eminent critics as Gippius and V. V. Zenkovsky. I believe, however, that the evidence is on my side.

As this is not a study in secondary sources, so it is not a study in influences. I have tried to keep my eye on the pages before me without indulging in extraneous speculation. Some of the specific conclusions I came to surprised me (this is perhaps in the nature of exploration), but I did not see how I could, or why I should, avoid them. The reader may even occasionally find contradictions—that, too, is possibly a consequence of exploration and is unavoidable when dealing with such a writer as Gogol (it is a rare reader who would call his writing straightforward). I did not think it proper to resolve such contradictions as there are (and I believe they are minor) by forcing them into some preconceived mold that I might happen to find congenial; to have done so would have been to destroy my purpose. It also would have worked against my aim if I had considered Gogol in terms of literary or psychological categories, although many of both kinds are easily applicable. I have therefore deliberately eschewed the employment of jargon, which often seems to me to act more as a screen than as a means of communication anyhow.

I have assumed an acquaintance on the reader's part with those of Gogol's works that are available in English (almost all) and have therefore desisted from outlining his writings, with one exception. The reader who finds such outlines necessary is referred to the bibliographies mentioned above. This exploration is also not intended to be a biographical study, despite what was, to me, an unexpected conclusion in chapter 11. Finally, I have not spelled out all the implications of the suggestions I have made (for example, in the interpretation of "The Overcoat"), because I wanted to leave the reader free to follow his own inclinations.

In the long run, I hope that I have provided a fresh way to read one of the great accomplishments of literature. This is not to say that I claim complete originality in all things; I do not. The hope is simply that the framework will provide a different orientation. My thesis is that Gogol was primarily interested in the nature of reality, which he identified with beauty. If we take Gogol seriously and believe that he said what he meant to say—many critics, from his day to ours, notwithstanding—what I suggest is not only a valid conclusion to reach, but is, I believe, a necessary one. It is in this thesis that my basic difference with the more recent books on Gogol lies.

A word on technical matters: all translations are my own unless otherwise noted. References to Gogol's fictional works and to his articles and essays are to the Academy of Sciences edition (Moscow, 1940–52); they are indicated by volume number and page number in the text. The letters *SP*, followed by page numbers, refer to *Selected Passages from Correspondence with Friends*, translated by Jesse Zeldin (Nashville, Tenn.: Vanderbilt University Press, 1969). The letter *P*, followed by page numbers, refers to *Letters of Nikolai Gogol*, selected and edited by Carl R. Proffer, translated by Carl R. Proffer in collaboration with Vera Krivoshein (Ann Arbor: University of Michigan Press, 1967). The letters *ML*, followed by page numbers, refer to Gogol's *Meditations on the Divine Liturgy of the Holy Eastern Orthodox Catholic and Apostolic Church* (New York: Orthodox Book Society, 1960). All other references are in the notes. Transliterations from the Cyrillic are aimed at an approximation of Russian pronounciation.

1
At First

Although Nikolai Gogol is generally regarded as one of the greatest masters of Russian prose and although his only works that are usually read were written in prose, still his first public tentatives were formally poetic—the hymn "Italy," published anonymously in the review *Son of the Fatherland* on 23 March 1829, and "Hanz Kuechelgarten, an Idyll in Pictures," privately printed under the pseudonym V. Alov in June 1829. The first has attracted no attention at all (books on Gogol uniformly ignore it), and the second, while mentioned, is usually dismissed as of little value. As works of art, there is little doubt that these poems deserve the oblivion into which they have fallen. What is primarily interesting about both for our purposes is that Gogol began his career thinking of himself as a poet devoted to beauty, a beauty whose embodiment was to be sought in the lands of art—Italy and Greece. In this sense, Gogol started with a quest, as he ended.

This quest for beauty is the constant theme of the unfortunately entitled "Hanz Kuechelgarten," a name that grates even on the German ear. That Gogol held high hopes for his poem and for the career it was meant to launch is evident from the Preface to it:

> The composition here offered would never have seen the light of day if circumstances of importance to the author alone had not impelled him to it. This is a work of his eighteenth year. Without undertaking to judge either its merits or its faults, we will but say that many of the pictures of this idyll unfortunately have not survived; they probably connected the now uncoordinated fragments more closely and delineated a portrayal of the main character. At least we are proud of the opportunity to assist in acquainting the world with the creation of a young talent. [1:60]*

---

* Citations in this form refer to volume and page in the Academy of Sciences edition of Gogol's works (Moscow, 1940–52).

The important thing about this poem is not that the author's hopes were disappointed, to put it mildly; rather, our concern lies in the interest evinced by the main character, who may be regarded as an idealized alter ego of Gogol himself.[1] Young Hanz wants nothing more than to live with beauty,[2] a beauty he conceives in terms of the monuments of ancient Greece that he has read about. He wanders to a land that his creator has never seen and but little understands, then returns, of course disillusioned with the material reality he has found, to settle down to a peaceful life on the farm with the girl who has been patiently awaiting his return. As any reader of the romantics, particularly the Germans, knows, there is hardly anything original about this; *Weltschmerz* and *Sehnsucht* are constant themes in their work. More important, however, is the point that this highly sentimentalized story in lyric form outlines the lifelong quest of the author himself. The young Gogol had a vision before him that he was never to lose, a vision of a harmoniously created universe—that is, of beauty itself—that he believed to be real, even though material phenomena seemed to deny it. Like Hanz, he would search for an embodiment of that beauty and never find it, because, as he quickly become convinced, Hanz had been looking in the wrong place, looking for the true in the realm of the false.

In his book on Gogol, Victor Erlich asks:

> Is it [the disenchantment] an indictment of the dreams or of the dreamer? Has the goal of Hanz's journey actually proved deceptive, or is it rather that this particular pilgrim was too tame to meet the challenges of the arduous journey? To put it differently, is the dream illusory or merely elusive? Did the confrontation with reality unmask the ideal, or did it simply suggest that the "given" is necessarily grubby, coarse, nauseating, and conversely, that anything worthy of admiration and enthusiasm is inevitably beyond one's reach?[3]

In answer to Erlich's questions: The "dream" was never indicted by Gogol, nor was the dreamer, only he who ceases to dream. The dream is neither illusory nor elusive; it is for Gogol a reality that demands devotion and is always present to the man who grasps the truth; the journey may be arduous, but only in the sense that the artist's journey is so. It is not a "confrontation with reality [that will] unmask the ideal," but a confrontation with the false that should reveal the true. The "given" is what is "worthy of admiration and enthusiasm" and is within everyone's reach, whereas illusion and deception are "grubby, coarse, nauseating."

The quest for beauty was thus a quest for what ultimately is, for an "ideal" only in the Platonic sense of ideal, not in the colloquial sense of a never-realized and unrealizable end.

Gogol's career was to be spent working with palimpsests, removing the layers of deception and restoring erasures; destroying idols, in the quest for the icon. From this point of view, Hanz made the error of putting his trust in the columns, pediments, and statues of ancient Greece. This romantic youth (whose successor will be Piskaryov in "Nevsky Prospekt"), looking in the wrong place, could not fail to be discouraged. For Gogol, however, despair was inadmissible. As his teaching mission grew, he began an exploration of those wrong places, which meant a deepening and more subtle exposure of ugliness as the consciousness of his own vision increased. In other words, Gogol, like most great artists, was single-minded, devoted to a truth that remained absolute and unchanging and that he aimed at in his fictional work. The goal remained beauty itself; but at the same time, being human and an artist, he was intensely concerned with man in relation to beauty. He seems to have believed, somewhat like John Milton and Plato, that if men once became cognizant of the false, they would the more vehemently demand the true; that once the ugly was shown for what it was, they would the more humbly devote themselves to beauty— a beauty that both the artist and the man of faith intuitively knew (although sometimes forgot, as Plato's Meno but forgot); that this beauty is the "given," and the material is the illusory, rather than the other way round.

Another way to say this is that Gogol never seems seriously to have believed in the reality of the physical world he physically inhabited. Like Hanz Kuechelgarten, he found it ugly, while he "knew" that the real was beautiful. He also seems to have believed, as is implied by much of his last published book, *Selected Passages from Correspondence with Friends*, that transfiguration was possible. Not to have believed so would have meant falling victim to deception, to the Prince of Lies. In this sense, many of his works stand as both a warning and an encouragement, as well as a plea. Also, of course, Gogol was engaged in a process of purgation; as he said:

I love the good, and I search for it and burn with it; but I do not love my abominations . . . ; I do not love those meannesses of mine which separate me from the good. I struggle, and will struggle, with them, and with the help of God I will expel them. . . . When I confess myself before He Who commanded me to come into the world and free myself from my faults, I see many vices in myself; but they are already not such as they were but a year ago: a holy power has helped me to tear myself away from them. [*SP*, 107–8]*

Public service combined with private service—Gogol wished to actualize reality in himself while warning, pleading, and encouraging other men to actualize it in themselves and in their relations with one another. The "quest for beauty" was thus not a quest of discovery nor a quest for an "ideal." It was rather a quest for embodiment, in both life and art. There is little doubt that in his last years, looking back over the corpus of his work, Gogol was convinced that he had failed, personally as well as publicly. There is no way of knowing whether he was right or wrong personally; on the public side, however, one may say (granting his notion of reality) that he expected too much too soon of too many. In this, Hanz Kuechelgarten was a disillusioned Nikolai Gogol; in this, the quest for beauty was the quest that failed, and the writer whose fiction has been a source of humor for so many turns into a figure of tragedy.

---

* Citations in this form are to Gogol's *Selected Passages from Correspondence with Friends,* translated by Jesse Zeldin (Nashville, Tenn.: Vanderbilt University Press, 1969).

order to indicate that these matters should be taken seriously, but rather to indicate a certain absence of those elements that give meaning to life. Indeed, the devilish activity that we do witness can easily be taken as but a sign of the loss of contact with reality of some rather unintelligent persons who are superstitiously inclined.

But we do discover one thing: evil, whether imagined or real, is ugly, in direct contrast with the God-created beauty of the landscape and the good-naturedness (in the literal rather than colloquial sense) of the characters. The setting that Gogol describes in his first paragraph is a purely natural, God-made world of spring loveliness. It is almost a garden of Eden, into which Gogol will introduce innocent, albeit fearful, characters:

> How entrancing, how luxurious is a summer's day in Little Russia! How languishingly warm when midday glitters in stillness and burning heat and a blue immeasurable ocean, bending over the land like a voluptuous cupola, seems to have fallen asleep, sunk in sweet bliss, embracing and hugging the beauty in its airy arms! . . . Bent by their heavy fruit are the branches of cherries, plums, apples, pears; the sky a pure mirror, the river in green, its frame proudly raised—how full of voluptuousness and sweet bliss is a Little Russian summer! [1:111–12]

The technique used is a cinematic one: a long, panoramic shot that slowly focusses down onto the persons who are to inhabit the story. The landscape is peaceful, beautiful, languorous; the characters introduced are on the whole innocent. Confusion and disruption, although treated lightly, occur only when evil—or the suspicion of it—intrudes. And the evil is in truth ugly, even though it attempts to appear otherwise. It is deceptive, not real.

The first statement of this point is made when we are told of a *tumble-down* old barn where "devilish tricks are always occurring" (1:117). Decay, the devil, and deception are connected. Then there is the gypsy who hints at his magical powers:

> There was something malicious, caustic, mean, and at the same time arrogant in the gypsy's swarthy features: any man looking at him would immediately have recognized that great qualities seethed in that strange soul, although their only reward on earth would be the gallows. Completely swallowed between

nose and pointed chin was a mouth eternally twisted in a malicious smile, the little eyes alive as fire, and the lightning flashes of enterprises and designs constantly alternating on his face—all this seemed to call for the unusual, strange costume then covering him. The dark brown caftan, which it seemed a touch would convert to dust; the long black hair falling in tangles to his shoulders; the shoes that dressed his bare bronzed feet—all seemed to be a part of him, his very nature's composition. [1:21]

Finally, the devil is believed to have assumed the shape of a pig. At last—when all is well, when the boy has got the girl—"everything," Gogol tells us, "was turned . . . to unity and converted to concord" (1:135). At the end of the story the landscape returns to the aspect it possessed at the beginning, although now tinged with melancholy through the absence of the joy that characterized Gogol's preceding scene of human celebration when the devil was defeated. At the same time, the melancholy mood hints at a knowledge that the devil will return, that his defeat is not a permanent one, in short, that the innocent loveliness of the opening has been corrupted.

Every time that evil appears here, it appears in an ugly guise. This is not the evil of Milton's Satan, Goethe's Mephistopheles, or even of the later seedy country gentleman of Dostoevsky. There is no grandeur, no intellect, no mockery here. These devils are closer to the horrid little pitchfork-wielders of the Middle Ages, distinguished by their noses meeting their chins or their pig snouts. In short, they are ugly, repellent creatures that do not really belong to our world. The world inhabited by people is still gay and good: nobody seriously wishes harm to anyone else, and life is enjoyed. But falsity has been introduced, and its intrusion is a little like that of the serpent in the garden of Eden, so that the final paragraph contains a note of regret. Still, as though in hope, the story itself ends happily, in the sense that life and beauty have won out and no one is seriously compromised.

"St. John's Eve, A True Story Told by the Sexton," the second tale in the collection, has another emphasis, fulfilling the melancholy possibilities of "The Fair at Sorochintsy." There is an implication that we are no longer in the realm of legend, for the sexton, who tells the story, says, "The main thing about Granddad's stories was that he never lied in his life and whatever he told us was exactly as it was" (1:44). He told it, in other words, "like it is." The devil is not conquered here, and blood and destruction result. The young couple do not get married and live happily ever after. But there is good reason for this negation: for the sake of beauty a young man consorts with the ugly; for the sake of the good he agrees to evil. And evil here is far more sinister, for it is capable of stealing a man's soul. In other words, where "The Fair at Sorochintsy" hints, "St. John's Eve" fulfills the hint.

It would also appear that in modern times the face of evil has changed, that now evil and ugliness go unrecognized, a theme that Gogol will develop in his later works. Where "The Fair at Sorochintsy" is set thirty years in the past, "St. John's Eve" takes place more than a hundred years ago, when faith was still possible:

> I know [the storyteller says] there are lots of know-it-alls who scribble in law courts and even read legal documents, but if you put a simple Book of Hours in their hands, they could not make out the first thing about it, while they still think grinning at disgrace is clever! Whatever you tell them they laugh at. Such unbelief has spread all over the world! Why— God and the Holy Virgin defend me!—even you might not believe me: once I mentioned witches in passing and guess what? there was a nut who didn't believe in witches! Here, thank God, I have lived a long time and have seen unbelievers who find it easier to lie at confession than it is for us to take a pinch of snuff, but even they cross themselves at witches. May they dream—I don't want to say of what, let's not talk about them. [1:139]

In short, it is difficult in these days to recognize falsity for what it is, as difficult as it is to attain to truth. Again in this story the ugliness of evil is emphasized: this devil, Basavriuk, scowls with "his bristly eyebrows," has "a friend from the swamp with horns on his head" (1:140), has "hair like bristles, eyes like a bullock's" (1:143), takes the young man to a place where "tall, black, wild weeds stifled everything by their thickness" (1:144), looks "blue as a corpse," enters the form of a roast lamb with "sly black eyes" and a "black bristly moustache," and so on and so forth. The hero, who at the beginning of the story only needed new clothes to "outshine all the lads of those days" (1:141), turns gloomier and gloomier as a result of his acceptance of materiality. "He became unsociable, was coated with hair, began to look dreadful, . . . was angry and bad-tempered, . . . was overcome by fury, . . . would gnaw and bite his hands like a madman, and in spite tear his hair to shreds" (1:149). Finally, he vanishes, and "where Petro had stood was a heap of ashes from which smoke in places still rose" (1:150).[4]

The fate of Petro seems to intimate another kind of ugliness that Gogol will develop in his later work: the ugliness of emptiness. Petro, having lost his soul, no longer *is*: life itself has deserted him, so that emptiness in itself is a sign of death. One might say that certain facets of *Dead Souls*—the chef-d'oeuvre on which Gogol would start work a mere five years after *Evenings on a Farm near Dikanka, Part 1*—was already in his mind. That the narrator's grandfather never in his life told a lie is meant very seriously, for as Dostoevsky was later to discover, the mark of evil is, above all things, the lie. The beautiful world is God's world, and thus is real; while the ugly world, the world of Satan, is false and destructive, as ruinous of the future, despite its promises, as it is of the present. In "The Portrait," ugliness will even obliterate the past.

"A May Night: or, The Drowned Maiden" is a story divided into six parts, each with its own subheading: "Ganna," "The Mayor," "An Unexpected Rival," "The Young Men Make Merry," "The Drowned Maiden," and "The Awakening."[5] The general structure resembles that of "The Fair at Sorochintsy," with a serene opening and a serene close, two general statements enclosing the ugly events of the story itself.

It must be pointed out that, at least at this time, 1831 (and I believe that he never seriously changed his mind), Gogol thought of beauty almost entirely in terms of harmony, as well as in terms of the good. In 1831 he wrote four essays: "Woman," "Sculpture, Painting, and Music," "On Contemporary Architecture," and "Life." In each of the four he evinced his concern with beauty as a harmonious balancing of elements in order to constitute a whole. The concept he had first spoken of in "Hanz Kuechelgarten" remained with him, although perhaps less obviously expressed. Interestingly enough, the first of the essays depends, as we have pointed out, on Plato; the middle two are concerned with artistic expression; and the last turns to Christianity as the highest vision of the truth.[6] Beauty and goodness can only be achieved if things are seen in their unity, a heavenly unity that ugliness and evil attempt to disrupt. It was to be Gogol's constant quest to express this harmonious wholeness in his fictional works. In this concern he was at one with many of the romantics (and their successors, in particular the Russian Symbolists) and with many of his more Slavophile contemporaries.[7]

Another essay of this time, "Boris Godunov," on Pushkin's play, expresses much the same idea—namely, that the glory of Pushkin's verse lies in its harmoniousness and that the glory of Pushkin himself lies in his all-inclusiveness (8:148–52). The real world for Gogol is a beauteous entity,[8] and discord, disruption, egoism, and chaos are real only in the sense that a lie is real. In "A May Night," for example, we find that the happy ending occurs because disruptive, warring elements have been defeated—that is, recognized for what they are—so that harmony may be restored. Things go wrong—and *only* go wrong —when the devil or his surrogate (a witch or sorcerer) intrudes upon and seduces those who live in, but do not recognize, beauty, calm, and innocence. Finally, the true triumphs over the false: "There was the same triumph on high, and the night, the divine night, glowed majestically" (1:180).

Actually, there are two kinds of deception in this story: that of the actual devil in the tale of the drowned maiden and that of the hero, Levko, who pretends to be the devil in order to frighten the mayor into acknowledging the truth. In the former, the result is death and a restless weeping soul; in the latter, we have a game played by one who knows reality and wishes to reveal it: the mayor, one may say, has gone astray and must be made to see the light, even if it means making a fool of him. However, only when the serious evil is defeated (and here the two parts of the story come together) can a happy ending be reached. Gogol seems to have been working on two different levels, but with a single governing aim, which was, in the long run, to celebrate the human life that is lived in God's real world.

This is not to say that a concern with truth and falsity, beauty and ugliness, life and death, was necessarily in the forefront of Gogol's mind when he was writing these stories (although the essays do indicate that it formed a part—one might say the major part—of his outlook). There is no doubt that current fashion and exploitation of it, leading to fame for himself, were Gogol's conscious motives. On the other hand, he seems to have been unable to escape the quest of Hanz Kuechelgarten, regardless of particular circumstances. The contrasts are too blatant and the revulsion at deception is too clear to be ignored by the reader. Only a Christian accent was lacking for the tale to be completed. That accent was supplied by the last of the stories in the collection, "The Lost Letter," which mixed together the elements of knowledge and falsity to the triumph of the former. It constitutes a nice capstone to the volume, and it was probably placed at the end precisely for the summary it contains.

Except for Rudy Panko's "Preface," "The Lost Letter" is the shortest of the pieces in *Part 1* of *Evenings on a Farm near Dikanka,*[9] and it is perhaps fitting that it should be so, since from Gogol's angle the point it makes needed no elaboration.[10] The narrator says:

> "Oh, the old days, the old days! What joy, what gaiety comes to the heart when you hear about long ago, so long ago that the year and month are lost! And if a kinsman is involved in it, a grandfather or great grandfather, it's hopeless: may I choke on the hymn to the martyr St. Barbara if you wouldn't think you were doing it all yourself, as though you had crept into your great grandfather's soul or your great grandfather's soul were playing tricks on you." [1:181]

A short time later, towards the end of this opening paragraph, we are told that the narrator's grandfather could not only read, but "on a holy day he would snap out the Acts of the Apostles in a way that would make a priest of our time run away and hide" (1:182).

Without going too far—without, that is, reading too much into the story—one may say that Gogol has emphasized, first, the contemporaneity of his theme ("The Lost Letter" is the only one of the tales in this volume to make such an emphasis) and, second, its Christianity. Indeed, it is only the hero's faith that saves him; he is a good son of the Church, although, like all human beings, he is subject to frailties. Having been sent as a representative of his people to carry a letter to the tsarina, Catherine II, he meets on the way a man who has sold his soul to the devil, to which news he replies: " 'Is that so unprecedented? Who in his time has not associated with the evil one? That's why you must make merry, as they say, while you can' " (1:183). He decides to help this man, because "he'd sooner have the forelock cut off his own head than let the devil sniff his dog's snout at a Christian soul" (1:183–84). But the letter is stolen, presumably by the devil, and the hero must deal with creatures with "pretty mugs" in order to get it back. He is surrounded by ugliness, falsity, and deception. But he wins out by making the sign of the cross, obtains the letter, and delivers it to the tsarina, who "was sitting in her golden crown, in a new gray gown and red boots, eating golden dumplings" (1:191). The Christian act and the Christian sign bring a happy conclusion, although we do receive a warning at the end: because the hero forgot to have his hut blessed (even Grandad could make a mistake), "every year, just at that same time, a wonderful thing happened to his wife—she would dance, and that's all there was to it. No matter what she did, her legs would do their own thing, and she was forced into her dance" (1:191).

We thus have a statement, although couched in naïve and simple terms that make no intellectual appeal, of the dependence of truth and beauty upon Christian faith. In this sense, the volume ends on an optimistic note, and it is noteworthy in this respect that in only one of the stories, "St. John's Eve," is the hero doomed, and his doom is a result of material obsession. The victory of "The Lost Letter" comes about, however, as a result of spiritual affirmation,[11] even though danger, as the last paragraph indicates, always remains. Thus early was Gogol exhibiting the didactic tendency that was to inform so much of his work, both fiction and nonfiction.

After all, early in 1831, even before the publication of *Part 1,* Gogol had already begun an official teaching career, although not yet at the University of St. Petersburg. By the spring he had several additional projects on hand: a continuation of the historical novel *Hetman* and first drafts of the short stories "The Portrait" and "Nevsky Prospekt"; and by summer he was working on *Part 2* of *Evenings.* By March 1832 he was also doing a good bit of essay writing, much of which was in accord with his teaching vocation—to that year belong "On the Teaching of Universal History," "A Glance at the Composition of Little Russia," "Schloezer, Müller, and Herder," and "A Few Words on Pushkin." In all these essays the romantic principle of unity is strongly stressed. All aim to convince the reader of the inseparability of things, of the oneness of truth. To divide things, and to leave them divided, is to falsify. This is made particularly clear in "On the Teaching of Universal History," where Gogol tells his audience that the history of mankind is all of a piece, that universal history "should collect into a whole all the peoples of the world broken up by time, situation, mountains, seas, and unite them into one harmonious whole: [it should] compose a majestic complete poem out of them" (8:26). This "poem" will present the truth about history and mankind, in contrast with the usual division and disharmony (hence ugliness) that constitute the false picture normally presented. This is the same aesthetic-religious view that we have already noted in *Part 1* of *Evenings on a Farm near*

Dikanka. For Gogol, as for many another, the designation of Satan as the Prince of Lies is taken very seriously indeed.[12]

Part 2 of *Evenings on a Farm near Dikanka,* published in March 1832, once again consists of a preface followed by four stories: "Christmas Eve" (first draft, spring of 1831), "A Terrible Vengeance" (first draft, summer 1831), "Ivan Fyodorovich Shponka and His Aunt," and "A Bewitched [or Enchanted] Place." These years were obviously very busy ones for Gogol; indeed, between 1829 and 1836 he accomplished the vast majority of his creative work, with the exception of *Dead Souls,* in at least first draft.[13]

"Christmas Eve" repeats the general atmosphere of "The Fair at Sorochintsy" in the sense that it is a boisterous, gay tale with no real harm—or horror—in it. There is one important difference, however: the malicious devil that we have here is a genuine one, while the one in "The Fair at Sorochintsy" was not. But this one is equally ugly and equally false. Indeed, it is he who—on this last night when he may roam, for the next day is the day of Christ's birth—steals the moon and brings darkness upon the earth, although light will soon, inevitably, return (the symbolism is obvious). On the whole, the tale is an episodic one that piles up farcical situations for the amusement of the reader.[14] Again the good Christian defeats the devil, the hero meets the tsarina, and the young couple get married and live happily ever after. In the end it is the devil who is put in Hell, not the good Cossack, even though, as one Cossack tells the tsarina, "We are not monks, . . . but sinful people. Like all honest Christians, we are susceptible to lewd things" (1:238). Although the Cossack may fall into sin, still, so long as he retains his faith, evil will be conquered; and the story ends as it began, with the praising of the Lord: the harmony that the devil tried to disrupt is restored.

The tone and style of "Christmas Eve" is generally one of good humor, with a kind of Marx Brothers quality to some of the scenes. The devil is more disgusting than anything else; in fact, he is referred to as "kaka" at the end. The fantastic element still rules, and Gogol makes no attempt to delineate character realistically. Indeed, he never did, which gives us at least an oblique reason to classify him as a romantic, despite numerous attempts to make him the "father of Russian realism" by such socially disaffected critics as Belinsky and his followers.

Gogol was also much interested at this time in pursuing his teaching vocation, in particular with reference to the history of the Ukraine, which he interpreted almost entirely in terms of the Cossacks of the Dnieper, forgetting, perhaps for exotic reasons, the other inhabitants of Little Russia. He had started two fictional works—*Hetman* and *The Terrible Boar*—meant to deal with these matters. He had plans to write a multivolume history of the Ukraine, and he did in fact finish two essays on the subject, "A Glance at the Composition of Little Russia" and "On Little Russian Songs," the former completed in 1832, the latter in 1833. This interest was to last through the writing of *Taras Bulba* (first published in 1835), after which Little Russia disappeared from his works, except for revisions and rewritings for later editions. In any event, the Little Russian stories and essays exemplify the teaching method that Gogol emphasized in his article "A Textbook of Literature for Russian Youth," written some time between 1831 and 1842: namely, statement illustrated by example. By the time of *Arabesques* in 1835 the two were combined in the same volume by an inclusion of many of the essays that he had written separately when he was composing the Ukrainian tales.

Certainly, Gogol was to think of himself in this teaching capacity for most of his life, and from this point of view, the only surprising thing about *Selected Passages from Correspondence with Friends* in 1847 was the reception that was accorded it. If those who criticized— and condemned—the work (the vast majority) had but referred to what Gogol had published earlier, they would have realized that any obtuseness lay on their side, not on Gogol's.

So far as Little Russia was concerned, while part of Gogol's aim was to teach about it (stressing his own intuitive grasp of "spirit" to the detriment of "fact"), he also had more general and ambitious goals, as the second tale of *Part 2,* "A Terrible Vengeance," makes clear. This is the one real horror story of *Part 2,* unrelieved by either humor or lyricism. It is pervaded by the false and the ugly, indeed, the obscene, even unto incest, with but rare touches of even natural beauty. It is a greater descent into the depths than any that Gogol had previously undertaken. Many scenes occur at night; days are often either sunless or have clouds drifting across the sky. Thick mists appear and fade. The sorcerer often works in wavy blue or pink light emanating from some unnatural source. Ugliness has more than just the goblinesque quality of mere pig snouts that we noted in the tales of *Part 1.* When icons were lifted before him, the sorcerer's "nose grew out and bent to the side, his rolling eyes turned from brown to green, his lips turned blue, his chin began to quiver and became pointed as a spear, a tusk zoomed out of his mouth, a hump arose behind his head, and the [sorcerer] turned into an old man." When he vanishes, he is "hissing and clacking his teeth like a wolf." The hubbub he leaves behind him is "like the sea in bad weather" (1:245). Tormented corpses rise out of the earth. The hero, Danilo, is killed by the sorcerer, his father-in-law, who then murders his own grandson, his daughter, and a hermit. Finally, the sorcerer himself is destroyed by a ghostly horseman who drops him down a precipice; and "dead men rising up from Kiev, from the Galician land, and from the Carpathian Mountains . . . leaped down the precipice, seized the corpse, and thrust their teeth into him" (1:278).

Only in the epilogue, to give the last section of the story its proper name, is the reader told that the tale is really only the last incident in the working out of a curse that had been pronounced on an ancestor of the sorcerer for a betrayal that ancestor had committed long ago. We are also told, however, that the one who had pronounced the curse will never enter the Kingdom of Heaven, because of the punishment he devised. Vengeance is done, but the conclusion leaves the strong implication that vengeance is really the Lord's.

Once more we note the connection between falsity and evil, the unnaturalness and hence unreality of the sorcerer's activity. We are in the presence, not of the truth, but of the lie. It was, after all, betrayal that brought on the curse to begin with, and the sorcerer continually tries to deceive others in the course of the tale. Indeed, Gogol goes out of his way to stress the perverted nature of the sorcerer's lust for his daughter. The evil, the ugly, the false, the nonnatural, are *not* normal; and those who are possessed by these negative qualities are not creatures who are as God made them, living in His world. Gogol the teacher is indeed pointing a moral, even if this all happened "long ago." Without wishing to make an allegory out of the story and without indulging in unwarranted symbolism, one must nevertheless recall that the original betrayal was of one brother (although not of the flesh) by another, and it was motivated by envy. Also, this is the first time that Gogol allows the innocent—Danilo, his wife Katarina, their son, and the holy hermit—to perish along with the guilty, Katarina's father. The reader need not be a biblical scholar to draw conclusions about Gogol's concept of sin.

A different approach to the problem that Gogol had set himself—

an exploration of another, or perhaps merely more subtle, realm of unreality (although the same premises prevail)—is indicated in the third tale of *Part 2,* "Ivan Fyodorovich Shponka and His Aunt," which is in fact more a fragment, the beginning of a story, a setting of the scene, than it is a completed tale in itself. The tone and approach will be developed in works to come, but not the form. In the short explanation of how the narrator came by the story, Gogol makes a point of the unfinished character of the tale: the ending, we are told, has been lost, although "if anyone has an irresistible desire to know what is told further on in this story, he will find it worth his while to make a special trip to Gadyach and ask Stepan Ivanovich. He will take great pleasure in telling it all over again from beginning to end. He lives near the stone church" (1:284). Furthermore, there is a strong implication, since no "granddad" is involved here, that the story, as Stepan Ivanovich originally told it and is willing to repeat it, is a contemporary one, that is, that it involves really living people in a world such as the one we inhabit. "Shponka" is the first of Gogol's fictional works to make this contemporary claim.

As Erlich points out, the core of the story is triviality. "For the first time," Erlich says, "we are treated to what was to become an essential Gogolian genre—the comedy of inanity, the enactment of pathetic stupidity through verbal incoherence and incongruity."[15]

Nothing, in fact, happens in the course of the tale. We are told of Shponka's childhood, of his army service ("in a short time, eleven years after receiving an ensign's rank, he was promoted to second lieutenant"; 1:286), of his return to his farm at his aunt's request and his meeting with a neighbor on the way, of the single-minded materialistic character of the aunt, and of his aversion to marriage. There really is not much more than that. Shponka is a kind of floater in the story; he is of so little substance until the end of the fragment, when he has a nightmare about marriage, that it is difficult to feel any sympathy, much less empathy, for him. Only once, when he was a schoolboy, did Shponka ever do anything that might indicate his possession of a personality: he tried to eat a forbidden pancake in class. Of course, the teacher caught him and he was punished. Gogol tells us that "from this time forth the timidity that had always somewhat marked him was increased still more. Perhaps this same incident was the reason he never had any desire to enter the civil service, having learned by experience that one cannot always manage to conceal one's misdeeds" (1:

285–86). He never really has any experiences again. His world—if it can be called that—is not only trivial; it is empty. One may say that Gogol has made the discovery, a logical conclusion of both "St. John's Eve" and "A Terrible Vengeance," that emptiness is as much the opposite of beauty as is ugliness, indeed, that emptiness is a species of ugliness. The very fragmentary nature of the story, its lack of rounded form, and its fading out, so to speak, indicate this, for given the nature (or absence of it) of the central character, there was no place to go. What do you do with a soul that has refused existence?

While Shponka himself is totally empty, each of the other three persons introduced into the story in detail—the neighbor Grigory Grigoryevich Storchenko, Shponka's aunt Vasilisa Kashporovna, and Grigory Grigoryevich's friend Ivan Ivanovich—has that specific characteristic of material vulgarity that Gogol had stressed in some of the preceding stories and was to stress even more in succeeding works as the degradation, if not to say destruction, of the human personality. Grigory Grigoryevich, so fat that his cheeks are like pillows, becomes a pillow himself, interested only in stuffing. Vasilisa Kashporovna is possessed by physical strength and the spirit of accumulation: her vision of her nephew's marriage is one of herself "fondling little grandchildren" (1:303). Ivan Ivanovich is a collector of data: he seizes the opportunity to sit down next to Shponka, "mentally rejoicing that he had someone to whom he could communicate his information" (1:299). Not one of these persons—or anyone else who turns up—stands in any real relationship to anyone else. Each is an isolated ego, and an ego so one-sided, so possessed by material, by fact, that it is incapable of moving outside itself, and thus is incapable of recognizing truth and is blind to beauty.

An even greater air of unreality hangs over this tale than over the fantastic stories of *Evenings,* in the sense that it is impossible to say that anything here meaningfully exists. It is a world that no sensible, sensitive person would have anything to do with. The falsity and vulgarity here pictured will later become the hallmarks of Gogol's work, in contrast with that truth, beauty, and reality in which he so deeply believed.

The last of the stories in *Part 2* is both a farewell and a return to "granddad," in a sense a repeat of "The Lost Letter," although "A Bewitched Place" cannot serve as the capstone that "The Lost Letter" did. After the real devil of "Christmas Eve," the devastation of "A

Terrible Vengeance," and the emptiness of "Shponka," boisterousness coupled with falsity returns. Furthermore, this time the tricky devil, whom we never see, wins out. The entire emphasis is on deception, not for good, but for evil, and Gogol cannot resist ending it with a little moral:

> That is how the evil one's power may fool a man. I know that ground well: later some neighboring Cossacks rented it from Dad for a melon patch. It's splendid ground! Its crop was always wonderful. But there has never been anything good on that bewitched place. It may be sown just right, but you never know what will come up: watermelons are not watermelons, pumpkins not pumpkins, cucumbers not cucumbers . . . the devil knows what it is! [1:316]

The point is that people do have a tendency to lose sight of the truth, to accept the unreal for the real, so that all is turned upside down, even to the laws of nature being upset: "watermelons are not watermelons, pumpkins not pumpkins, cucumbers not cucumbers." This is chaos, not God's world. Nor is it a real world, for man is tricked, lied into it, and can make nothing of it. Now it is a matter of man's mere error; later men will deceive themselves.

The last of Gogol's Ukrainian stories, again a set of four, divided into two parts consisting of two stories each under the general title of *Mirgorod,* was published in 1835. There is neither a general preface nor a preface to either part. Rudy Panko has said farewell, and evidently he meant it. Only the first of the tales, "Old World Landowners," has a narrator who pretends that he is personally acquainted with the characters and details of the story. Gogol did add a footnote to the third tale, "Viy," which claimed that he was but recording folklore in the terms in which it had been told to him. Gogol is thus far the only person who has heard of this story outside the pages of *Mirgorod,* however.

The period between the summer of 1832 and March 1835 was occupied by a number of things other than fiction, although Gogol did conceive a dramatic comedy, *St. Vladimir's Cross,* of which he wrote only some scenes. He also had probably conceived, as early as the fall of 1832, "Old World Landowners"; was at least thinking of his short play *Marriage,* an early version of which he read in the spring of 1834; composed "The Nose" and "Diary of a Madman"; and, in August

1833, read to Pushkin "The Quarrel of Ivan Ivanovich and Ivan Niki-forovich," which was published in the spring of 1834 in the journal *Northern Bee*. At the same time that he was engaged on these projects (both *Mirgorod* and *Arabesques* were published in 1835 within a few months of each other, although I have reserved *Arabesques* for discussion in the next chapter), Gogol busied himself with various nonfictional essays, since he was also taking himself very seriously as a historian and, in fact, received a post as lecturer in Medieval History at the University of St. Petersburg. In connection with these interests he wrote the essays "On the Middle Ages" (delivered as the opening lecture of his course), "Al-Mamoun," and "On the Movements of Peoples at the End of the Fifth Century." He also revived a project to write a history of the Cossacks of the Ukraine (he even published an advertisement asking for materials for such a history in January 1834), as well as formed the idea (it never advanced to the status of a plan) of writing a universal history and a universal geography, under the general title of *Man and His World*. It is as though Gogol were feverishly trying to get it all out at once, rapidly turning from one thing to another, shifting back and forth between fiction and nonfiction, remembering his folkloristic success but becoming increasingly concerned with the contemporary scene in his tales.

Mirgorod at least partially reveals this situation, since it is split among the recent past, the folkloristic, the historical, and the contemporary. Given this sequence and movement, the total, like *Part 1* of *Evenings on a Farm near Dikanka*, may be considered a whole, despite the variety in subject matter.

"Old World Landowners," the first story in the volume, continues the trend set in "Ivan Fyodorovich Shponka and His Aunt," with a significant absence, however, of the humor with which Gogol had endowed the latter. In the strict sense, there is no more story to "Old World Landowners" than there was to "Shponka"; again we have something closer to a mood piece, an evocation of an atmosphere, bearing much in common with the lyrical digressions (descriptions of the steppe, of the Dnieper, of moonlit nights and sunny days) that sprinkle much of his work. He makes it clear that what he is here relating is not a special case having to do with certain persons; it is, on the contrary, typical. It is, he says, concerned with "the life led by the old, typically national, simple-hearted and at the same time wealthy families" (2:15). While the general mood is one of sadness, it is that kind of nostalgic sadness that, while recalling the past somewhat fondly, does not wish for it to return. The world of "Old World Landowners" was not a real one, nor was it inhabited by living people. It was instead a world of routine in which habit had replaced life. The theme of emptiness is with us once more, an emptiness acquired through lack of will, so that both the husband and his wife have depersonalized themselves, become but terms in a relationship without the possibility of independent existence. They have become things, in other words. Habit has removed reality from their ken; they have deceived themselves. This becomes clear in the utter lostness of the husband after his wife's death. He may be a gentle man, and the scene may be touching, but only out of a sense of regret at what might have been. The narrator, observing the old man's reactions, says:

> At that time all our passions seemed to me childish next to this long, slow, almost insensible habit. Several times he struggled to utter the name of the deceased, but halfway through the word, his quiet and ordinary face distorted convulsively and his child-like wailing struck me to the heart. No, those were not the tears of which old men are usually so lavish when they display their pitiful situation and their unhappiness; they also were not the tears they shed after a glass of punch. No! These were tears that flow uninvited, of themselves, accumulated by the caustic pain of a heart already turning cold. [2:37]

As V. V. Zenkovsky points out, the theme of "Old World Landowners" is death.[16] It is not just death at the end; death imbues the entire story. It is not simply physical dissolution that Gogol has in mind either; it is the death of the soul, that anonymity that comes from submission to routine, sapping the will and clouding the sight. Finally, when physical death does arrive, it is because of inability to pierce through deception and because of refusal to break with custom. Sign has replaced meaning. The wife has been convinced that her cat's desertion of her (an endless circle of routine has been broken) is a signal that she will die, and so she does. The husband then dies because of the overwhelming force of years—the deception so long practiced finally achieves its victory:

> He surrendered completely to his sincere conviction that Pulkheria Ivanovna was calling him; he surrendered with the

freedom of an obedient child, pined away, coughed, melted like a candle, and finally died down, as a candle does when nothing remains to support its poor flame. "Lay me beside Pulkheria Ivanovna" was all he uttered before his end. [2:37]

Once the physical deaths are accomplished, it is as though the old couple had never been. They leave nothing behind except a narrator who remembers their typicality. In the long run, perhaps regretfully, they didn't really matter, in the sense that meaning, hence reality, has been banished.[17]

In a way, the most important character in the story is neither the husband nor the wife, but the narrator, who is both author and audience. He is the one who suffers the shock of recognition at the end and passes it on to us:

"God!" I thought, looking at him, "five years of all-destroying time—an old man already unfeeling, an old man whose life never seemed to have been stirred by a single strong feeling, all of whose life seemed to consist simply of sitting in a high-backed chair, of eating dried fish and pears, of good-natured stories—and such long, such passionate grief! Which has more power over us—passion or habit? Or are all the powerful impulses, all the storm of our desires and seething passions, only the consequence of our bright youth, and is it only because of that that they seem deep and shattering?" [2:36]

These were very important questions to Gogol, who was at this time trying to decide his own future, which meant a conscious attempt to define his talent and his quest. It was at the end of 1833, after the conception of "Old World Landowners," that he wrote his short note "1834." There Gogol calls upon his genius to indicate the path for him to follow. "This," he says, "is that fateful, irresistible border between memory and hope. Memory is already gone, . . . hope is already over-powering it" (9:16). Although he seems unsure of what his future is to be, there is yet a strong indication that it will be different from his past, and that he must, questing, move forward into it. Life and accomplishment consist in movement, never in stagnation.

I would suggest that this personal statement of Gogol's is applicable to much of his fiction. The difficulty with the old-world landowners is that they are old, that they are past, and only past. Because of habit, because their souls have been drained, because they have chosen the void, and because they have refused the quest for beauty and have settled for appearance, for deception, they can do nothing but disappear, leaving ruin behind. The estate is put in the hands of trustees and they "shortly removed all the chickens and all the eggs. The huts, which had been almost level with the earth, completely collapsed; the peasants started drinking heavily and most of them became runaways. The real master . . . very rarely came to his village and didn't stay long" (2:38). The void can only leave a void behind, because the very movement towards the actualization of beauty has been destroyed. Nobody cares, and it is for this reason that the story is pervaded by death. The great pity (if pity is the word) of "Old World Landowners" is that the central characters, gentle and sweet though they appear to have been, have given up their humanity, as surely and disastrously as had Petro in "St. John's Eve." Gogol's theme was deepening, his search broadening, as he began to realize that times had not changed that much after all.

Still the historical past and Little Russia intrigued him, and he made a final fictional attempt to evoke them.[18] The long story that followed "Old World Landowners" in *Mirgorod*, "Taras Bulba"—a story that is unjustly famous in my opinion—marks his last attempt at historical fiction. Actually, Gogol essayed a number of versions of the subject: "Taras Bulba," as first published in *Mirgorod*; "A Glance at the Composition of Little Russia," written in 1832 and published in *Arabesques* in 1835; the revised version of "Taras Bulba," published in 1842 in the second volume of a collected edition of Gogol's works; the two aborted fictional efforts already mentioned, *Hetman* and *A Terrible Boar*; and one nonfictional attempt that never even got to the stage of abortion, *A History of the Little Russian Cossacks*. His attitude toward history is best exemplified in the remarks on Sir Walter Scott that he made in his article "On the Movements in Journal Literature in 1834 and 1835," printed in the *Contemporary* in 1836. There he called Scott "a great writer of the heart, of nature, and of life, the fullest, broadest genius of the nineteenth century" (8:171). Of course, admiration of Scott was widespread at the time in a Russia that was searching for its identity. Gogol saw his task, thus, as an evocative one rather than as a setting down of data; it was the moral essence of the epoch that was of importance—and it must be felt, not just described. What finally resulted, unfortunately, was a simplistic tale well suited to Hollywood.

That Gogol retained some interest in the fictional aspect of his subject is obvious from the fact that the version of "Taras Bulba" printed in 1842 is a good two-thirds longer than the 1835 version in *Mirgorod*. There is little difference in the thrust of the two versions, however, and since the version usually printed in translation is that of 1842, I will make my remarks on the basis of that one.

The story itself is a highly romantic one whose characters, as is usual with Gogol, are meant to be typical rather than individual, exemplars of virtue or the lack of it, meant to appeal to a reader's exotic imagination while Gogol attempts to recreate what he imagines to be the way of life and historical movements from the fifteenth (the tale is technically set in the fifteenth century) through the first part of the seventeenth century. Time, however, is compressed, as would be normal in a tale of this type, so that it all takes place within a period of a few years. Anachronistic details are of minor importance; what mattered to Gogol were the flavor and what he thought was the character of the epoch, not the "factual reality" of specific events. "Taras Bulba" is sprinkled, even more liberally than is Gogol's wont, with digressive passages (some of them in fact paralleled by others in "A Glance at the Composition of Little Russia") that concentrate on Gogol's real purpose.[19] If one examines the characters in "Taras Bulba," he will find them to be really no more than typical, rather clichéd (even in Gogol's time) romantic heroes, larger than life, somewhat exotic, who live by the primitive code of a far-off time. On the whole, they are exceedingly noble types (with an occasional traitor thrown in, and stock Poles and Jews for villains—it is possible that Gogol misread *Ivanhoe*), exalting the virtues of a patriarchal society that Gogol thought was peculiarly Russian.[20] At the same time, however, there is a religious emphasis on the Orthodox Cossacks' struggle against Roman Catholic Polish oppression of the true faith. At the end, when Taras has become a martyr and is being burned alive by the Poles, he cries:

> Farewell, comrades! . . . Remember me and return next spring and make a really good time of it! What have you won, you Polish devils? Do you think anything in the world could frighten a Cossack? Wait, a time will come, there will be a time when you will learn what the Orthodox Russian faith is! Even now do peoples far and near scent it: from the Russian land will their ruler arise, and there will be no power on earth that will not submit to him! [2:171]

Then Gogol adds in his own voice: "The fire was already above the pyre, it gripped his legs and spread its flame around the tree [to which Taras was bound]. But nowhere in the world is there fire, torment, and power enough to master Russian might!" (2:171).

What Gogol has done, of course, is to make the Cossacks and their struggle symbolic of (if not parallel to) Russia and its struggle, as Gogol perceived it, against the West. His continued interest in the Ukraine was not, thus, a fascination with the Ukraine for its own sake, but for the sake of his interpretation of it as a spiritual model.[21] In this sense, the story is both nationalistic and religious, although, perhaps, in a crude way.

Thus far, it might be said that *Mirgorod* shows the simultaneous concern of Gogol with the themes of beauty, Orthodoxy, and Russia. The three are in the process of merging into one as Gogol pursues his quest.

The third tale in the collection, "Viy," is of a different genre from "Taras Bulba," though in his footnote to the story, Gogol does appear once again to be trying to give the past a vote: "Viy is a colossal creation of the common people's imagination. It is by this name that the chief of the gnomes, whose eyelids go down to the very ground, is called among the Little Russians. This whole tale is popular legend. I did not want to change it in any way, and I relate it with the same simplicity that I heard it" (2:175).

The story is, of course, anything but simple. It is, instead, clearly the product of a literary man trying to make a point, even if he is not always sure of how to do it. It is certainly doubtful that Gogol ever meant the pretense of the footnote to be taken seriously: it is, rather, a literary device used to separate the author from his work and to place that work within a context that the reader may find alluring.

Much of the tale is written as though Gogol could not make up his mind about what tone to use, jocularity or horror (perhaps this is the reason for the footnote, since it appears to absolve Gogol of responsibility). The principle of harmony, of concordance of elements, which he had extolled as essential to a work of art in his essays on Pushkin, on the painter Bryulov, and in "A Textbook of Literature for Russian Youth," is missing here, and the climactic horror, when it finally appears, seems a bit tired. One even wonders why the story is called "Viy," since the "chief of the gnomes" only enters on the scene a page and a half before the end of this tale of forty pages and since he is *not* built up to, or even mentioned, before his entrance. The reader, or at least this one, may also be puzzled by Gogol's insistence that Viy is a gnome, since the only gnomish quality about him or his cohorts is the black earth that clings to them. A more fitting title would have been "The Philosopher," for it is only by centering the story on this personage that unity may be attained, although the split in tone remains. If this is done, the tale becomes an attack, at times satirical, on philosophic pretension, an unmasking of falsity, in the earlier portions of the story, through humor.[22] It seems to me that it is enough for Gogol to characterize his central figure as "the philosopher" for his point to be made; he need not examine the character's thought, merely mention his profession (unlike Dostoevsky, Gogol was never a very good analyst). Like most of Gogol's personages, the philosopher stands for and exemplifies something, rather than being an individual in his own right. The point is, so far as the story is concerned, that there are more things in heaven and earth than are dreamt of in *anybody's* philosophy, and these things are real. What is *un*real is the world that the philosopher thought he knew, which is indicated at the end of the story when Gorobets, the former rhetorician graduated to philosopher, says: "I know why he was done for: because he was afraid. If he had not been afraid, the witch could not have done anything to him. You have only to cross yourself and spit right on her tail, and nothing will happen. I know all about it. Why, among us in Kiev, all the old women who sit in the market are witches" (2:218). In reality—and the ironic twist strikes the reader—Gorobets knows no more about it than his former comrade did; the kind of old-woman-witch he has in mind is very far from the one that the philosopher met and that Gorobets himself may meet, but fail to recognize, some day. This is, however, more than mere obtuseness or superstition. It is an agreement with falsity, accomplished by an airy dismissal of knowledge, by a refusal to see and acknowledge truth.

More interesting for purposes of the present discussion is Gogol's treatment of beauty in "Viy." At first sight it would appear that he has changed his attitude, that evil can indeed take on the guise of beauty, since the young woman who is a witch is very beautiful indeed when the philosopher first sees her in her coffin.

> Never, it seemed, had a face's features been formed in such
> sharp yet harmonious beauty. She lay as though alive. The
> lovely forehead, delicate as snow, as silver, seemed deep in

thought; the thin, even brows—a night in the midst of sunshine—proudly rose up above the closed eyes, while the eyelashes, which fell like arrows on the cheeks, glowed with the warmth of secret desires; the lips were rubies, ready to smile. [2:199]

When, however,

in them, in those very features, he saw something terribly penetrating, his soul began to ache painfully, as though suddenly, in the midst of a storm of gaiety and whirling crowds, someone had begun singing a funeral dirge. The rubies of her lips looked like blood boiling up from her heart. There was suddenly something dreadfully familiar in her face. "The witch!" he cried out in a voice not his own. [2:199]

What he sees now is the witch with whom he had had an adventure early in the story, ugly and old when possessed, beautiful and young when herself: that is why there is "something dreadfully familiar in her face." Night after night, from this point on, ugliness becomes more and more the girl's characteristic, for she appears to him more and more as one possessed. It is not that beauty in itself may be evil, or even that it may conceal evil. When the girl is in repose, when she is herself (in this case, dead), she is beautiful—that is, she is as she is meant to be. Only when she is animated by a spirit not her own, by the Prince of Lies, does she turn ugly. But, we remember, the girl has chosen to be a witch—she herself, of her own will, has refused truth. Thus, it is not beauty that deceives, but the denial of beauty. By becoming a witch she has denied her own aesthetic validity. When she is dead as a person, she is beautiful; when she rises from the coffin, in obedience to her hellish refusal, she is horrible. It is in the assertion of hellish horror, in the acceptance of the false, that real death comes: when Viy arrives—the ugliest of the ugly, covered with earth, arms and legs like roots, his eyelids hanging down to the ground, and with a face of iron—the philosopher, we are told, "lifeless crashed to the ground, and his spirit flew out of him in terror" (2:217). The church where the philosopher died is abandoned, "with monsters stuck in the doors and windows, overgrown by the forest, by roots, by tall weeds and wild thorns, and no one can now find the way to it" (2:217). Aesthetic refusal (the philosopher looked upon the face of Viy and took him for truth) has reaped its reward in death. For this reason the philospher ends as the witch ended, for she too denied beauty (one wonders if he may not have just such a false resurrection as hers, appearing alive, but in reality dead).

This is possibly the strongest statement that Gogol ever made—regardless of the strength or weakness of the story as such—of the opposition between beauty and ugliness, good and evil, truth and falsity.[23] When he turned to the contemporary world, however, he was to find ugliness and falsity more subtly expressed and obsession not so easily detectable; he was also to find that the jocular, satirical tone of the first part of "Viy," which is reminiscent of the tone of "Ivan Fyodorovich Shponka and His Aunt," could be sustained throughout a story that would at the same time, without a change of tone, without indulgence in overt horror, reveal ugliness and fulfill Gogol's aesthetic mission. Humor, rather than fear, was to be the weapon used to make his point, seducing his audience rather than shocking it.[24]

A step in this direction is taken in the last story in *Mirgorod,* "The Tale of How Ivan Ivanovich Quarreled with Ivan Nikiforovich." Here Gogol depicts an ugliness of soul that is all too common in the world we know.

The story portrays the deterioration not only of the relations between the two Ivans but of the soul of each of them, the change from life to death. Gogol even emphasizes this in his use of seasons in the tale. After a first chapter that gives character sketches of the two Ivans —character sketches that subtly point out the importance to each of his own ego, despite their ideal "friendship"—the story proper begins: "One morning—it was in July—Ivan Ivanovich was lying under his awning. The day was hot, the air was dry, and currents of air were flowing" (2:228). The generally fair weather continues through the few days of the main body of the story. Then, towards the end, a much more serious narrator than the one we had at the beginning intervenes: "Five years ago I was passing through the town of Mirgorod. I was traveling at a bad time. It was autumn, with its melancholy damp weather, mud, and fog" (2:274). In the last paragraph the narrator leaves town:

> The gaunt horses . . . pulled wearily, their hoofs making an unpleasant sound as they sank into the gray mass of mud. The rain poured onto the matting-covered Jew who sat on the box. The damp pierced me through and through. The dismal barrier, with the sentry box in which an invalided veteran was cleaning his gray equipment, slowly swept by. Again the same

fields, in places pitted and black, in places greening, the wet cows and crows, the monotonous rain, the tearful sky without a shaft of light. This is a tedious world, gentlemen. [2:276]

The very face of the land has changed from those beautiful, sun-filled Ukrainian days that Gogol was so fond of describing to a gray, monotonous, muddy landscape. Symbolically, both Ivans have become bogged in the mud, in a materiality that smothers them. It is indeed "a tedious world," tedious and heavy, made so by the extraordinary concern with the self, with the ego, that is evinced by both Ivans.[25] The quarrel started, after all, because Ivan Ivanovich fancied that his *amour-propre* had been insulted. Ivan Nikiforovich, astonished at the offense taken, because it has never occurred to him that he *could* insult anyone, promptly invented an offense against *his* ego that had been committed by Ivan Ivanovich. Not dignity, but self-esteem is in both cases wounded, as well as, each thinks, his esteem in the eyes of the world. Rank and position, rather than genuine value, bother both of them. Because of their egos, the harmony and serenity that seemed to reign at the beginning of the story are destroyed, and confusion, disturbance, and perturbation set in. Balance is lost; proportion disappears as each of the Ivans is obsessed, possessed. This is a story, above all, of aesthetic denial.

This does not mean that the relation between the Ivans at the beginning was in reality a beautiful one, although to the ordinary, banal citizen of Mirgorod it appeared so. That is precisely the point: it was an appearance, not a reality. The reality is revealed in the course of the story: the goodness of both Ivans, so praised at the beginning, is shown to be false, not even rising to the level of hypocrisy, for neither of them is willing to recognize the truth. An example is Ivan Ivanovich's attitude towards beggars. He loves to talk to beggars, to ask them questions about their lives, to appear to be considering their situation; and he clearly believes that he is being kind in doing so. It never occurs to him that he is raising false hopes, that he is, indeed, torturing them. This saves him from sadism, as it does from hypocrisy: he simply refuses to move outside himself, so that he cannot see things in proportion and relation to one another. His ego is such that he does not even know himself.

This is a point that Gogol makes many times in his works, as we have already indicated: difficulties arise and disasters occur because of a loss of perspective and because of a loss or lack of the ability to construct balanced wholes—through a loss, in other words, of artistic judgment, a loss that often has its source in an inordinate emphasis upon some material thing, an emphasis that in turn leads to the isolation of the ego. This is exactly what happens in "The Tale of How Ivan Ivanovich Quarreled with Ivan Nikiforovich."

Ivan Nikiforovich's housekeeper is airing out a number of her master's things that have been in the attic for years. Among the other items that she hangs out on the line is a gun that, the reader can guess, probably would blow up if anybody tried to fire it; in fact, we later learn that its lock is ruined. Ivan Ivanovich has been observing the airing process:

> "What does this mean?" thought Ivan Ivanovich. "I have never seen a gun at Ivan Nikiforovich's. What's the point? He never shoots, but he keeps a gun! What use is it to him? It's a splendid little thing! I've wanted to get one like it for a long time. I'd very much like to have that little gun; I love to forget all about things with a little gun." [2:230]

The last sentence is a clear indication of Ivan Ivanovich's *desire* to be possessed, that is, to deny his personality (whatever that personality may be) in favor of thingness. Why does he want the gun? For no other reason than that he wants it, that with it he will "forget." On the other hand, Ivan Nikiforovich wants to keep the gun, for he, too, identifies with it. Thence arises the quarrel. The final insult to Ivan Ivanovich's self-esteem comes when Ivan Nikiforovich calls him a gander. From that point on, the two are irreconcilable: the one attempt on the part of the townspeople to bring them together (the townspeople also have their egos to worry about) founders on the rocks of the egoistic obsessions of the two Ivans.

This theme of materiality is not a new one for Gogol—we are reminded of the search for treasure in some of the Ukrainian stories and the supplying of gold by devils in others, as well as of the acquisitive spirit of Vasilisa Kashporovna in "Ivan Fyodorovich Shponka and His Aunt"—and it will crop up again in the Petersburg tales and in *Dead Souls*. Indeed, so strong is the theme that V. V. Zenkovsky comes close to calling it an anticapitalist attack on Gogol's part.[26] I do not think however, that Gogol was sufficiently interested in either economics or politics to take a stand in these terms. Rather, he seemed to see attachment to things, whatever those things might be, as contradictory to both beauty and personality. The thing becomes in itself deceptive and has a tendency to reduce the person to anonymity,[27] to make him a thing himself, to turn him from a subject into an object. This is precisely what happens to the two Ivans: the gun leads to the insult, which leads to the endless litigation, which, in its turn, possesses each of the two Ivans to such a degree that they become, not persons, but mere puppets in a game that they cannot control but in which they must, perforce, perform their parts. This is the loss of the soul, which is well symbolized by the landscape and by the narrator's remarks at the end. Further, loss of soul is concomitant with loss of relationship, which brings with it the destruction of harmony, although we know, if we have read the character sketches of part 1 of the tale attentively, that the harmony itself was false—that is, that it was an illusion held both by the Ivans and by their neighbors. Instead of a proportionate balancing of parts, instead of real beauty, it was an invention that had nothing to do with the truth. It was thus *un*real, despite the first narrator's enthusiasm. Only at the end does the second narrator understand the truth and the wasteland become apparent.

That all of this is involved with *poshlost'* is, of course, correct.[28] But *poshlost'*, despite all the discussion of it by commentators, appears to be a surface manifestation for Gogol of something deeper. Certainly, the Ukrainian stories indicate that he was not a realist in the colloquial— or even in the literary—sense of the term, simply because he did not believe that material in itself was qualitative (except in a negative sense). If there is one thing that the realist (as we are using the term, rather than as a philosopher might use it) must believe, it is that the physical world he inhabits is a solid ground, is a reliable "given." It is not only there, to paraphrase Dr. Johnson, because it hurts, it is there because it means in itself. Gogol's reality, however, was of a different order; it was close to, if not identical with, that of Plato, and is described in this phrase: "And God saw all the things that he had made, and they were very good."[29] Precisely this world is what those possessed by the devil and obsessed by material deny. The Paradise of Dostoevsky's Father Zosima is indeed already here, if we would only see it.

Gogol could no more describe this reality, however, than Dante could. He could only hint, because the beauty that he believed in, while apprehensible, eluded both sense and thought. Sense had a tendency to deceive; and as for thought, Gogol's approach was intuitive rather than argumentative: he felt none of that dialectic urge which marks the great works of Dostoevsky. What he was left with, then, was the portrayal of negation, seeking the true through the portrayal of the false, while constantly emphasizing the falsity of what he was presenting.

If we take the Ukrainian tales as a whole—that is, both parts of *Evening on a Farm near Dikanka* and *Mirgorod,* both the more or less Gothic tales and "Ivan Fyodorovich Shponka and His Aunt," "Old World Landowners," and "The Tale of How Ivan Ivanovich Quarreled with Ivan Nikiforovich,"[30]—we find that Hanz Kuechelgarten did not die in the fire that Gogol had set for him, although he was considerably transformed. That young man had searched the world for material exemplifications of beauty and had found his discoveries disillusioning at best. Poor as that work is—the clichéd attempt of a young, overinfluenced provincial who possessed little facility in the form (the incredible bad taste, unless it was done for a joke, of rhyming "Aristophan" and "Winkelmann" is sufficient evidence)—still it does indicate what I take to be Gogol's lifelong concern. That Hanz did not find true beauty in ancient ruins did not mean, for the author, that the quest must be abandoned. The failure of Hanz, and of so many in the tales, implied a lack in them, not an absence of beauty itself. The negative, to which Gogol devoted so much of his creative career, indicates the positive, just as fear of Satan necessarily implies belief in God.

3
Petersburg

The division of Gogol's stories between "Little Russian Tales" and "Petersburg Tales"—common as the division is and despite the fact that Gogol made such a division himself—is an artificial one, if one wishes to discuss Gogol's career in terms of his literary development. While the stories that we have so far explored all take Little Russia for their setting, they were written after Gogol's migration to the capital and while he was thinking of and composing some of the Petersburg tales. I would suggest that his left hand knew very well what his right hand was doing and that what he saw, he saw in an intuitive flash and completely. What remained was to work it out; this he tried to do in every way he could devise.[1]

The Petersburg stories were written over a long period of time in relation to the shortness of Gogol's activity as a whole: from the spring of 1831, when he wrote the first drafts of "The Portrait" and "Nevsky Prospekt"; through 1833, when he was working on "The Diary of a Madman" and "The Nose" (in January 1835, before the publication of *Mirgorod,* "Nevsky Prospekt," "The Portrait," and "The Diary of a Madman" were published in *Arabesques,* along with the two never-completed Ukrainian fragments and thirteen articles, mostly on historical subjects); through April 1836, when he read "The Nose" to some friends; through the summer of 1839, when he did new versions (actually revisions) of both "The Portrait" and "The Nose"; through December 1839, when he accomplished the first draft of "The Overcoat," another version of which he finished in the summer of 1840, completely redid in the fall of 1841, and finally published in volume 3 of the collected edition of his works in 1842.[2]

It would seem best, for present purposes, to consider these stories in the order of their conception, although it is to the texts of the final versions that I will refer. The sequence then is: "The Portrait," "Nevsky Prospekt," "The Diary of a Madman," "The Nose," and "The Overcoat."[3]

"The Portrait" is split into two parts, of which the first logically follows the second, given minor changes at the beginning of the first and at the end of the second in order to make a smooth transition. Gogol had used this device before and was to use it again in *Dead Souls,* where we are given Chichikov's background only at the end. It is as though Gogol had immediately grasped the consequence and then went back to find some reason for it—for the reader's sake, one suspects, more than for his own.

Although the story is set in Petersburg, it bears a certain resemblance to the Gothic Little Russian tales in that we once again have a satanic force, now, however, only half-personified, that destroys a man's soul. But this force is far more grimly malevolent than any we have found previously, and there is no relief of humor. In addition, the satanic force here is set in *overt* opposition to beauty and to art.[4] It is also more openly symbolic than the devils we encountered earlier. Indeed, here—and more and more in the stories that follow—evil, ugliness, and falsity are externalized; increasingly they become manifestations evoked by perverted human will.

The above applies most particularly to Part 1; Part 2, however, is more in the nature of an explanation, an essay, than it is organically a part of the story, although it is interesting as well for the ideas that Gogol expresses on the nature of the artist, ideas that he also expressed in articles written at various times during his career, notably: "Boris Godunov" (1831), "Sculpture, Painting, and Music" (1831), "A Few Words on Pushkin" (1832), "On the Last Day of Pompeii" (1834), "A Textbook of Literature for Russian Youth" (some time between 1831 and 1842), "On *The Contemporary*" (1846), and various of the essays printed in *Selected Passages from Correspondence with Friends* (1847). Certainly, the evidence is sufficient to indicate that what he had to say in Part 2 of "The Portrait" was not simply a result of Gogol's revising the story when he was increasingly preoccupied "with religion, morality, and the horrible wages of sin."

A reading of these essays and of "The Portrait" yields a set of principles which Gogol seems to have thought should govern the production of art; in fact, if these principles are not kept in mind by the artist, the result may be an object, but it will not be an *art* object. First of all, the artist is a teacher whose concern is to pass on, not daily trivia, but the same sort of verities that fathers pass on to sons, as he puts it in "A Textbook" (8:470). The arist, therefore, must be sincere, depicting as clearly and briefly as possible what he himself has perceived, felt, experienced. There is a clear moral connotation here: the more "moral," the "better" the artist is, the loftier will be the content of his art; and the more "moral," the "better" he will make his audience. The artist is not only a teacher; he is also a prophet. Gogol made much of this in his later years, when he insisted that he must purge himself of all baseness and meanness, must himself become "better" before he could go on to the completion of *Dead Souls,* since, after all, Parts 2 and 3 were to portray the regeneration of Chichikov. This was not a matter of religious fanaticism or madness on his part, however; it was simply the conclusion of the position that he had held from the very beginning which had always insisted on the artist's sincerity. If the artist is not sincere, his work will be false and thus will run the danger of deceiving his audience.[5] He will be talking about something about which he has no knowledge. By knowledge, further, Gogol did not mean merely acquaintance with outer details (his own lack of acquaintance with the small-time provincial life that he depicted in *The Inspector General* and *Dead Souls* is well known). The preception, feeling, and experience that he had in mind referred to what he would have called the soul. Somehow (probably because of incomprehensible divine selection) the artist's soul "sees" more clearly than other men's souls do.[6] The artist's devotion to truth, further, is part and parcel of his devotion to beauty. Gogol would have agreed entirely with Keats's dictum that "Beauty is truth, Truth beauty," but he would have added "Good" to complete the platonic trinity, even if the good that he had in mind was as much a moral one as it was the form of forms.

The artist, thus, stood in a very special relation both to truth and to his fellow men. To both he had an obligation to fulfill, at peril of his soul—Part 1 alone of "The Portrait" makes this point. The artist Chartkov, however, not only betrays his own obligation, which is embodied in his talent, he goes berserk and tries to destroy the works of artists who have fulfilled their obligations: having lost his own soul, having falsified himself, he turns to an assault on beauty and truth themselves. At the same time, Gogol makes it clear that Chartkov's betrayal came about through an act of will—that is, Chartkov chose (although tempted) to follow the path most advantageous to his material ego; obligation was rejected in favor of this ego.

As is usual with Gogol, concentration upon the ego is symbolized in the accumulation of material riches, which are deliberately pursued. Chartkov, after all, was given a choice when he first discovered the roll of gold coins: he could have used the gold to relieve himself of material cares in order to devote himself to his art, or he could have decided to use it to advance his material comfort and gain worldly admiration.[7] He chose the latter course, thus ceasing to fulfill his role as a devotee of beauty and a teacher of truth. In this way, Chartkov became "possessed," by an act of his own will, not simply because Satan took him over—Gogol was too good a Russian Orthodox ever to controvert the doctrine of free will. This "possession" meant loss of his distinctive personality, of that which made him what he was—his talent—as Chartkov discovered when he tried to paint honestly again: he no longer is what he was; he no longer sees clearly; and his brush can only depict the falsity to which he has devoted himself for so many years. In short, he has become the very lie that he chose.

Part 2 of "The Portrait" really does no more than spell out the implications of Part 1. Here we have an artist who is tempted but who, by an act of will, recovers from the temptation and fulfills his vocation. Here, also, the symbolism is made doubly obvious: the roll of gold coins of Part 1 is replaced by a usurer of foreign extraction (he might be "an Indian, a Greek, or Persian, no one could say for sure" [3:121]). That he is foreign is of immediate significance—evil is destructive of the native order, not a part of things as they should be.[8] We are told openly that poets bring "peace and perfect calm to the soul, not agitation and grumbling" (3:114). Invariably, those to whom the usurer lends money turn selfish and vicious. However, the painter who painted the usurer's portrait refused to finish it, recognized the malevolence of the now-deceased usurer, and withdrew from the world to become a monk; through mortification of the flesh and prayer he made himself "better," that is, more worthy of his talent, and finally put his talent to proper use by painting the Nativity. A real work of art, fulfilling the principles that should govern the artist as well as the work of art, was produced:

> The feeling of divine humility and gentleness on the face of
> the Immaculate Mother inclining over the Child; the profound

intellect in the eyes of the Divine Child, as though they perceived something afar; the triumphant silence of the Magi
struck by the Divine Miracle as they are prostrated at His feet;
and finally, the holy, inexpressible calm that pervaded the
entire picture—all this was presented with such harmonious
strength and mighty beauty that the impression was magical.
All of the brothers fell on their knees before the new icon,
and the affected prior pronounced: "No, it is impossible for
a man to produce such a picture solely by human means: a
holy, higher power guided your brush, the blessing of heaven
rested upon your labor." [3:134]

Later the artist tells his son:

An intimation of the divine heavenly paradise is in art for man,
and that is why it is loftier than all else. . . . Without it a man
is powerless to raise himself from earth, and he cannot make
the wonderful sounds of peace. . . . For the lofty creations of
art descend to the world for the peace and reconciliation of all.
It cannot sow grumbling in the soul, but, like a resounding
prayer, it aspires eternally to God. [3:135]

The portrait he painted of the usurer, thus, because it inspired "rebellious feelings, uneasy feelings, not the feelings of an artist, for an artist
breaths peace into unease" (3:136), was not a work of art. The painter
therefore sends his son forth to find the portrait and destroy it. Unfortunately, the son fails, and the portrait is still in the world.

This theory of art and the artist was for Gogol a complete one,
repeated time and time again in his essays throughout his career. In
no story, however, was he to state it so overtly as he did in "The
Portrait," whether in the first version or the second, even if it must
be admitted that the second version is plainer than the first, insofar as
the points are made more emphatically.[9] Gogol's statements about art,
however, are the same, and they are meant very seriously. But, one may
ask, is there anything new here; is there any great originality to what
Gogol has to say on the subject? Obviously not: much of his view
can be traced back through various sources to the ancient Greeks. Regardless of sources, however, Gogol does seem to have been convinced
of the notion that harmony is essential to beauty and truth—and it is
to a revelation of this harmony that art aspires. Further, art, so far as
it has an effect upon mankind, brings peace, tranquillity, and, perhaps
most important of all, reconciliation. Art accomplishes, both within

the individual and in the relations of individuals with one another, the great service envisioned by Plato in *The Republic*.[10] On this ground, Gogol could justify his own artistic activity, for in his mind he was performing as real a service as the most highly placed functionary in the Russian state. The profession of letters, which was only just becoming established *as a profession* in Russia,[11] was a very high calling indeed, for the poet is not only a counsellor of kings in the tradition of Roman and Renaissance writers, he is also a prophet to all mankind.

This attitude towards art must involve a writer in the question of reality. So was Gogol consciously involved, in both the story "Nevsky Prospekt" and in the essay "Petersburg Notes of 1836." From one point of view, his subject in both cases is a specific one: the city of St. Petersburg—its atmosphere and meaning both as a city and as the capital of the Russian Empire.[12] From another point of view, the one that I have adopted for the purposes of this essay, the city is a mere excuse, an image that can be used for the expression of ideas of far-wider import than the city itself, or even than the city as symbol. This is not to state, or to imply, that the city—not only in "Nevsky Prospekt" and "Petersburg Notes of 1836," but in all the other writings of Gogol's that dealt with the image—had no importance. Certainly, the city had a strong impact on him, as it did, for example, on Pushkin before him, on Dostoevsky, and, later, on Andrey Biely and Alexander Blok. Indeed, from the time of its founding by Peter the Great until the transfer of the capital back to Moscow by the Soviets, St. Petersburg was in political and ideological terms the symbol of a great traumatic split in the consciousness of Russian intellectuals. So it was for Gogol. But it also, as I think "Nevsky Prospekt" and "Petersburg Notes of 1836" demonstrate, served as a symbol for his prime concern with the nature and location of reality.

"Nevsky Prospekt," again a story divided into two parts, one solemn and the other humorous, emphasizes the enormous difficulty we encounter when we assert with certainty what is real and what is not. The first part is still involved with the search for beauty, and the reader is reminded of the deception practiced in "Viy," where the beautiful young woman turns out, in reality, to be an almost indescribably ugly witch. Now Gogol is more subtle, although the possible falsity of physical beauty is again made apparent. Contrary to medieval theory, a fair exterior does not necessarily mirror a fair interior. For Gogol, as we have already pointed out, the physical world, the illusion in which most of us choose to live, is not the real one. Dr. Johnson, to put it another way, did not genuinely know what pain was.

Despite the division of "Nevsky Prospekt," Gogol succeeds in accomplishing a unity by enclosing the entire tale within a frame. We open—as was often Gogol's usage—with a panoramic view of the avenue, accomplished in a rather realistic fashion. The scene, although somewhat satirically presented, is easily acceptable as a picture of what the street is like, at least for an "objective" observer. A proper fashionable boulevard that changes its clientele according to the hour of the day, it is quite recognizable to the reader, for most properly brought-up large cities have at least one prospect of this kind. In short, the description appeals to the way we normally view the world; there is nothing in it that either shocks us or calls into question our everyday concept of reality.

The other part of the frame, however, the conclusion of the story, while it returns to a general statement after the details, is quite another matter. Nothing, particularly reality, is so simple as it would seem: "Everything is a fraud, everything is a dream, everything is not what it seems! . . . everything breaths fraud. It constantly lies, this Nevsky Prospekt" (3:46). Not only have both main characters in the story been deceived; so have we. If everything we have been led to think of as real is a dream, then what about those things that we have been led to think are dreams? Where are the real and—in the first part of the story—beauty to be found?

The moment that we know that Piskaryov, the hero of Part 1, is an artist, we know that Gogol's theme again is beauty, for Gogol clung persistently to the view that beauty is the artist's realm. Piskaryov, however, is still young, still struck by concrete appearance, still capable of accepting that appearance for the thing-in-itself. To this extent, he makes the same error that Hanz Kuechelgarten had made. But he goes further than Hanz—he thinks that he can remold the physically beautiful prostitute so that she will inwardly be what her outward form promises, so that, Pygmalion-like, he may create the harmony essential to beauty itself.[13] Of course, he fails; indeed, the prostitute laughs at him for even suggesting such a possibility. No Liza Doolittle she, she has no intention of helping to actualize Piskaryov's dreams, which are, for her, mere nonsense. It was to be left to Dostoevsky (following the Bible) to invent the saintly prostitute, and to Bret Harte to invent the golden-hearted one. For Gogol, the law of contradiction unfortunately holds. Piskaryov, his mind clouded, showing signs of madness, commits suicide. The devotee of beauty kills himself because beauty is not what or where he thought it was after all, because the "reality" of the prostitute destroys what he thought was the truth; the beauty he had dreamt of does not exist. Neither did it, we remember, for Hanz Kuechelgarten.

But does it really exist? Did this artist fail for the right reasons? Is his conclusion that beauty is unattainable a correct one? He himself says, "God! what a life is ours! Eternal strife between dream and reality!" (3:30). A good third of Piskaryov's story takes place outside the realm of physical reality and in that of dreams. In these dreams the prostitute appears in complete and harmonious beauty, no longer the contradiction that she is in physical life. Obviously, this can all be viewed in psychological terms along the lines of wish-fulfillment and frustration, and such an approach is clearly valid within its own domain. I should like to suggest, however, that this approach is neither a necessary one nor the only valid one, especially if we subscribe to V. V. Zenkovsky's proposition that Gogol was a portrayer of types rather than of individuals. Viewed, therefore, in terms of the problem of reality, it may well be that Gogol was reversing the usual perception, that Piskaryov's dreams represent the truly real, while the prostitute's world is the falsely real. For it is in the former that beauty exists, in the latter that it does not; the former that tells the truth, the latter that deceives (we are reminded of the narrator's remark at the end that it is on Nevsky Prospekt that "everything is a dream"); the sight of the former that is especially vouchsafed the artist, the sight of the latter that is seized upon by most. The device of the dream is here used, in other words, less to make a psychological point about the workings of the human mind than it is to emphasize Gogol's idea of what constitutes truth. The story's pathos lies in Piskaryov's failure to realize that it is the artist's job to convey reality, not to invent it.[14] This does not mean that the artist has no obligation to attempt to change human life. On the contrary, that is the very reason for his conveyance of reality, so that men may be brought to live in it. The difficulty is that most people either do not know, or they deliberately reject, the real; they choose, as "The Portrait" and "Nevsky Prospekt" show, what is false. The prostitute is false to beauty, and Piskaryov, not realizing that the beauty he sees in his dreams is real beauty, betrays it also. His suicide, indeed, occurs as a result of his final collapse in the face of his own inadequacy.

The opposite side—the more "normal" side, the side of those who have never even considered truth but live and deceive within deception—is portrayed in Part 2 of "Nevsky Prospekt." Gogol is at great pains to inform us of the everyday nature of his other hero, Pirogov, in this section of his tale. Piskaryov, we have earlier been told, "belonged to a class that is rather an odd phenomenon among us, and he no more belonged among the citizens of Petersburg than a face appearing to us in a dream belongs to the world of fact" (3:16). Although he is a member of a rare group, still he carries "in his soul sparks of feeling, ready at the right moment to be converted into flame" (3:18). Pirogov, on the other hand, is far more ordinary, far more the sort that one might meet any day, one of those "officers who form a kind of middle class of society in Petersburg" (3:31). Gogol informs us of all the typical activities of this sort of person, what he is likely to say, how he is apt to react, what a lack of genuine concern undistinguishes him, how shallow and, indeed, nonexistent he is. While Piskaryov thinks of beauty, and in his dreams sees it, Pirogov thinks only of appearance and dreams only of playing a role. He and his adventure are fitting subjects for laughter, and so Gogol treats them, for the deceiver who deceives himself deserves no more. From his sympathetic handling of the failure Piskaryov, Gogol changes to mockery when he comes to the blind egoist Pirogov. The quest for beauty that drives Piskaryov has never had any meaning to Pirogov; all this young army officer is interested in is normal premarital seduction before settling down to the usual, banal, superficial—and false—existence of a thing.

Highly significant are the names that Gogol gave to the husband of the dumb blonde whom Pirogov is pursuing and to his friend: Schiller and Hoffmann. He says of the former that he was "not the Schiller who wrote *William Tell* and the *History of the Thirty Years' War*, but the famous Schiller, the tinsmith of Meshchansky Street" (a well-known street in Petersburg that was given over largely to trades-men of various kinds, most of them, interestingly enough, non-Russians; the word *meshchansky* refers not only to a tradesman, however; it may also mean "vulgar," "narrow-minded," "Philistine"). Of the latter, Gogol remarks that he was "not the writer Hoffmann [that is, E. T. A. Hoffmann], but the rather high-class bootmaker from Ofitsersky Street [literally, 'Officer's Street'; Pirogov, we remember, is an officer], a great friend of Schiller's" (3:37). This is more than mere irony. These persons, because of the very names they bear, are deceptive; their names should indicate a connection with the world of art, and thus with the world of beauty and truth;[15] but they are, in fact, living contradictions of their names, just as the prostitute's inner corruption is a contradiction of her outer beauty. They are as false as Pirogov himself; but because they are false, they do not recognize the deception in which they are involved, any more than he does.

Pirogov's adventure stands in remarkable contrast to that of Piskaryov in that here no one is in the least concerned with truth, even though the tale is far more "realistic" than Part 1, in the sense that the actions seem more "true to life," more "authentic," in the vulgar sense of the term. Amusing as it all is, there is really nothing either extraordinary or important about either the persons or what happens to them: it is "realistic comedy." There is none of the vision or yearning or pathos of Part 1, for what *appears* to be real in Part 2 is constantly accepted *as* real by the characters concerned; there is none of that sense of betrayal and failure that pervades Part 1, for no one here is either conscious of or cares about the truth. The only conclusion we can reach is that this world, the common world, is not what Gogol meant by reality, that it is as much a dream as Piskaryov's attempt to play Pygmalion. This may be precisely the warning that the teacher Gogol was trying to get across to his readers.

This second part of "Nevsky Prospekt" does also, of course, contain a satire on banality, on *poshlost'*. Indeed, it may be—and often has been—read as a social attack on the mores and the emptiness of the Russian capital in Gogol's day. Such satire—enjoyable as it may be and no matter how agreeable to various prejudices—appears, however, to have been a secondary aim to Gogol, not a primary one. As he said so often, his subject was the "soul of man," not society. The point is that it is all a lie, that in Petersburg, and elsewhere, we may presume, "a demon lights the street lamps to show everything in a nonreal way" (3:46).

There is another point, however: Pirogov gets himself involved with a German girl, her German husband, and the husband's German friend. In "Petersburg Notes of 1836," composed, it is true, after "Nevsky Prospekt," Gogol, contrasting Petersburg with Moscow, wrote that, while Moscow "still has a Russian beard, [Petersburg] is already a precise German [the word Gogol uses, *nyemets,* while it literally means 'German,' might also be translated as 'foreigner']. . . . How the dandy Petersburg has progressed, how it stands at attention! . . . Petersburg is a sprightly chap, he never stays at home, always dresses up and [preens] before Europe" (8:178). The essay goes on to emphasize the foreignness of Petersburg and the native Russianness of Moscow. Gogol ends the first section of the essay with the statement that "the distance [between the two] is enormous!" (8:179). A bit further on he tells us that Petersburg is "something like a European-American colony" (8:179). Everything about it, in short, is in imitation of the West; it possesses no reality, no truth of its own. Gogol finally ends with an expression of his yearning to be elsewhere, in lands of beauty, "under another sky, in southern green groves, in a country of fresh, crisp air." Indeed, he imagines the "likenesses of the mountains of the Caucasus or the lakes of Switzerland, or Italy crowned with anemones and laurels, or Greece beautiful in its wilderness . . . painted at the end of a Petersburg street" (8:190).

I would suggest that Gogol was already unhappy with the praise of those critics, like Belinsky, who lauded him for his social conscience, for what they saw, because they wanted to, as his attack upon conditions in Russia. Both "Nevsky Prospekt" and "Petersburg Notes of 1836" are, on this level, anti-Western rather than anti-Russian statements, for in both cases, Russianism is what is being denied. Gogol is very close to an assertion that the peculiar essence of Russianism is an attachment to beauty, as though, like many Russians of his time, he took the story of the conversion of Russia in the *Primary Chronicle* very seriously.[16] Furthermore, in both cases the loss of identity is sharply stressed.[17] As we have seen, the theme of personality loss was not a new one for Gogol, and it was to be repeated, in various ways, in his later work.

When we turn to "The Diary of a Madman," on the surface we seem to have a straightforward, comparatively modern portrayal of schizophrenia, the degeneration of a poor downtrodden clerk who thinks that he hears two dogs talking to each other. Later, he reads what he takes to be letters—composed by Lord knows who—between them, and he finally imagines himself to be the king of Spain. He is a little man who has been crushed by a cruel, unfeeling world, one of the "insulted and injured," who has been driven out of his mind by the pressures of the Russian milieu. The account of the treatment accorded Poprishchin (whose name is only mentioned one time, towards the end of the story) in the madhouse, coupled with his pathetic appeals to his mother, might well be taken as an attack on a system that refuses to give people a chance—a kind of Russian *Oliver Twist* without a happy ending. Technically, Gogol accomplished a feat by telling the story in the first person, so that the impact, from the point of view just outlined, is all the greater. For once, it can be claimed at the same time, Gogol was not being typical, because what are depicted are the particular processes of one mind. Considered on this level, "The Diary of a Madman" is certainly more successful than Dostoevsky's more famous *The Double*.

No such story, however, can escape being involved in the problem of reality; it could be said that the schizoid has simply chosen a different reality from that of the rest of us. The curious thing here is that Gogol gives no reason categorically to state, no matter what our inclinations may be, that the dogs did *not* talk to each other and that they did *not* exchange letters; the assumption that they did not is simply based on the audience's different perception of what is real. Are those genuinely the wanderings of a sick mind, as the reader automatically assumes and as Gogol's title indicates, or, once again, is reality not quite so simple as the reader would like to think? Is it not possible, rather, that reality, while "objective," is not material? The device of narration in the first person here assumes additional significance, since it is the *narrator's* reality that we are involved in, the *narrator's* point of view that the reader must accept—and it is the point of view, the reality, of a man who is completely alone, in a state of utter separation. The frightening thing is that once we grant Poprishchin's premise that things are not what they seem to be, that no one sees the truth about him, and that he lives in truth, whereas everyone else lives in falsity, then everything makes sense—the absurdity, the grotesqueness that so many critics have commented upon, disappears. If the madman is one who has lost touch with reality, then we have a right to ask what reality is. And this question is precisely the one that is posed for us here.

This does not mean that for Gogol reality is relative. Perhaps neither of Poprishchin's worlds—either that of his office or that of his madness—is the real one; perhaps everything in the story, in short, is mad. The officials, without exception, are more interested in their positions and ranks than in what they are. It is on the basis, indeed, of position and rank that one man speaks to another. One might go so far as to say that this emphasis on rank is what teaches Poprishchin to become the king of Spain. He is, after all, officially only a titular councillor, the equivalent of a captain, ninth on the Table of Ranks. This defines him, as the others' ranks define them. It is like being defined by a piece of clothing or a hairdo or a particular kind of mous-

tache (Gogol often, in fact, uses inanimate objects to define his characters). But what does this definition have to do, Poprishchin asks, with
what a person is in reality: "I have many times wanted to discover why
all these differences occur. Why am I a titular councillor and on what
grounds am I a titular councillor? Perhaps I am some count or general,
and only seem to be a titular councillor? Perhaps I myself don't know
who I am" (3:206).

The last sentence is of particular significance—does anyone, even
granted that all the characters are seen through Poprishchin's eyes,
know who he is? As he says, "Give me a fashionably cut coat, and let
me tie on a necktie like yours—and then you wouldn't hold a candle
to me. No income—that's the trouble" (3:198). And later: "Everything that's best in the social world is gotten either by court chamber-
lains or by generals. You find some poor treasure, you think you've
got it in your hand—a court chamberlain or a general snatches it away
from you. . . . I'd like to become a general myself. . . . I'd like to be
a general only to see how they would try to get around me and do
all their court tricks and *équivoques* and then say to them: I spit on
you both" (3:205). When reading the dog's letter, he makes a comment that applies to his entire world: "How can anyone fill a letter
with such foolishness! Give me a man! I want to see a man. I ask for
food to nourish and pleasure my soul, and instead these bagatelles"
(3:205). But no one knows, nor cares, even about himself, much less
about Poprishchin. No one is a man.

Poprishchin's fault, for which he is called mad, is his attempt to
find a personality, to become somebody. And he is the only one who
makes such an attempt. He suffers, as his colleagues do, from what
most Western readers would regard as a normal and legitimate desire:
he wants to be regarded, to be noticed, to be paid attention to; his
complaint is the same as that of Dostoevsky's Devushkin in *Poor Folk*
and of Golyadkin in *The Double,* not to mention the line of buffoons
that Dostoevsky trailed behind those two. Once Poprishchin decides
that he is king of Spain, he is aware that people have a different attitude
towards him; now they pay attention. He may be tormented, but at least
he is there, which is more than can be said of anyone else. He is there,
that is, except for one brief moment at the very end of the story when,
tormented in the madhouse, he cries out: "They do not heed me, do
not see me, do not listen to me. Why do they torment me? What do
they want of poor me? What can I give them? I have nothing"

(3:214). Then, calling upon his mother, he laments, "Press your poor orphan to your breast! There is no place in the world for him! He is persecuted! Mother, pity your sick child!" (3:214). There is indeed no place in this world, or in any world, for him. Poprishchin seems to have an intimation of the truth, but no more than that; he is as much isolated at the end as he was at the beginning. The king of Spain is as egocentric as Poprishchin's colleagues in the office. Value remains on this false level. From this point of view, there is no serious difference between Poprishchin mad and Poprishchin sane; both of his worlds and both of his "states of soul" are denials of reality—one as empty and meaningless as the other—so that his "thereness" turns out not to exist after all. The point is that while Poprishchin may have a mind that is susceptible to such terms as sanity and madness, it is his soul that is lost; and for one moment at the end of the story he knows it, as surely as did Chartkov, the philosopher, and Petro.

One of the strangest things about "The Diary of a Madman" is the humor with which Gogol treats his central character. This is not the good humor or the jocularity of some of the Little Russian tales; on the contrary, Poprishchin is meant to be laughed at, not with. The laughter is meant to put a distance between reader and character, not to enlist sympathy. Not only is Poprishchin's world wrong; *he* is wrong. His and his world's falsity is being unmasked, as a warning to the reader; and from this point of view the story is relentless. Like all Gogol's humorous tales, this is a horror story—not because we are witnesses of the crushing of the "little man" (after all, Poprishchin's ambitions are only to be superior to others, as he thinks they are superior to him; to crush as he is crushed), but because we are witnesses of the loss of humanity by those who do not see the truth—we are witnesses of the void.[18] As Poprishchin himself says, he has nothing to give. This statement is a far more profound one than Poprishchin realizes.

We know that whatever reality we choose in "The Diary of a Madman," it will be false, for they are all vulgar and, thus, ugly. Nowhere do we find Gogol's touchstone of beauty and harmony, and nowhere do we find reconciliation. The office that Poprishchin works in is a jangle of discordant elements, each isolating itself: things everywhere are struggling with things. It is marked by separation rather than by unity, even though nobody really cares who he is. Only Poprishchin for a moment realizes the loss, as he says, as much of himself as of others: "Give me a man! I want to see a man. I ask for

food to nourish and pleasure my soul, and instead these bagatelles."
This might well be the complaint of Gogol himself. This is not only a
tedious world, but an insane one, outside the asylum's walls as well as
inside them. The one thing we can be certain of is that it is not in this
insanity that the truth will be found.

It would appear that this interpretation would lead to a condemnation of the central character as well as of the milieu he inhabits; it
would seem that Gogol has gone Swift one better. I do not think that
this was Gogol's intention, for condemnation without an alternative is
meaningless. The difficulty was that the beauty that Gogol had already
implied in his essays and stories as being the reality transcending and
capable of transfiguring material appearance had not yet been actualized
in human affairs and thus was incapable of being depicted. Even Gogol
had to recognize that his later attempts to do so in *Selected Passages*
and in the destroyed portion of *Dead Souls* were failures. But those
were endeavors undertaken in desperation. At this stage the only immediate material for the pen of an artist—or at any rate, of an artist
like Gogol—was the false, in the belief that the exposure of the false
would lead at least to a realization of its opposite. His teaching vocation was to be accomplished through the unmasking of the void. In
this sense, Gogol's great talent—and a most unusual one it was—
consisted in the portrayal of meaninglessness rather than of meaning, not
because Gogol despaired and thought the world absurd, but because
truth, like Plato's Good and Dante's God, was ineffable, even though
real.[19] Poprishchin, after all, was meant to be laughed at, not to be
pitied, because of what Gogol regarded as a false sensibility. I would
suggest that Gogol was here confronting the reader with problems
that the reader did not previously know existed, problems of the ordinary and everyday that the reader has always taken for granted—
"Things are not what they seem" is over and over again his point. What
is real and who is sane, if anybody is, in "The Diary of a Madman"?
If we are men like Poprishchin's colleagues, the answer is plain—
Poprishchin is the one who has lost touch with reality. Few readers,
if any, will willingly identify with them, however—they are obviously
far too shallow, too petty, too vulgar for us to do so; we know that their
perception of reality is false, that they do not have souls. Does that
mean that we must identify with Poprishchin, the "victim"? The same
objection arises; otherwise there would be no reason for our laughter.
Where, then, does reality lie? Or is it all false, and are we?

The point is doubly emphasized by the upset in time when Poprishchin discovers that he is king of Spain. Before that, the dates of the entries in the diary all make perfectly good "sense," running from October 3 to December 8 (and including, in this "normal" sequence, the episodes of the talking and letter-writing dogs). Then time begins to disappear—from "2,000 A.D., April 43"; through "Martober 86 between day and night"; "no day—the day had no date"; and so on, and so forth; to utter temporal gibberish for the last entry, which is "February" written upside down and backwards. This last entry, interestingly enough, is what returns us to lucidity, with Poprishchin's call to his mother. The very notion of the stability of time has been called into question, while a reality transcending time has been indicated.[20] Time, in short, is irrelevant, so that it is not only Poprishchin's world that is disturbed, but our own. We too, despite our laughter, are involved in the problem. Indeed, Gogol the teacher is telling us that it *is* our problem.

In "The Diary of a Madman," Gogol approached his subject without resorting to the fantastic. "The Nose" is another question entirely. Here the grossly improbable, if not to say impossible, reigns—from the reader's point of view, be it noted, not always and necessarily from the point of view of those within the story.[21] At most, those in the story feel a momentary sense of shock at being presented with something—namely, Kovalyov's loss of his nose—that is outside their range of experience.[22] The immediate reaction of the barber, at the very beginning, is to disembarrass himself of the experience, to pretend that it never happened and that he had no part in it. One must also be struck by what occurs in the Kovalyov household when the Major, as he insists upon calling himself, discovers himself to be noseless: he *commanded* a mirror, *ordered* some water, and *ordered* his clothes (literally, "ordered himself to be dressed"). To whom, however, did he direct these requests? One presumes that they were directed to a servant or servants, but Gogol does not tell us, and the Major's valet, Ivan, does not turn up until much later. In any event, we think it must be someone; yet, whoever carries out the commands takes no notice of the absence of the nose. Gogol deliberately left out, perhaps *cut* out, normal reality, so that anything fantastic, abnormal, or nonhabitual is not to be recognized within the context. Kovalyov, like Poprishchin, is out of touch with truth. Before proceeding with the story, Gogol pauses to record a short character sketch of his central figure. Kovalyov is on the whole rather an unremarkable person who prefers to appear other than what he is. He is actually a collegiate assessor, one rank above Poprishchin in the Table of Ranks, but he prefers the military equivalent of his title—Major—"to give himself greater weight and dignity." Further, he is out of a job and is looking for one "befitting his rank"; he also has hopes of discovering a bride with a large dowry. Again, things are not what they seem: outer form replaces inner substance, Gogol's favorite theme. Poprishchin's demand for a man still receives no response, and the deception that is so widespread in the Little Russian tales and "Nevsky Prospekt" continues.

When Kovalyov first sees his nose in the street, the nose is wearing the plumed hat of a councillor of state, which is three ranks above Kovalyov's rank of collegiate assessor and is the equivalent of a major general. Kovalyov is the only one who thinks (he has his own egoistic reasons for doing so) that there is anything unusual about this councillor of state who (or which) maintains his own residence, takes a carriage, piously goes to church and prays (Kovalyov finds prayer impossible), and finally declares himself to be, not Kovalyov's nose, but simply himself.[28] None of Kovalyov's efforts to have the matter of his lost nose treated as an affair of importance succeeds. Even the newspaper office refuses to accept an advertisement offering a reward for the return of the nose, on the grounds, first, that the loss of a nose is absurd (which Kovalyov denies; even he evidently believes that while such a thing is embarrassing, it by no means violates ordinary experience); second, that this is a matter for a physician, not for the personal columns of a newspaper; and third, that it wouldn't do Kovalyov any good anyhow. The police inspector is not interested, both because he is about to sit down to dinner and because such things do not happen to respectable people (evidently they *do* happen to disreputable people, which may be Gogol's point). Then a policeman, simply doing his duty and seeing nothing unusual in it, returns the nose, which he has recovered from the barber in whose loaf of bread it turned up at the beginning of the story. But Kovalyov cannot get it stuck back on his face, and the physician he finally manages to consult tells him that while it could be done, it would be better to let nature take its course (evidently nature *has* been taking its course). There is some bustle in the city when the news of Kovalyov's experience gets out, but only among the sort of sensation hunters and curiosity seekers who would attend public executions, interested in spectacle that fulfills law rather than spectacle that violates it. They are all anonymous, and no one cares in the least about the collegiate assessor himself. Finally, the Major wakes up one morning, and there is his nose, right where it is supposed to be—in the middle of his face. The narrator winds it all up: "Where are there not incongruities? . . . Still, when you think it over, there really is something in all this. Whatever anyone says, occurrences like these do happen in the world. Not too often; but they do happen" (3:75).

The most extraordinary thing about this fantastic story is that nobody in it thinks it is fantastic. Unusual possibly, maybe even incongruous—but incongruity, as our narrator tells us, is everywhere, even if most people prefer not to notice what is as plain as the noses on their faces.

The question of reality has been raised again, along with the themes of isolation, the ego, and outward form versus inner substance, the last of which was so emphasized, in another context, in "Nevsky Prospekt." Nowhere is anyone, not even Kovalyov himself, concerned with the essence of the man himself—appearance is always what matters; and appearance, as we know from the other Petersburg stories, is very deceptive—it is often, indeed, a fraud.

I do not think, as Evdokimov does, that this is because of devilish possession, that Satan is behind it all. For Gogol, this was never more than a device to be used in the Little Russian stories, but the loss—or absence—of soul here seems to be a subtler matter. Here Gogol deliberately brings in a certain rational element; that is, everybody brings his reason to bear on the problem and solves it in a way that is satisfactory to his own peace of mind. We are even given a good reason for the barber's being involved in the affair (although not for his loaf of bread's) before the story is over. After all, a barber handles a man's nose quite often—what more natural than that his hand should slip, take a swipe, and cut a nose clean off? When one loses something, what more reasonable than to advertise for it, go to the police about it, and accuse someone of having taken it? Should not a physician analyze, diagnose, and prescribe?

All reactions to the situation are perfectly sane. But the situation is such that sanity, or rationality, is useless; things are *not* as they should be, and rational answers are no answers at all. In this world, reason is the fraud, for it is a world beyond reason's power even to recognize, much less understand. From reason's point of view, whatever happens, no matter how strange, cannot be contrary to law; therefore, it is not, to reverse Hegel. Even Kovalyov regards the affair as more of an inconvenience than anything else, one to get over as rapidly and sensibly as possible. He does not wonder at it so much as fret about it. He wants to know how it could have happened, what it might mean; he speaks to his nose when he meets it in church in the normal terms of his world—and is answered in exactly the same terms. At this point, Kovalyov sees a pretty girl, thinks of picking her up, and then, in after-thought, remembers the blank space in the middle of his visage. This reduces him to despair, because he is prevented from being himself, that is, from being the fraud he has always been.[24] Of course, Kovalyov does not know that he is a fraud (he would have to have a sense of reality for that), so that when he is confronted with his own emptiness, he refuses to recognize it for what it is.[25] When his nose ("his" nose, he insists) is restored to him—as suddenly as it was taken away— "Major Kovalyov . . . sauntered about as though nothing had happened, on Nevsky Prospekt, in the theaters, and everywhere" (3:74–75). The nose, as though it has given up, sticks to his face "also as though nothing had happened, showing not even a sign of any difference at the sides" (3:75).

Rationality is restored, and nobody need ever worry again, except for the warning in the last lines that occurrences like this "do happen in the world." On the whole, however, the failure of the experiment must be emphasized, as the narrator indicates when he says: "In the first place, there is decidedly no profit of any kind to the fatherland; in the second . . . but there is no profit in the second either" (3:75). What he means is that no one is likely to take any profit from the and it certainly did not do anybody in the story any good. The false, now connected with the rational, appears to reign everywhere.[26]

Part of the reason for the failure, within the story, is the egoistic concentration of the participants. This is nicely exemplified in the policeman who returns the nose. His conversation constantly slips away from the subject at hand and reverts to himself and his own particular concerns. Having been asked by Kovalyov how he happened to come by the nose, the policeman replies that he caught it in the guise of an official on the coach to Riga, which was very lucky, because the police-experiment, for the world of the audience is much like that in the story, man, who is very near-sighted, just happened to have his glasses with him. "My mother-in-law," he says, "that is, my wife's mother, doesn't see anything either" (3:66).

When asked where the nose is, the policeman tells of his suspicions of the barber, whom he took into custody. As a sort of afterthought, the nose is given to Kovalyov. Then, when asked to tea, the policeman replies: "I would consider it a great pleasure, but there is just no way. From here I have to go to the penitentiary. . . . Everything has got very expensive. . . . My mother-in-law, that is, my wife's mother, lives at my house, and there are the children; the eldest, in particular, shows great promise: he's a very intelligent boy, but there's no way to get the means for his education" (3:67).

No one asks—nor does Gogol indicate—how the nose grew to the stature of an official, then shrank back to a size proper to fit into a pocket. Such questions are quite beside the point of the actual possession of the nose; it is property. The nose is valuable because, like the title of Major, like a wife with a large dowry, or like the wearing of a medal (after the nose is restored to him, we are told, Kovalyov bought the ribbon of an order "for some unknown reason, since he was not a knight of any order himself"; 3:75), it lends a certain status to its owner, or, to be more accurate, its absence deprives him of a certain status, he believes. Other people have their possessions: the policeman his mother-in-law; the physician his "noble carriage"; the newspaper clerk his officiousness. And each defines himself in terms of his possessions. Since possessions confer standing, or "position," one would expect a certain amount of cohesiveness among the possessors, one would expect them all to "belong." But cohesiveness does not occur, because there is nothing to cohere with.[27] Unity, in Gogol's view, could not be realized in this way, for unity can be accomplished only in the realm of spirit, not in the realm of matter. Matter, indeed—and this was also true of his Little Russian tales—is illusion at best, fraud at worst.[28] This is not to say that Gogol was taking a Manichean stance, since the contest is not between two hostile powers, but between what is and what is not. The fault lies in the acceptance of the fraudulent for the true; and Gogol, the teacher and servant, is trying to point out the distinction for the sake of the realization of spiritual unity and harmony, of beauty, of salvation.

As we have suggested, each of the individuals who appears in "The Nose" lives, if it can be called that, in isolation, a separate element who is unaware of, or denies, his own spiritual essence, trying materially to "get ahead." It is indeed extraordinary that no one in the story is changed in the slightest by the experience, as Gogol hoped at least his audience would be. This does not, however, make Gogol a social writer in this tale. It is not social justice that he is interested in, not a revision of a political or economic system, and certainly not revolt.[29] Rather, he is attempting to accomplish a spiritual recognition of beauty, truth, and reality. By withholding this recognition from the people in his fictional works, he stressed its necessity to his readers.

The last of Gogol's Petersburg tales, in terms of both composition and publication, is "The Overcoat," a story that has been even more anthologized, in English as well as in Russian, than "The Nose." We have often been told that this story started the theme of the "little man" in Russian literature; and the apocryphal remark by Dostoevsky that "we all crawled out from under Gogol's overcoat" has been cited time and time again, even while those citing it have pointed out the absence of any such remark in the known writings of Dostoevsky. One must note, first, that it is one of Gogol's last stories, written after *The Inspector General* and after a good deal of *Dead Souls,* Part 1, had been finished. It is therefore what critics like to call a "mature" work.[30] Since it is generally regarded as "Gogol's most remarkable short narrative," as Erlich puts it,[31] a few words about its critical reception, in general terms, may be in order.[32]

The most popular reaction, until comparatively recently, has been to regard "The Overcoat" as a great humanitarian expression of Gogol's concern for the poor and the downtrodden, an appeal to the conscience of society—in the same class as Dickens's more sentimental passages, so that Akaky Akakyevich becomes a kind of middle-aged Russian Little Nell.[33] Most contemporary scholars who are acquainted with Gogol's social opinions are in agreement: whatever Gogol intended, that was not it; and this opinion is more suited to the critics' prejudices than it is to Gogol's (it is still the standard Soviet view).

Second is the more common contemporary interpretation, since *poshlost'* has been rediscovered, that the story is an attack, in what is presumed to be the usual Gogolian vein, on triviality. Akaky Akakyevich is here analyzed as a man who is eternally attached to things that do not matter, such as calligraphy; and the overcoat itself is considered an object too minor to be worthy of a man's serious and wholehearted concern, even though Gogol emphasizes the cold of the winter that Akaky Akakyevich must face.

Third is the view that, while Gogol himself seems to have been peculiarly sexless, the story is full of erotic imagery which, paradoxically, emphasizes the failure of Akaky Akakyevich as a human being. There is the further implication that Gogol, the eternal pessimist, is attacking the triviality of most human pursuits. From this Freudian angle, Akaky Akakyevich turns out to be a kind of negative hero.

Fourth is the approach of the formalist critics who concentrate on Gogol's style, the extraordinary twists and turns of his language, from which the meaning arises. Unfortunately, brilliant as these analyses are, they cannot be of much help to the reader of English (Gogol is often far from easy stylistically even for a Russian). Allied to this approach is the discussion of Gogol's art in terms of the grotesque. Ordinary life, normal perception, is here accepted as a precarious reality, and what happens in this story is that the delicate balance is upset, or thrown into confusion, by the powers of evil with which Gogol was obsessed. This view, which has of late become very popular, makes Gogol a writer, like Kafka, whose fiction is imbued with the absurd. As Erlich puts it, "the grotesque effect occurs when what seemed familiar and natural suddenly turned out to be strange and ominous. . . . [The world has been] unmasked as chaotic and absurd, vulnerable to the dark, demonic forces."[34]

Last is what might be called the religious attitude, according to which Gogol is concerned to show the nature of evil: he made a "descent to hell," à la Dante, and returned to tell us of what he had seen and thus save the world.[35]

All of these approaches, and combinations of them, can be—and have been—well argued. As the reader will discover, my own interpretation is by no means independent of several of them. What we must first recognize is that Gogol's primary aim was to expose the fraudulent, which must of necessity appear trivial. But the trivial is a consequence of the fraudulent, not its cause. Furthermore, Gogol's persons are typical because of their fraudulence, not because of their reality, for they have lost themselves. This point is made at the very beginning of "The Overcoat," where Gogol writes:

> In the department of . . . but it's better not to name the department. Nothing of any kind can get more irate than departments, regiments, offices, and, in short, any kind of official association. These days, every private person considers all society insulted in his person. It's said that not long ago a

petition from a certain police superintendent—I don't remember from what town—was received, and in it he clearly set forth that government institutions were perishing and that his sacred name was absolutely being taken in vain. As evidence he appended to the petition a huge volume of some romantic work in which a police superintendent appeared on every tenth page, in some passages even completely drunk. So, to avoid any unpleasantness, we had better call the department that is our setting *a* department. [3:141]

This lack of specificity implies a lack of humanity, for it implies the same identification with "things" that we have already observed in Gogol's work. The approach is Gogol's usual one of exclusion of specificity for the purpose of *in*clusion of the general, and thus of the typical. By informing the reader that he is is not discussing anyone in particular, Gogol lets us know that he is discussing everyone in general.[36] This is reinforced by the description of Akaky Akakyevich, who is far from being a remarkable man, despite his rather odd appearance, which, we are told, is not really so very odd, because of the "Petersburg climate" (3:141). His rank is, of course, of importance, because you cannot mention anyone in Russia without his rank; and his rank turns out to be a very common one, the same as Poprishchin's: he is a titular councillor. As for his name, although at first sight it may appear to be unusual, yet it turns out to have been an inevitable choice, Gogol tells us. When we turn to his position in the office, he is the original faceless man, the symbol of the "silent majority." Akaky Akakyevich remains this "average man," rather than "little man"—much to the unadmitted chagrin of the reader, who is himself "average"—until he acquires his new overcoat. To one symbol is added another.[37] With the overcoat, Akaky Akakyevich—Everyman—puts on flesh. He enters the physical world, as though passing through a second birth, so that the faceless one acquires a face; the silent, a voice; and *akakos* becomes acquainted with *kakos*. Still Akaky Akakyevich is bewildered, as the work that he does emphasizes, for he is a copier of documents. When once asked to write a report based on a document he had been given, he was incapable of doing so, even though "the work consisted only of changing chapter headings and in some spots changing pronouns from the first person to the third" (3:144).

Indeed, the entire description of Akaky Akakyevich in these early passages, before the overcoat is acquired, makes a point of his inability to enter into physical life, of his nonmateriality. He is the Everyman who has not yet experienced, who has not yet been tempted and then fallen. Assuredly, there is no malice, much less evil, in him. This is the uncorrupted silent majority, unattached to the world of ambition and physical pleasure. I would suggest that "The Overcoat," if considered this way, is Gogol's greatest tale of corruption, not by spiritual forces (to Gogol, "corruption by spiritual forces" would be an absurdity), but by physical ones. In this sense, "The Overcoat" is the story of man's fall. It is a fall that occurs, however, through lack of clear perception on the hero's part, through a lack of appreciation of his own innocence; he loses his innocence because he did not know he had it.

Akaky Akakyevich did not wish to buy a new overcoat. All he wanted originally was to patch up his old coat, which was so ragged that it was transparent in places; it has never occurred to him that his "self" should be obscured from the world, that he should deceive. To be regarded, to be singled out, has never been his desire. But then he meets the tailor, Grigory Petrovich, who has come to be known simply by his patronymic, son of Peter.[38] Through Petrovich, matter enters Akaky Akakyevich's life; through him, Akaky Akakyevich loses innocence. "The Overcoat" becomes a kind of *Paradise Lost,* with Books 11 and 12 unfortunately missing. But Gogol's entire career was a quest for that Paradise lost, and one could conclude that he died hoping that in that way, divorced from matter, he would attain it.

Akaky Akakyevich's old overcoat has been getting more and more threadbare (ancient) year by year; still he would like to hang on to it. But Petrovich refuses to mend it; Akaky Akakyevich must have a new one. This is not only something unexpected; it is not real: "At the word 'new' there was a cloud before Akaky Akakyevich's eyes, and everything in the room was confused. . . . 'What? a new one?' he said, as though finding himself still in a dream" (3:151). When Akaky Akakyevich leaves Petrovich, who feels "gratified that he had not discredited himself and had not betrayed the tailor's art" (3:152), he walks off "completely in the opposite direction" (3:152). The policeman he bumps into asks, "What are you poking into my mug for, isn't the sidewalk enough for you?" (3:152). Akaky Akakyevich has entered the material world, and when he gets home, for the first time in his life he begins "to collect his thoughts, he [sees] his position in a clear and genuine way, [begins] to converse with himself not jerkily but sensibly and candidly, as with a prudent friend with whom one can talk about serious and intimate matters" (3:152).

Although he makes one more effort, there is no escape, and Akaky Akakyevich begins to hoard his money, not simply putting by two kopeks for every ruble spent, as he had done for years; he now bends all his efforts, depriving himself of the barest necessities, in order to collect "the capital for the overcoat" (3:153). His privations become habitual, but he puts up with them because "he was nourished inwardly by carrying the eternal idea of the overcoat in his thoughts. From this time forth, his existence became, so to speak, fuller, as though he were married, as though he felt another person with him, as though he were not alone and some pleasant girl friend had agreed to walk the path of life with him" (3:154).[39] The female imagery of this passage is deliberate, not, however, because of "the incongruously erotic quality of its imagery," not because the images "suggest a displacement of the libido," as Erlich puts it,[40] but because, following the symbolism suggested in notes 38 and 39, the Whore of Babylon is replacing Mother Church. At the same time, they indicate Akaky Akakyevich's entrance into the false everyday world.[41] After this passage, Gogol describes the change that came over Akaky Akakyevich in terms that emphasize his being in this world and, at long last, capable of dealing with it; he now exhibits the qualities usually thought to be necessary for cutting a figure, for being a man among men: "He became, as it were, more alive, even firmer of character, like a man who has made a decision and set up a goal for himself. Doubt and indecision of themselves vanished from his face and conduct—in short, all hesitant and indefinite features. At times a fire appeared in his eyes, and the boldest and most daring thoughts flashed through his brain" (3:154–55). Akaky Akakyevich, in other words, feels that he is capable of taking a place among the buyers and sellers, the seekers for power, the confident actors in the world. So risen is he, so much more esteemed (despite the fact that he is, rather interestingly, more prone to make mistakes in his copying than he used to be), that he receives a material reward: he is given twenty rubles more as a bonus than he had any reason to expect, which means that the overcoat can be made immediately. It is, and Akaky Akakyevich's colleagues look at him with new eyes. For the first time in his life, in celebration of his acquired status, Akaky Akakyevich goes to a party, to his rebaptism. Curiously enough, although Akaky Akakyevich's new overcoat instigated the agitation for a party, the party is given by another clerk whose birthday it happens to be—the identity that Akaky Akakyevich thought he was gaining is in reality a loss of identity. Gogol spends only a few lines on a description of the party itself, but many on his hero's passage through the city on his way to and from the party—the lively streets, the physical movement, an advertisement in a shop window, and so forth. Akaky Akakyevich, although he does not yet really know what to do with this world, is pleased. Having "put on the flesh," he enjoys it; he even comes close to chasing after a woman he encounters on his way. As he passes on, however, the streets that he walks along become increasingly empty, until he finally reaches a huge square with only a lonely sentry box on the far side. The former innocent is alone, resting on his own resources, trusting to the magic of his new faith, a magic that is fulfilled in the ultimate of physical expressions, violence: he is beaten, and the overcoat is stolen from him. However, the sentry in his box, who witnessed the incident, saw nothing of robbery and assault—to him it was a meeting of friends, as indeed, from the viewpoint that I have been trying to suggest, it was. Akaky Akakyevich is conquered by the very materiality that he had been seduced to espouse. Even when he returns after death, it is in a fleshly guise rather than in the spirit, in the guise of corruption rather than purified (we are reminded of figures in the Little Russian tales who returned after death). Gogol tells us very carefully that it is Akaky Akakyevich's *corpse* (*mertvyets*), not his spirit or ghost, that has appeared to snatch overcoats from passersby; he repeats, even perpetuates, the very violence that he himself suffered—it is inherent in his changed nature, the nature of *akakos* become *kakos*, of Adam become Cain. This might have been a tragedy, but Akaky Akakyevich was lowered, not elevated. Instead of being illuminated by reality, he was blinded by falsity.

But Akaky Akakyevich's adventure has a further result in the figure of the Person of Great Consequence, who is changed, after suffering, in exactly the opposite direction from that taken by Akaky Akakyevich. The life of the Person of Great Consequence had been a fraud. He, like "everyone in Holy Russia, was infected with imitation"; like "everyone, [he] mimics and poses as his superiors" (3:164) and demands this kind of behavior from those below him. But now, after being grabbed by the corpse and after throwing his overcoat from his shoulders (rather than waiting for the corpse to snatch it, thus indicating a reversal, spiritually, of Akaky Akakyevich's action when he lost his overcoat), the Person of Great Consequence is greatly altered in his relations with others: "Far more seldom did he say to his subordinates, 'How dare you? Do you understand who is in front of you?' and he never uttered them at all without first having sounded out the entire affair" (3:173). If we want a moral from the story, it is that the path of the Person of Great Consequence is the more proper one: spirit should be gained, not lost; material fraud should be rejected in favor of spiritual truth. Suffering should ennoble, not demean.

Seldom did Gogol so explicitly speak of the loss of innocence as he did in "The Overcoat." Akaky Akakyevich falls prey to a falsity that destroys him, symbolized by the overcoat and the attitude that he adopts towards it. That overcoat becomes as important to him as his nose did to Kovalyov. It means, and brings, a new life—one like that of other men, unfortunately, for Akaky Akakyevich is accepted; and this, because it is riveted upon the material world—and only the material world—means the loss of innocence. Harmony, beauty, and truth are traded for material deception; integrity is exchanged for appearance in the eyes of others.

In direct contrast with most of the Petersburg tales stands the fragment "Rome," which was first published under this title in the collected edition of Gogol's works in 1842. However, it was probably conceived some time around the summer of 1839 as a tale or novel to be entitled *Annunziata*. Certainly, this is the title that Gogol used when he read it to friends in Moscow early in 1840. He read a revision of it in February 1842, and it was published under the title "A Fragment" one month later in the newly founded journal *Muscovite*. It is the only story (after "Hanz Kuechelgarten") set outside the confines of Russia. More important, however, it was conceived and worked on at the same time that Gogol conceived and wrote "The Overcoat" (it also coincides with the latter portions of *Dead Souls,* as well as with revisions of various other works, in particular the one that resulted in the final version of "The Portrait"). It would therefore be too much to ask that there be radical changes of ideas among these works. Rather, what should be expected is the same, or similar, ideas attacked from different angles. This is precisely what happened.

Since "Rome" is probably one of the least known of Gogol's works to readers of English (I am not acquainted with any translation of it), a short outline would seem apropos. The story begins with a vision of loveliness, Annunziata, with whom a young Roman prince is in love, although he has only seen her, not met her (one is reminded of Dante's *La Vita Nuova*). After the description of Annunziata, Gogol uses a flashback to tell us how the prince's love came about. Of an old patrician Roman family, he was first tutored by a monk, then sent to the University of Lucca, which was at the time under strong French influence. His great desire was to go to the country beyond the Alps, there to learn of the true Europe, which is so attractive from afar. In France is supposedly all the vitality of the modern world. The young man's desire is fulfilled, and he is sent to the Sorbonne to continue his studies. Actually, Gogol's description makes him sound more like a Russian than an Italian coming to the capital of civilization, Paris, that "bazaar of Europe," which completely fascinates him at first by its very confusion. He becomes a Parisian—that is, as Gogol makes clear, a superficial dandy. He is delighted and excited by the lectures at the Sorbonne, brilliant intellectual exercises that send his brain in a whirl. What a wonderful place it is, "where you grow taller, where you feel you are a member of a great universal society!" (3:226).

But with the passage of time the prince becomes disillusioned. All the activity of the city "vanished without issue, leaving no fruitful spiritual sediment" (3:227). Here are many words, but no acts, a search for novelty at any price, even in commerce. Everything has a lack of proportion, and the prince recalls a poem by Alfieri:

> Tutto fanno, nulla sanno,
> Tutto sanno, nulla fanno,
> Giravolta son Francesi,
> Piu gli pesi, men ti danno.[42]

He decides that France is but "a light vaudeville, engendered by itself" (3:228). Finally, the prince returns to Italy, investigates his own country, and discovers a harmonious fusion of the centuries in Italy's history and an august serenity in its people. In particular is he struck by the works of the Renaissance—and this reader, for one, believes that here Gogol is speaking for himself. The genius of Italy is artistic, while its people is imbued with dignity. After having reached these conclusions, accompanied by a certain grave inner calm, he sees Annunziata, the very incarnation of all he had discovered; and it is in quest of her that the fragment ends, as it began.[43]

The tale seems clear. In one sense, it is obviously a return, if return were needed, to Gogol's early essay "Woman."[44] Its celebration of immaterial value, of unity and harmony, of beauty, both in history and art, establishes a link also with various of Gogol's other works, from "The Portrait" (which in one French edition of Gogol's works is printed in a separate section along with "Rome")[45] to "The Overcoat," in that the same scale is established in them all: the falsity of immediate earthly concerns; the deceptions; the fraudulence, indeed, of monetary material considerations, which is exemplified finally by France; and the superiority of general harmonious truth and beauty, which is exemplified finally by Italy, in its history, its art, and its people. It would be well on this score to keep in mind the much-ignored essays on both art and history that Gogol published in *Arabesques* in 1835, as well as the articles that he was to publish in *Selected Passages from Correspondence with Friends* in 1847. In all these cases Gogol was pleading for a recognition of his vision. The teacher, in quest of beauty himself and possessed of a vision, was convinced that this beauty meant salvation for mankind in general as much as for his Italian prince.

In "The Diary of a Madman," "The Nose," and "The Overcoat," Gogol had tried to approach his subject indirectly; but despite the impact of these stories, from his point of view, he failed to get his point across. In "The Portrait" and "Rome," as in his essays, he tried the direct approach, and because of the lack of impact, he failed again. The failures came about because the very thing that Gogol was protesting against—materiality—was also the very thing that interested— he would have said seduced—his readers. The laughter, meant to unmask and convert, instead confirmed convictions of superiority and righteousness in the very ones whom he was attempting to teach. It might be said that he was too good for his own good.

In short, Hanz Kuechelgarten, reincarnated in the Italian prince, sets out on his quest once again. He does not return disillusioned, because he is older and because Annunziata, the significance of whose name hardly bears comment, still flits before him. As Gogol said in "Nights in a Villa," his lament over the death of a young friend which was written in 1839, "How horrid are all these riches and honors, these resounding enticements of the puppets we call men." And he proceeds to recall an innocent youth, now gone.

4

The Theater

As is well known, Gogol was interested in the theater from his school days in Little Russia. He even, we are told, got a tryout as an actor when he first arrived in Petersburg, and many who knew him later have testified to his acting abilities. Through much of his career, furthermore, he tried to write plays. As with his prose fiction, however, he wrote only one full-length piece,[1] *The Inspector General*, which is usually regarded as the greatest comedy ever produced in Russian. Like his prose works, further, the plays underwent constant revision. Here it might be helpful to give a table of the plays, with such dates concerning each as are appropriate:

1. *The Cross of St. Vladimir, Third Class*, the first that we know of, was probably conceived in 1832. All that we have, however, and probably all that were written, are four scenes:
   a. "A Morning of a Man-of-Affairs," written in 1834 or 1835, published in the *Contemporary* in April 1836, republished in the collected edition of Gogol's works in 1842
   b. "The Law Suit," read by Gogol in October 1839, published in the collected edition of 1842, first performed in September 1844
   c. "The Flunkeys," probably written in late 1839 or early 1840, published in the collected edition of 1842
   d. "A Fragment," published in the collected edition of 1842
2. *Marriage* was probably conceived with the title *The Suitors* in mid 1833; read, with this title, by Gogol in the spring of 1834; redone, shifting the scene from a small town to Petersburg, in the spring of 1835; again read by Gogol, under the title *Marriage*, in September 1835; revised in 1836, 1839, 1840, 1841; pro-

duced in Petersburg in December 1842; published in the collected edition of 1842; produced in Moscow in February 1843.

3. *The Gamblers* was begun in the autumn of 1834, worked on
intermittently until a complete revision was accomplished in the
spring of 1842; published in the collected edition of 1842; produced in Moscow in February 1843, in Petersburg in April 1843.

4. *Alfred,* a play about the English king, was begun in the summer
or fall of 1835. All that we have of the play is a beginning fragment. It was not published during Gogol's lifetime.

5. *The Inspector General* was, according to Gogol, suggested to
him by Pushkin in 1835, in the fall of which year he wrote the
entire first version; produced in Petersburg, 19 April 1836,
before the tsar; in Moscow, 25 May 1836; revised five times
over the next seven years before its publication in the collected
edition of 1842. There is evidence that Gogol was thinking of
another revision shortly before his death in February 1852.

6. *Leaving the Theater after the Presentation of a New Comedy*
was written in May 1836, revised in the spring of 1842, and
published in the collected edition of 1842.

7. *The Dénouement of "The Inspector General"* was written in
late 1846 along with a preface to *The Inspector General;* it was
read by several persons over the next few years, but was not
published during Gogol's lifetime.

8. *A Zaporozhian Tragedy* was conceived in 1839/40 as a play
based on Zaporozhian Cossack history. There is a report that
Gogol read the beginning of it to Panov in September 1840;
there is a further report that he read it to Zhukovsky, who fell
asleep during the reading, in September 1841. After this second
reading, Gogol destroyed the work; all that we have is a few
notes for dramas taken from Ukrainian history.

In its way, this is a strange history, filled with false starts and
endless reworkings, while the one complete full-length piece was, at
least in its first version, completed in a few months. On the other hand,
the idea for *The Cross of St. Vladimir, Third Class* was certainly a good
one: the central character was to be so obsessed by the ambition to
attain the decoration that he would go mad at the end and imagine
that he had turned into the cross himself. It was as good a comic (and
serious) concept as Gogol had ever had, similar in its aim and atmosphere to "The Nose," "The Overcoat," and "Diary of a Madman." Indeed, some elements of it seem to have been transferred to these stories.
But the play itself was never achieved, and one may speculate that it

was because Gogol could not here bring form and content together. The reader finds it very difficult even to connect the four scenes as fragments of a united whole, which is doubly strange when we consider that Gogol thought of the drama as a tightly knit, precise form. In the section of "A Textbook of Literature for Russian Youth" devoted to the novel, Gogol also tells us how he thinks of the drama. The novel, he says,

> like the drama, . . . is an extremely structured composition. It also contains a strict and sensibly thought-out plot. All persons obliged to act, or, better, among whom the action must take place, must be set up . . . by the author. . . . Whatever is there, is there only because it is closely connected with the fate of the hero. . . . [It must be] unified by a vivid interest in the persons of the main incident in which the dramatis personae are entangled, . . . which . . . compels the dramatis personae to develop and disclose their characters. [8:481]

The drama, thus, must be tightly constructed on the basis of plot and character. Gogol's detailed stage directions and, in the case of *The Inspector General,* character sketches indicate just how seriously he took his dramatic principles. In addition, he played close attention to all details of production. It is precisely these details that he could not work out for *The Cross of St. Vladimir, Third Class.* Instead of a plot, he had an idea and several incidents. Instead of character development, he had a number of separate, static styles. One might also say that the intrigue involved too many levels for them to be brought together and straightened out.

"A Morning of a Man-of-Affairs" was clearly intended to be the opening scene of the play. Here, situation, some characters, and theme —the pursuit of the decoration—are set. Each person lives under a mask and believes that his mask has succeeded, while at the same time he thinks he sees through the masks the others are wearing. The great theme of reality and truth is proposed, without, however, any serious hint as to how it will be resolved. Perhaps Gogol himself did not know how to resolve it. The scene stops just as we are informed that something is to follow which may well make life different for the central character, but that is all.

"The Law Suit" seems to have little connection with "A Morning of a Man-of-Affairs." It is, rather, a sketch or skit that would find a proper place in a revue,[2] although the central character might be either of the main persons introduced in "A Morning of a Man-of-Affairs." It also might be a new beginning, since without great, and probably unwarranted, inventiveness on the part of the reader, it advances nothing. In effect, we have a repetition of the themes of deception and ego, with truth being no one's concern. Nor does either of the other two fragments advance the intrigue. They, too, are set comic skits as they stand, rather than discernible parts of a larger whole.

Obviously, these fragments, while amusing, at times biting, and always displaying a great command of dialogue, are not in themselves vital pieces of theater.[3] Their importance lies, rather, in that they demonstrate Gogol's continual preoccupation with the subject of dehumanization through deception. The characters display neither dignity nor compassion, they are only isolated voids attempting to assume various guises. Only in his great works will these egos appear as false as the masks they wear, or, in other words, will the "hollow men" come on stage.

Marriage: A Thoroughly Improbable Incident in Two Acts, made its point in its first title, *The Suitors;* for each of the persons in the play, empty in himself, is suing for material status, for position in the world of matter. Marriage is an excuse for something else: a dowry, social position, comfort, self-esteem, revenge, social legitimization (for the girl), and so forth. Thus we are again in a situation involving masks and deception, of self as well as of others. There is no hypocrisy, for until the end, there is no recognition of truth. On the other hand, *Marriage* is one of the few of Gogol's works after some of the Little Russian stories to have a happy ending.[4] This happy ending occurs, however, through rejection rather than through assertion. The hero, Podkolyosin, finally recognizes that he is a person after all, and he revolts against pretense and returns to his bachelor life. Everyone else may be discomfited at the failure of plans; he, at least, has escaped. It is in this that the ending is happy; it would have been unhappy if the marriage that Podkolyosin was being pushed into had come off.

Fortunately, or unfortunately, the subtitle also describes the play. Like so much of Gogol's work, it is episodic; that is, despite Gogol's strict view of what constituted a drama, there is little plot movement or character development. In a sense, the play is remarkably successful in keeping up our interest by making us wonder *if* there will be any such changes. In fact, what we get is at best a return to the *status quo ante*—a device that Gogol was to use again, although much more skill-

fully and pointedly, in *The Inspector General*. Rarely, perhaps because
he viewed the truth as absolute and nonmaterial, did Gogol indicate
change coming about because of action, since action takes place in the
realm of matter.

The great themes still remain unresolved. Lies and deception are
exposed, but truth is not revealed in anything but a superficial sense.
Podkolyosin's recognition is, in the final analysis, a recognition of fact—
that is, where his own advantage lies—and no more. In this sense, he
is as empty as the others, and his "truth" is equally pretentious. The
escape, despite what we said above, is no escape at all, so that the play
cannot be resolved. Gogol was still unable to say "how"; he could only
say "what." The final result is thus more exposure than it is revelation,
pointing out error of judgment, but not asserting reality. Despite the
lack of love interest, it is a traditional work in which the intriguers are
all foiled at the end, so that the audience can leave the theater without
any feeling of discomfort: as in traditional comedy, we are superior to
the characters; we can be rather smug gods who are never seriously
involved.

The Gamblers is also a "slight" play, despite its epigraph, "An
affair of days long past," which was taken from Pushkin's *Ruslan and
Ludmilla,* a poem that has nothing at all to do with *The Gamblers*.[5]
Interestingly enough, when it was published in the collected edition of
1842, this was the first work to be printed in volume 4, under the general title of "Dramatic Fragments and Separate Scenes." Gogol himself
apparently did not think of it as a complete, full-length piece.

Again, the action is dominated by deception, with an additional
twist in that at the end the deceiver is deceived. Unfortunately, this does
not mean the defeat of deception itself, or even a recognition on the
part of the central character, Ikharev, that there was anything wrong
with his own attempts at fraud beyond their having failed. His last
lines, and the last of the play, are:

> That such swindlers should exist is a shame and an abuse of
> mankind! I'm simply ready to go out of my mind—how dam-
> nably it was all played! How subtly! . . . To be crafty after this!
> To be subtle of mind! . . . It's not worth the noble zeal, the
> effort! A cheat will sidle up and outcheat you! . . . What an
> underhanded country! Luck only comes to stupid dopes who
> understand nothing, think about nothing, do nothing—all

they can do is play boston for pennies with secondhand cards!
[5:100–101]

The play, in short, is about a wise guy who gets his comeuppance, for Ikharev had shortly before said, "To spend your life as a fool spends his life is no trick, but to spend your life with subtlety, with art, to deceive everyone without being deceived yourself—that's a real mission and goal!" (5:98). What he does not understand, of course, is that he has already deceived himself, and is continuing to do so.

But virtue does not triumph from the other side either, for the "winners" are merely greater cheats than the cheat whom they cheated. In this sense, this little comedy lays a trap for the audience, for the only people we are likely to identify with are the outstanding cheaters, who are not by any means lovable rogues. We are left with the uneasy feeling that the lack of profit in crime depends upon the criminal; at the same time, we have the pleasant feeling (unjustified) that we would do better. There is nothing to offset the spiritual ugliness of being possessed by greed and deception. In this sense, *The Gamblers* is as cynical and depressing a work as any that Gogol wrote.

Equally important, however, is the play's demonstration of Gogol's mastery of theatrical technique. Here we do have change occurring carefully and increasingly rapidly, building to a prepared but unexpected ending. Still, the audience believes it has escaped, for the blow seems to fall upon a character in the play rather than upon the audience itself. It would take *The Inspector General* for Gogol to manage the trick of having the blow fall equally upon both, without either being able to avoid it.

The Inspector General is certainly Gogol's theatrical masterpiece, both from the point of view of technique and from the point of view of theme. But from the time of its first productions in 1836, Gogol insisted that he had been misunderstood: his revisions over the years were aimed at making his meaning clearer.[6] Immediately after its production he wrote to Pushkin (although the letter was never sent and was not published, as "A Letter to a Writer," until the 1841 edition of the play), complaining about the reception that his work had received, because, he said, even those who liked it, liked it for the wrong reasons.[7]

The main revisions of the play really change little of the original of 1836. They are contained in the material that Gogol inscribed for the second edition of 1841: the drunken monologue of Khlestakov towards the end of act 3; the whole beginning of act 4; the Mayor's explosion toward the ends of act 5; the living-statue scene at the end; and two scenes that had been suppressed in 1836 (and separately printed in 1841) because they "held back the action." For the collected edition of 1842 Gogol redid the closing living-statue scene; added the Mayor's famous line, "What are you laughing at? You're laughing at yourselves," to his explosion; and added the epigraph, "Don't blame the mirror if your mug is off-center." In 1851, marking a copy of the 1842 edition, Gogol changed Khlestakov's "Beautiful codfish! beautiful codfish!" just before he passes out in act 3. The definitive edition, and the one usually used for translations, includes all the revisions except the two "suppressed scenes" (the first of which fits into scene 3, act 3, and the second between scenes 6 and 7 of act 4).[8] None of the revisions, save possibly the living-statue scene and the emphasis that Gogol placed upon it, seriously changes either the direction or the impact of the play (in my opinion, the "What are you laughing at?" line, although much has been made of it, merely makes Gogol's point more obvious; it does not change it).

Certainly, *The Inspector General* is the most solidly constructed of Gogol's theatrical pieces, and given the professional control of plot and character development, one cannot help but wonder if Pushkin, whom Gogol acknowledged as the source of the idea for the comedy, did not help Gogol with more than just the idea. There is no evidence that he did so, but neither before nor after *The Inspector General* did Gogol display such command of his material in the drama.

Gogol was disappointed not only in the reception accorded his play but also in its production. For him, for example, the central character was Khlestakov, but the stars of both the Petersburg and Moscow productions, two of the best-known actors of the day, chose to act the part of the Mayor. In addition, the work was played for its farcical possibilities, and farce was the furthest thing from Gogol's mind. In a note to the edition of 1841, which was not, however, published until 1889, he said: "Above all, one must be careful not to fall into caricature; nothing must be exaggerated . . . even the smallest roles. . . . The less the actor tries to make people laugh, the better the comic in his role will come out" (4:371). In his "Letter to a Writer" of 1836, Gogol had already complained that Khlestakov was being played for farce, or for vaudeville, which was exactly the wrong way to play him.

As Gogol further implies, the point about Khlestakov, central character though he may be, is that he is an *excuse* for the action rather than an actor himself.[9] He is, in a very profound sense, anonymous—the central void around which the others circle, revealing in this not only their own banality, their *poshlost'*, but their incredible degree of deception, so that they deceive even themselves. They have become so dehumanized as to be parodies of human beings, men turned upside down, not as they are in reality but as they have falsified themselves. I would suggest that much of the humor of the play arises precisely from parody rather than from realism or, for that matter, from incongruity.

One of the difficulties with *The Inspector General,* as well as one of its marks of greatness, is its susceptibility to a variety of interpretations. Depending on the critic's particular bias, these interpretations range from social criticism, to a political attack, to Freudian complexes, to metaphysical revelations, to good, not-always-so-clean, fun. In the context of Gogol's own interests, prejudices, and statements, however, it is still highly likely that he remained concerned with his vision of truth and beauty as immaterial absolutes to be sought, rather than as concrete manifestations. Satan continues to be the father of lies.

This is not to imply, as Evdokimov, for one, does, that Khlestakov is an agent of the devil, a deceiver who, Mephistopheles-like, attempts to entrap people. His role is catalytic rather than deliberate, for what happens, happens because of decisions to falsify, decisions that have been made long before the play opens. In other words, Gogol is not dealing here with people as they are in reality, but as they have falsified themselves. For this reason, he could with justice claim that not one character in the piece was based on anything in the real world. He does not mean for the audience to see itself on stage as it really is, but as it might convince itself it is. It is all a lie, in short, but so obviously one that the truth should be revealed. This is the reason that no one in the play acts in consciousness of either himself or of his relations with others. Yet each person's ego is of vital importance to him, although in reality no one has a true self, only an obsession. Instead of being real, these selves are imaginary. In this sense, the events of the play constitute a fantasy, constructed by the imaginations of those within it—a diary of madmen.

It seems to me that this imaginary quality in the play is the crux of the matter, for the implication is that the world that is presented on stage—the world that some members of Gogol's audience in outrage identified themselves with; the world of deceit, which they thought real; the one that they thought they lived in—is not real at all. It is entirely fantastic, not only for the author of *The Inspector General* and for the characters in his play, but for those in the orchestra, loge, and balcony who, being less perspicacious than the author, failed to realize how far off the mark, how false, that world is. The joke was on those who thought they saw the joke.[10] This is an imaginary world, further, because it is a man-made world, one based on refusal to comprehend, rather than the real created world, which is true and beautiful.[11] Thus, what we are faced with in *The Inspector General* is not only the triviality and banality—the *poshlost'* that Gogol himself referred to and that Nabokov, among others, made so much of—but also a much deeper ugliness. What Gogol was doing was holding up a mirror to his audience's imagination, not to what they are but to what they think they are; this is what *we* imagine reality to be, not what Gogol does, for he did not believe that he had any imagination at all. Like many imaginary constructions, further, this is a parody, a turning upside down. Gogol's hope was that once the parody was exposed for what it was, it would be abandoned as being too ridiculous, too laughable, and too much at variance with what is known to be true for it any longer to be taken seriously and indulged in. Consequently, this lie that imagination had made would be discarded, and men would return to their proper harmonious home.

Hence Gogol's emphasis upon the living-statue scene at the end and upon the character—or lack of it—of Khlestakov. Surely Gogol was experienced enough in the theater to know that a minute and a half of immobility on stage, which is what he called for, is a very long time.[12] The scene is there for additional clarification, to inscribe the point as emphatically as he could, despite its difficulty dramatically. Because Gogol is so precise in the way that he stations his characters, he must have thought that the audience needed the time in order to realize what the scene meant. In his note preceding the first scene of the play he wrote:

> The actors must pay attention in particular to the last scene. The last word pronounced [by the policeman, that another Inspector General has arrived] should produce a sudden electric shock among them all. The whole group should change position in the twinkling of an eye. An astonished

sound should escape all the women at once, as though from a single breast. If these directions are not followed, the whole effect may be lost. [4:10]

The last scene itself is described as follows:

The Mayor in the middle like a post, with arms outstretched and head thrown back. On his right side, his wife and daughter, concentrated upon him by the inclination of their bodies; behind [or beyond] them the Postmaster, reduced to a question mark addressed to the audience; behind [or beyond] him Luka Lukich, lost in utter innocence; behind [or beyond] him, at the very edge of the stage, three lady visitors, leaning towards one another with the most satirical expressions on their faces aimed straight at the Mayor's family. On the Mayor's left side: Zemlyanika, his head bent somewhat to the side as though he were listening to something; behind [or beyond] him the Judge, with arms spread wide, squatting almost to the ground and making a movement with his lips as though he were going to whistle or declare, "That's all we needed!"; behind [or beyond] him, Korobkin, turned to the audience with eyes screwed up, caustically hinting at the Mayor; behind [or beyond] him, at the very edge of the stage, Bobchinsky and Dobchinsky, their hands reaching out to each other, mouths wide open and goggle-eyed at each other. The other visitors simply remain like posts. For almost a minute and a half the petrified group holds this position. [4:95]

Following Gogol's directions, there are two possible ways that the main characters could be positioned, either of which is suggestive:

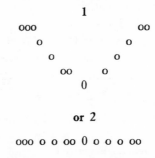

First, and most obvious, is the fact that Gogol gives directions for precisely twelve persons, plus the central figure (carefully made central) of the Mayor. Second, the characters are not arranged evenly: there are five on the Mayor's left hand, and seven on his right; in addition the groupings are slightly different. All this is sufficient to make the whole picture seem somewhat uneven, somewhat discordant, as though something, somewhere, somehow has gone wrong. The elements are deliberately not arranged to compose a harmonious whole. Certainly, the number of persons (twelve plus one) chosen for the tableau was a conscious decision (the policeman, for example, could easily have been included, thus making an even fourteen. But this would have made the Christ and Disciples analogy impossible).[13] Given the expressions on people's faces and the attitudes of their bodies, we have, in arrangement 1, the Crucifixion; or, in 2, the Last Supper, but in parodic rather than real form. The scene itself is a deception, but is meant to be seen as such. These are a false god and false disciples, all of them living in a false world. And instead of the harmonious reconciliation that either of the events should signify, with the promise of the eternally beautiful life to come, we know that the announcement of a new Inspector General, who may or may not be a genuine one, means a return to the cacophonous falsity that has reigned throughout the play. The parody remains exactly that.

When we turn to Khlestakov, we find ourselves in the same unreal world. He is not only a parody of an inspector general, he is also a parody of a human being. Gogol describes him as follows in the character sketch preceding the comedy:

A young man of twenty-three years, thin, slight, somewhat foolish and stupid, one of those people who in offices is called "good-for-nothing." He speaks and acts at random. He is incapable of concentrating on any thought for any length of time. His speech is jerky, and words fly out of his mouth completely unexpectedly. The more the one filling this role shows sincerity and simplicity, the more he will succeed. Fashionably dressed. [4:9]

In his "Letter to a Writer" of 1836, complaining about how Khlestakov had been played, Gogol described him thus:

Khlestakov is not a swindler at all; he is not a liar by profession; he himself forgets that he is lying and almost himself believes what he is saying. . . . To lie means to speak a line in a tone so close to the truth, so naturally, so naïvely, that it

> could only be done when speaking nothing but the truth. . . .
> Khlestakov does not at all lie coldly, nor as a theatrical brag-
> gart; he lies with feeling; his eyes bespeak the pleasure he gets
> from it. It is the best, the most poetic moment of his life,
> almost a kind of inspiration. [4:99–100]

And in 1841, in a description that was not published until the edition
of 1889, Gogol said:

> Khlestakov in himself is a worthless person. . . . But the
> strength of the general fear has made a remarkable comic
> person out of him. . . . He who had hitherto been thwarted
> and snubbed in everything . . . felt elbow room and suddenly
> expanded, when he least expected it himself. Everything in
> him is surprise and unexpectedness. He cannot even guess
> why he is getting so much attention and respect. . . . The fur-
> ther he goes, the more wholeheartedly does he enter into what
> he is saying. . . . It seems to him that he really has done all
> these things. . . . Having himself been repeatedly blasted, he
> knows the speech for it perfectly; he feels a special pleasure in
> blasting others, even if only in tales. . . . On waking, he is the
> same Khlestakov he was before. He does not even remember
> that he frightened them all. As before, there is no understand-
> ing in him; there is the same stupidity in all his actions.
> [4:116–17]

It is quite clear, then, that Khlestakov is a figment of the imagination, a kind of wish fulfillment, an Inspector General who corresponds
to preconceived fantasies, both his and others', rather than a reality in
himself. There is little doubt, further, that the new Inspector General
announced by the policeman, regardless of what he really is, will also
immediately be transformed, in a parody of transfiguration, into an
imaginary being who will fit the fears, desires, and prejudices of the
imaginary inhabitants of the town. Reality, whatever it may be, will
once again be refused; the cacophonous ugliness of death (itself a
parody) will once again usurp the place of harmonious beauty.

The horror to Gogol was that his play and the characters in it
were taken to be portrayals of the world as it really is, while he knew
that it was Annunziata who was real, not Khlestakov. From Gogol's
point of view, his critics were in the same position as those who find
Milton's Satan powerful and his Christ pale; Dante's *Inferno* more
impressive than his *Paradiso;* Dostoevsky's Ivan more alive than his
Father Zosima.

Gogol's comment that Khlestakov's lies took on the semblance of truth, even for him, further emphasizes the parodic nature of the play.[14] Khlestakov, too, is a joke—but a very serious one, because he does not know he is. In this he goes beyond a Tartuffe, who at least has the virtue of hypocrisy, so that, avoiding parody, Tartuffe remains human.[15] Khlestakov, on the contrary, being parodic, is imaginary; he only gives the semblance of a man. It is no answer to say that Khlestakov in actuality is some irresponsible clerk from Petersburg who just happened to be passing through, because that does not clothe him in any more flesh and blood nor give him any more soul than he had before.[16] Even the letter at the end, by which the townspeople learn that Khlestakov is a fake, is of little help, for there is no revelation of truth in it at all, just that he is not what they thought he was. No one knows any better what he is.

The strange and shocking thing about the play is the persistence of the townspeople, their utter refusal to see anything in any light but the one that they themselves have provided. Their deception is thus entirely self-deception. Nobody foisted Khlestakov off on them; they foisted him off on themselves, as each of them foists himself off on the others. From this point of view, it is appalling that the information about Khlestakov's falsity does not result in a realization of their own falsity. They discover—perforce—that he is imaginary, but not that they themselves are. Indeed, one is struck by the remarkable stubbornness of these people, who are not in themselves terribly stupid. Gogol says as much of the Mayor, who is "very shrewd in his own way," while Zemlyanika, we are told, is a "wily scoundrel." The only one who we are definitely informed is stupid is Khlestakov himself. Untruth is not embraced because of a lack of reason; it arises, curiously enough, out of too great a trust in reason. The Mayor's tirade in act 5, for example, focusses on the original mistake made in taking Khlestakov for an inspector general; but neither he nor anyone else finds that the conclusions and actions based on that premise are amiss. If Khlestakov had been an inspector general, whatever was said and thought—all the townspeople's actions—would have been, to their way of thinking, perfectly proper. Not only do they lack substance; they do not even know that they lack substance. Khlestakov is not the only one who is worthless (Gogol also calls him "empty"); we have one example after another of egoism and conviction of rectitude (this applies even to the shopkeepers who bring complaints against the Mayor; we discover that they, too, are false) attached to vacuums, to substancelessness.

The absence of substance is pointed out twice in the course of the play, both times in reference to Khlestakov, and both times inadvertently. The first time this happens is in scene 4 of act 3. Osip, Khlestakov's servant, is asked if his master is not a general. He replies, "Oh, yes—he's a general. But in reverse." In answer to whether that makes him more or less than a genuine general, he says, "More" (4:44). The second instance is in scene 8 of act 5. The Postmaster, asked *what* (not *who*) he thinks Khlestakov is, responds in kind: "Neither this nor that; the devil knows what it is!" (4:90). In both cases we learn that it is whatness that is of interest rather than whoness—a thing rather than a person. In this connection, we also note (Osip has passed the information on to the audience in a soliloquy) that Khlestakov is a collegiate registrar (the lowest grade on the Table of Ranks). Osip's speech makes a point of this. The reader, or audience, has a right to ask *why* this particular rank is ascribed to him, since most of Gogol's officials are of more middling grade. There are two reasons for the choice: first, to make the enormity of the parody clear (how many television comedies have made comic hay out of the second lieutenant impersonating the general, or the shipping room clerk passing himself off as head of the company); the second is involved with the question of what a registry clerk does: he notes down, files away, "statisticizes," if I may coin a word. In short, his job, his vocation—if Khlestakov can be said to have one—is to abstract persons, to dehumanize them. And this is precisely what he does, by his presence alone, not by his action, in the course of the play. The trick that Gogol accomplished was to create a character who is unaware of his function even while receiving total cooperation in the exercise of that function. He who wishes to lose his soul loses it. Much of the greatness of the comedy rests on this ground of Khlestakov's unawareness; as Gogol pointed out, he doesn't know what is going on. He doesn't even know what he is doing while doing it, as his letter to his friend in which he describes the people of the town indicates. As others imagine him, so he imagines others, no more aware than they of this imaginary quality. According to the letter, in Khlestakov's "judgment" the Mayor is "as stupid as a grey gelding,"[17] and the "grey gelding" is repeated; the Postmaster is the "image of the porter Mikheyev; the scoundrel probably also hits the bottle"; Zemlyanika is "a pig in a skull cap"; Luka Lukich "stinks of onions";[18] the Judge, Lyapkin-Tyapkin, "is as *mauvais ton* as you can get" (4:91–92).[19] None of these descriptions really does any more than file its subject away and register it without concern for reality, for the descriptions do not really apply to anyone at all; they are as deceptive as their subjects.

Gogol in this play accomplished two very original things. First, he managed a play about deception without using a conscious deceiver. In such comedies about mistaken identity (and their number is legion), the trickster is usually a conscious rogue; one need but refer to the comedies of Plautus, Shakespeare, Jonson, and Molière for examples. In *The Gamblers,* Gogol wrote in this tradition. There, everyone is a conscious cheat. In *The Inspector General,* no one is, because no one, as we have noted, is a hypocrite.[20] It is a remarkable achievement, in this sense, of the portrayal of nothingness, of soullessness. These are all little men who aren't there.

From this point of view, Gogol was indeed acting as a teacher and prophet, giving warning of the pit that yawns and the fate that awaits those who see this as a real depiction of a real world: these are not persons; they are parodies of persons. Nowhere within the play is there a portrayal of the harmonious beauty that Gogol held so dear. On the contrary, he presents us with a discordant ugliness, the only release from which is laughter. In a return to an image for ugliness that he had used so often in the Little Russian tales, he has the Mayor say, when the full extent of the mistake that he has made has been borne in upon him, "I see only pig snouts instead of faces, nothing more" (4:94), thus repeating a remark made by Khlestakov and unconsciously putting himself in Khlestakov's class. It is the same horrid reversal of beauty and truth that we met in "A Lost Letter," for example. Furthermore, the remark is not addressed to anyone in particular, or it is addressed to everyone in general. There are no stage directions to indicate whether the Mayor is speaking to the other members of the cast, to the audience, or to his own imagination. For this one brief flash, Gogol holds out the possibility of redemption from the ugly and false, for the Mayor has just said that he has "been killed, utterly killed." Unfortunately, this is only a glimpse of the truth regarding others, not the truth about himself. Like everyone else, he cannot discard his mask, because there is only a void behind it. Gogol is more worried about his audience, however, than he is about the imaginary creatures of the play: those in the comedy have no future, but the audience may have, since Gogol still believed that the reality of the latter might be asserted. At this point, the future is still outside the work of art, on the other hand, rather than inside it. Only as *Dead Souls* developed did he realize that as he wrote, he must carry his readers into the future if his vision was to be communicated, if the quest was to involve them as well as himself.

The ugliness, and hence falsity (or falsity, hence ugliness), within the play is reinforced by the discordancy that we meet at every turn— it is a reversal of the harmony that Gogol felt to be essential: no one is interested in anything save his own skin; each tries to gain favors for himself, to maintain his face, to be regarded, to be singled out, not for what he is, but for what he imagines himself to be, just as Proprishchin, Kovalyov, and Akaky Akakyevich did. The Mayor's wife and daughter, Anna Andreyevna and Maria Antonovna, imagine that they are highly seductive females and that they are persons who are capable of holding their own in the most exalted circles; the Mayor imagines that he is a general, with a decoration on his breast, giving orders; Luka Lukich, the superintendent of schools, imagines that he is a clever boulevardier, superior to these country yokels; the Judge, Lyapkin-Tyapkin, imagines that he is a man of independent, well-considered thought; the Postmaster imagines that he is a man who keeps up with events, one who knows what is going on; Zemlyanika, the administrator of charitable institutions, imagines that he is a down-to-earth practical man; Dobchinsky and Bobchinsky, Gogol's Tweedledum and Tweedledee, imagine that they are persons of probity and intelligence; and so forth and so on. One cannot imagine what these imaginings have to do with reality. As with Poprishchin, Kovalyov, and Akaky Akakyevich, fantasy has usurped the place of truth. Like the Inspector General himself, everyone in the play—with the possible exception of Osip— is traveling incognito. It is not that the forms assumed are in themselves bad; indeed, as we have already pointed out, all the disguises make perfectly good sense in the unreal world in which the characters live. They fail because, although x plus y may equal z, or two plus two may equal four, they are only registrations without meaning.

For Gogol—and this applies to his view of the world as well as to his view of art—form without substance (and substance here is *not* a synonym for matter) is empty, is meaningless. In fact, the forms taken by these persons are material—x, y, and z notwithstanding—not spiritual. It is precisely spirit that is lacking in *The Inspector General*.[21]

To put it another way, this is a play without a soul: persons are not like this for the very good and sufficient reason that these are not persons. Indeed, to criticize *The Inspector General* on realistic grounds is to miss the point entirely, as Gogol himself was well aware. He was always careful to avoid the mistake of confusing fiction with truth (both Hanz Kuechelgarten and Piskaryov made that mistake and may serve as warnings of its consequences). The play may be the thing; but as in *Hamlet*, to indicate the truth, not to be the truth. Gogol, one of the greatest handlers of the Russian language, also knew that telling the truth is not so easy as many assume. The oath "I swear to tell the truth, the whole truth, and nothing but the truth" probably appeared to him as irresistibly comic, as, indeed, it is. We can imagine what would have happened if Pushkin had given *that* idea to Gogol![22]

Material (or rank, riches, esteem, prerogatives) is the mask that the dramatis personae assume; therefore, we may say that what they actually do, so far as Gogol is concerned, is de-form themselves, which answers the question we asked above about to whom the Mayor's remark, "I see only pig snouts," is addressed: it is addressed to all who have exchanged spirit for matter. Not only was this image used to characterize ugliness in the Little Russian tales, we remember; it was also used in specific reference to nonhuman monsters, all of whom are, from man's point of view, deformed (this gives them their grotesque quality, and from this their horror arises). They are also, therefore, soulless. Without hanging the entire interpretation of *The Inspector General* on one phrase, I think we can safely conclude that this comedy is Gogol's greatest horror story, so much so that it is bearable only because it is funny, and it is funny only because it is not real. This is not the laughter of Homer's gods whose wounds are healed overnight while men die, nor is it the objective laughter of Mozart shaking his head at mere folly. For Gogol, nothing could surpass the terror that he felt at the sight of deformed material emptiness, of chaos; his laughter is an exorcism of that terror, for the soulless, he believed, were without—or beyond—hope; and not to laugh would have been to condemn himself to black despair and deny his vision—that is, to become one of the characters on stage. What a blow, then, it must have been when some members of the audience protested that Gogol had put them on stage, while others praised him for giving a "realistic" picture of conditions in Russia. For both were casting the prophet-teacher—who was attempting to turn men's eyes to truth and beauty and thus to save them—in the role of a satanic destroyer. "For the sake of Heaven," one can hear him cry, "don't you realize that this is *not* what you are!"

Leaving the Theater after the Presentation of a New Comedy was certainly written after the reviews of the Petersburg production of *The Inspector General* came out, but probably before the Moscow production. Although revised later, it properly belongs to this time—it is not, in other words, a reinterpretation done seven years after the fact when Gogol was in the grip of some "religious mania."

The "play" (a more proper name would be "dialogue") is a discussion among a number of people about what they have just seen on stage. There is no plot, and the characters are static. What we have is simply the author listening to what these various, typical persons have to say about his work: two men *comme il faut,* two officers, two men of the world, a middle-aged civil servant, a man who is interested in literature, two "overcoats," two more officers, and so forth and so on. In general, the piece is a survey, often rather caustic, of reactions to *The Inspector General* upon its first presentation. And it is the author of the piece who has the last word. Since this speech by the author may be presumed to be Gogol's own opinion, it is worth quoting in full:

I have heard more things than I foresaw. What a motley heap of opinions! Happy is the comic author who is born in a nation where society has not yet fused into a single motionless mass, where it is not yet enveloped in the single crust of old prejudice which confines everyone's thoughts in the same form and standard, where there is an opinion for every man, where everyone is the creator of his own character. What diversity in these opinions, and how the firm, clear Russian intellect shines everywhere: in the noble aspiration of the statesman; in the lofty self-sacrifice of the civil servant who is lost in the backwoods; in the tender beauty of a magnanimous feminine soul; in the aesthetic feeling of connoisseurs; in the simple true instinct of the people! And how, even in the malevolent criticisms, there is much for a comic author to learn! What a living lesson! Yes, I am satisfied. But why has my heart become so sad? It is strange: I am sorry that no one noticed the one honest person in my play. Yes, there was one honest, noble person there throughout. This honest, noble person was— *laughter*. It was noble because it was resolved to come forward despite the base meaning given it in the world. It was noble because it was resolved to come forward despite the fact that it has caused an offensive sobriquet to be ascribed to the author —the sobriquet of cold egoist—and has compelled him to doubt even the fresh movements of his soul. No one has come forward in defense of this laughter. I am a comic author, I have served it honestly, and thus I must be its defender. No, laughter is more meaningful and more profound than is thought. Not the laughter engendered by a momentary irritation, by a bilious sickly disposition of character; and not the light laughter that serves people as idle entertainment and pastime; but the laughter that flies out of the luminous nature of man, that flies from it because in its depths is enclosed his eternally gushing spring, that deepens the subject, compelling whatever would slip by to come forth clearly, and without whose penetrating power the pettiness and emptiness of life would not frighten mankind so much. The contemptible and the worthless past that he indifferently walks by each day would not grow before him with such terrible, almost ridiculous power, and he would not, shuddering, cry, "Are there really such people?"—when, as he well knows, there are worse people. No, those who say that laughter incites are unjust. Only the dismal incites, while laughter gives light. Many things would incite man if presented in their nakedness; but illuminated by the power of laughter, they bring reconciliation to the soul. And he who wanted vengeance on a wicked man will almost be at peace with him when he sees the vile movements of his soul ridiculed. Unjust are those who say that laughter has no effect on those at whom it aims, that a cheat will be the first to laugh at a cheat on stage: the cheat's progeny will laugh, but the contemporary cheat will not have the strength to laugh! He perceives that there is in everyone an irresistible image and that one mean move on his part is sufficient for that image to give him an eternal sobriquet; mockery frightens even the one who has nothing to fear in the world. No, only a profoundly good soul can laugh with good radiant laughter. But he does not perceive the powerful force of such laughter: "What is laughable is base," says high society; only what is uttered in a stern and stilted voice is called lofty. But God! how many people daily pass by for whom nothing in the world is lofty! For them, whatever is created by inspiration is a trifle and a tale; for them, the creations of Shakespeare are tales; for them, the holy movements of the soul are tales. No, it is not the outraged petty self-esteem of a writer that makes me say this; it is not because my immature, feeble creations were immediately called tales. No, I see my flaws, and I see that reproaches are deserved; my soul could not indifferently support the abuse of the most accomplished works with the names of trifles and tales, the consideration of all the luminaries and stars of the world as creators of but trifles and tales! My soul moaned when I saw how many there are who, amid life itself, are dumb, dead automatons, terrible in the immovable cold of their souls and in the barren emptiness of their hearts; my soul moaned when not even the ghost of an expression quivered on their insensitive faces at the same thing that plunged a profoundly living soul into heavenly tears, and it moaned that their tongues did not stick to utter their eternal word: "tales." Tales! But centuries have flowed past, cities and peoples have been demolished—have vanished from the face of the earth, all whirled away like smoke—but these tales live and are repeated to the present day; wise sovereigns heed them, and profound statesmen and beautiful old men and youths full of noble aspirations. Tales! But the balconies and railings of theaters groan; everything is shaken from top to bottom, in one instant transformed into one feeling, into one man; and all the people receive one another like brothers in a single spiritual movement; and in the concerned applause a hymn of gratitude to a man who has not been in the world for five hundred years rings out. Do his rotted bones hear it in the grave? Does his soul, which suffered life's harsh woe, respond? Tales! But in the ranks of this shaken crowd comes one who is depressed by woe and the unbearable weight of life, ready to raise a desperate hand against himself; and suddenly cooling tears spurt from his eyes, and he leaves, reconciled with life, and anew asks woes and sufferings of heaven, if only he may live and anew may be flooded with tears at such tales! Tales! But the world would sink into stupor without such tales; life would run aground; souls would be covered with mold and slime. Tales! O let the names of those who have graciously heeded such tales be eternally holy for posterity: the miraculous finger of Providence is contantly above the heads of their creators. Even in moments of misfortune and persecution the most noble in the realm became their defenders before all men: the crowned monarch shielded them with his imperial shield from the height of his inaccessible throne.

Courage, then, on the way! And let not my soul be troubled by condemnations, let it, rather, gratefully take instruction for its faults, not even being darkened when they deny its lofty movements and sacred love for mankind! The world is like a maelstrom of opinions and doctrines eternally moving in it; but time mills all. Like husks do falsities fly away, and like firm kernels do immutable truths remain. What was deemed empty can then appear armed with stern meaning. In the depths of cold laughter can be found the burning sparks of eternal mighty love. And who knows, perhaps then all will own that it is by virtue of the same laws that a proud and powerful man is worthless and feeble in misfortune and that a weak man grows to gianthood amidst calamities, in virtue of the same laws that the one who sheds deep spiritual tears also seems to be the one who is the greatest laugher in the world! [5:168–71]

It seems to me that this statement is important for a number of reasons, even if portions of it may not have been written until some time after the event and although a separation of the reasons is somewhat artificial: first, because of the importance that Gogol attached to the literary art; second, because of the particular kind of artist that Gogol thought he was; third, because of the religious import of his remarks; fourth, because of the view that he had of what he was doing in *The Inspector General;* and fifth, because of the significance that he thought his play had. The first two points will be discussed in chapter 8, "The Artist," and the third in chapter 9, "The Christian." This is the place, however, for some discussion of points four and five.

Clearly, Gogol saw his work, not as the presentation of men as they are, but as they might be, in a negative sense. He had no illusions that the play was other than an artificial construction whose very content was, as such, artificial. This is not, in other words, a simple lopsided or distorted or grotesque vision of reality. Nor was he attempting to depict the impact of one kind of reality upon another. *The Inspector General* is, rather, a portrayal of negative potentiality. To take it otherwise would be, Gogol thought, to distort it grossly. He agrees that people have done so, and the fault is his own—an artistic fault, which he never, one might add, rectified successfully.

Gogol also wishes it to be known, in his passage on laughter, that solemnity is not necessary to seriousness, that comedy, particularly his comedy, has import. The laughter is meant to illuminate and, in its way, terrify. For this is one of the things that we would be like *if;* and the laughter is to bring recovery, but not anger on the part of those who see self-portrayal on stage or smugness on the part of those who either consider themselves superior or think, like Nicholas I, that Gogol has made a "good hit" (this despite his praise of Nicholas). What he thought he was doing, then, or what he wished to do, was to present, within a harmonious framework, the nonhuman abasement that man is capable of. *The Inspector General* is, in this sense, a contrast between form and content, rather than a blending of the two. And it is out of contrast, in the long run, that Gogol's meaning arises, because the play, possibly owing to the influence of Pushkin and his insistence upon purity, is almost classical in form. I would suggest that this desire for perfection of form, rather than any changes of mind regarding the meaning, dictated Gogol's constant revisions of *The Inspector General,* as well as of his other works. The remarks cited above concerning artistic failure seem to bear this out. The proper place to look for the truth was in the harmony and the beauty of the form of the play, not in the discord or the chaos of the content. It is there that the great endeavor was made, in his form, to indicate the vision that he held. This is why there is no change, why a full circle is performed, why the end returns us to the beginning. The parts fit together in harmonious relationship, much like musical movements, to form a whole that is in itself a beauteous construction—in direct contrast with the chaotic content. It was the contrast that was meant to raise the audience's awareness of reality. But Gogol failed, perhaps because he expected too much, particularly in a drama.

Gogol made a further attempt to explain, this time by a reinterpretation, when he wrote *The Dénouement of The Inspector General,* a quite late work. Critics and scholars have been in the habit either of ignoring this piece or of dismissing it, again, as "religious mania."[23] That Gogol goes too far in some statements is probably correct, but he did feel that he was in a battle, and he had long had the habit of exaggeration to make his point.

This "play" is of the same genre as *Leaving the Theater;* that is, it is a nondramatic dialogue in the course of which *The Inspector General* is discussed. In this case, the discussion takes place among those who have played the comedy—the actors—rather than among members of the audience. There is no certainty that the actors, to whose performances Gogol had objected when his play was first produced, are really voicing Gogol's thoughts throughout. I do think, however, that we can be certain of some remarks made at the end, where it is strenuously denied that a real Russian city is being depicted in *The Inspector General*: In short, there is no such town," we are told. "But what," the speaker continues, "if this is our spiritual town and exists in each of us?" An allegorical interpretation is thereupon tendered.[24] This interpretation indicates that the play is meant to reveal the negative possibilities that each of us has, to terrify us by informing us of the monsters we are capable of becoming. There is no intention of saying that this is what man is:

> Laughter, which was created to mock everything that defames the true beauty of man. . . . Just as we laughed at the vileness in another man, let us generously laugh at whatever vileness we may find in ourselves! . . . Let our spirits not be indignant if some angry mayor, or, more justly, the unclean spirit himself should whisper with his lips, "What are you laughing at? You are laughing at yourselves!" Proudly will we say to him: "Yes, we are laughing at ourselves, because we hear our noble Russian nature, because we hear the lofty command to be better than others!" [4:132]

The last statement of all is: "Let us in concord show all the world that in the Russian land, everything, whatever there is . . . aspires to serve the One Whom everything in all the land ought to serve and is raised . . . up, to supreme, eternal beauty!" (4:132–33). Repeated here is what Gogol had in mind from the very beginning of his career: harmony and beauty. Man is indeed made in the image of God, since his nature is in reality beautiful. The joke is on those who have taken the dismal view.

5

Dead Souls, Part 1

Dead Souls was begun in late summer, 1835, about seven months after the appearance of *Arabesques,* about five months after the issuance of *Mirgorod,* and about three months before Gogol started on *The Inspector General.* In a letter to Pushkin dated 7 October 1835, Gogol said that he was already on the third chapter of his "novel," as he called it at this time (10:374–75). By the following summer, when Gogol was in Germany, he was certain that he was engaged on a major project. Work continued in Switzerland and France. Finally, in March 1837, Gogol settled in Rome, where, perhaps distracted by his love for Italy, progress was intermittent. Perhaps, also, Gogol found the very length of the work difficult to handle, used as he was to short fiction (the longest piece he had thus far successfully completed was *The Inspector General*). There are also reports of bad health at this time, however. Still, he went forward, with frequent breaks to work on other pieces, some of them brand new, like "Rome" and "The Overcoat," some revisions of short stories and plays already written in at least first draft. We do know that it was not until May 1840 that he finished chapter 6 (out of a total of eleven in the final version of Part 1). By the beginning of 1841, however, he announced that he had not only finished Part 1, but had revised it and was already proceeding with Part 2 (11:322). He now saw it as a "colossal" work. The announcement was, however, a little premature, since a third revision of Part 1 was not finished until the summer of 1841. Finally, in the fall of 1841 a definitive text was submitted to the censor, who after some delay demanded the omission of the Captain Kopeikin episode, a change in title from *Dead Souls* to *The Adventures of Chichikov; or, Dead Souls,* and about thirty other "corrections." In April 1842 Gogol sent the manuscript to the printer, without Captain Kopeikin and with the title change. He had also designed the title page of the book, so that the largest, most prominent word on the page, which strikes the eyes even before the title itself, is "POEMA"—that is, "A Poem." In the meantime, he revised the Captain Kopeikin episode so as to make the captain a simple lawbreaker instead of a soldier who rebelled because of ingratitude shown him by his superiors. Finally, on 9 May 1842, the Petersburg censor passed the poem, and the first copies came off the press twelve days later.

The story of Gogol's constant work on Part 2 and of his burning of three versions of it, so that we have only the first four (probably) chapters and one of the later (possibly) chapters, is well known. Certainly, he was concerned with the "poem," his chef-d'oeuvre, until his last illness and death in February 1852. In short, for seventeen years *Dead Souls* remained in Gogol's thoughts, from the time he was twenty-six until he was forty-two. That it posed a multitude of problems for him seems obvious; I would suggest that these were problems of form, however, not of content. So far as content is concerned, Gogol's attitudes changed little over the course of time. He was as sure as he had ever been of what he wanted to say and of his vision; the question was— in view of what he thought had been his failure to be clear in other pieces that he had written and was writing—how to find and use the proper vehicle. This is what plagued him all through his "visions and revisions" of *Dead Souls*.

Gogol's first impulse was to write what he called a "novel." As he went on, however, it became clear to him that the novel, as he understood the form, would not serve his purposes. As we know from "A Textbook of Literature for Russian Youth"—the one place where Gogol gives a definition[1]—he thought of the novel as a tight, carefully plotted form akin to the drama, by which, given his description, he meant something like a well-made play. Despite the well-grounded and well-argued remarks of many commentators, according to his own testimony, Gogol did not have Laurence Sterne in mind. If he had followed his own prescription, he would have turned out something closer to the novels of, say, Flaubert (whom he probably did not know—Flaubert was eleven years younger than Gogol) than to that of his English predecessor. After all, when Gogol came to *Dead Souls,* he had little native tradition to guide him—the sentimental writing of Karamzin in such a work as *Poor Liza,* perhaps, and Pushkin's tentatives in *Eugene One-*

gin and *The Captain's Daughter* (other, minor writers of fiction, such as Vladimir Dal' and Faddey Bulgarin, have been mentioned by commentators). On the whole, the generation before Gogol was largely poetic, which meant—generally speaking and with exceptions—lyric, understanding lyric to include the ode. Even the picaresque novel—Sterne's or Fielding's—could not serve as a model, any more than *Candide* could, because while Gogol's work was to be a "wander" book, imbued with comedy, detailing the adventures of an ambitious man, and full of digressions and while it was meant to be such a work as would encompass all of Russia, it was also meant to be regenerative. The hero, unlike Khlestakov, was to be intelligent and was to possess a conscience that would, finally, be aroused.[2] Of course, Gogol could have chosen to write a tragedy in the style of the *Oresteia,* but as he well knew, his genius lay in another direction.

Gogol could not have gone too far before he perceived that the novel, as he conceived it, would not serve his purpose. The scope and approach, he realized, leaned more to the epic than to anything else. But his book was also to be comic. He did turn to a foreign literature for his models, and he turned exactly where one would expect, not to England, but to Italy, the country outside Russia that he loved best.

There is no need to argue the case for Italy's attraction for Gogol; it is too well known and too well documented for that. As it was for a Renaissance Frenchman or Englishman, Italy was for Gogol the very home of harmony and beauty.[3] Of more importance than the ruins of the ancient world, however, was the Renaissance, particularly as expressed in literature and in painting, which was exemplified for Gogol in Raphael. To Gogol, sixteenth-century Italian literature meant primarily Ariosto and Tasso, both of whom were quite popular in Russia in the early years of the nineteenth century.[4] Behind them both, of course, was the gigantic figure of Dante, as he was behind the Renaissance as a whole. Much as he admired Dante, however, much as Dante's tripartite division intrigued him, much as he was attracted to the heights depicted by Dante in *Paradiso,* much as the harmonious nature of an entire universe exemplified in *The Divine Comedy* may have excited him, Gogol realized that the Dantesque form was unsuited to his talent, just as the grand style of Tasso was unsuited to it. Once he had recognized that *Dead Souls* would go beyond the bounds of his conception of the novel and once he had acknowledged that the Homeric—whose images in the ancient world were *The Iliad, The Odys-*

sey, and *The Aeneid,* and in the Renaissance world was *Gerusalemme Liberata*—was outside his powers, was, indeed, foreign to his subject matter as well as to his talent (the epic in Russia would have to wait for Tolstoy), Gogol turned to the one Italian model that was congenial to his task.[5] His answer lay in that peculiar Renaissance form most successfully practiced by Ariosto in the *Orlando Furioso,* the ironic and comic romantic epic—the *romanzo,* or, as Gogol called it in "A Textbook of Literature for Russian Youth," the "lesser kind of epic." There he said of this form:

> A kind of narrative composition has been produced in modern times that consists of a mean, so to speak, between the novel and the epic, with a hero who, while a private and insignificant person, is nevertheless significant in many respects for the observer of the human soul. The author leads his life through a chain of adventures, and he is changed, in order that the author may at the same time present a recognizable, faithful picture of everything that is significant in the features and customs of the time he has adopted, an earthy, almost statistically comprehended picture of the deformities, abuses, vices, and everything he has noted in the epoch and time he has adopted that is worthy to attract the glance of every observant contemporary who seeks in the past, in what has gone by, living lessons for the present. Such phenomena have from time to time appeared among many peoples. Although many of them were written in prose, they can nonetheless be reckoned among poetic creations.
>
> It is not universal, of course, but the full epic extent of significant particular phenomena may be there, in proportion as the poet clothes it in verse.
>
> So Ariosto depicted an almost fairy-tale passion for adventures and wonder, in which a whole epoch indulged for a time, and Cervantes laughed at the inclination for adventure which after the rococo [*sic*] still remained in some people at a time when the age around them had changed; both identified with the idea they had taken. It filled their minds constantly and therefore acquired a carefully considered, strict meaning; it shows through everywhere and gives their compositions something of the look of the epic, despite the humorous tone, despite the lightness, and even despite the fact that one of them was written in prose. [8:478–79]

Whether or not the above is an accurate description of *Orlando Furioso* and *Don Quixote* is beside the point. More important is whether or not it applies to *Dead Souls,* Part 1. I submit that it does, up to the point that Gogol tells the reader of Chichikov's life before he came to the town of N. There a shift occurs, of which more below.

In any event, necessary to this kind of work are:

1. A central character, unimportant in himself, who goes through
2. adventures that
3. change the central character;
4. a picture of many aspects of the time, particularly the negative ones;
5. humor;
6. the *look* of an epic; and
7. a lesson for the reader.

Whether the work is in prose or verse is quite immaterial—it will still be a "poetic creation." Aside from all of the above, which obviously applies to *Dead Souls* (although a complete change in Chichikov does not occur, it is intimated that it will occur),[6] there is another element that Gogol would have found much to his taste—the digression. Digressions are not only legitimate in the romantic epic, they are required.[7] Gogol's use of them in *Dead Souls* (most of his prose works show a predilection for them anyhow) was much criticized by his contemporaries precisely because they were thinking in terms of a different form and because Gogol gave no warning other than the short passage cited above, although his letters and essays frequently make mention of both Ariosto and Cervantes, as well as of Tasso. I suggest that a good many of the questions concerning the form of Part 1 disappear, and a good deal of light at least is thrown on Gogol's problem of continuing his work if this matter of form is taken into consideration. As Gogol says, the work grew on him in the course of writing—I believe that it grew from a novel to a comic romantic epic, a shift that occurred fairly early; this would account for the speed with which Gogol accomplished the beginning as well as the slow pace of the rest of Part 1. By the time that he came to the end of Part 1, the problem, instead of vanishing, had grown even larger. Behind Ariosto stood Dante, whose great work is far from funny and whose hero, Dante himself, is anything but insignificant. On the one hand, Gogol's audience wanted to be amused (they had also been "amused" by *The Inspector General*);[8] they wanted more of the same, without, in Gogol's opinion, having understood what he was about in the first place. On the other hand, Gogol did not see how he could continue along the same path. The subject now demanded something else, something, perhaps, in the Dantesque vein. But how could Parts 2 and 3, demanding what they did,[9] be made to fit with Part 1? How, in other words, could an artistic harmony be attained? I suggest that this is the problem that Gogol never solved. It was not that he had gone mad, nor that his artistic powers had waned. The formal question, rather, is the one that stopped him, and it was his own critical sense that forced him to destroy Part 2. Even his harshest critics, many of whom believed that Gogol had become incomprehensible on some subjects, thought that he retained his critical literary faculties to the very end.[10] Despite the insolvability of the problem, the fragments that we have of Part 2, plus the end of Part 1, do indicate that he was trying to shift the focus in accordance with the original idea of reforming Chichikov's character; the difficulty arose, however, in that this was to be more than a mere change in the hero—it was to be a spiritual reawakening.[11] In addition, there would have to be an emphasis on virtue instead of vice, which also meant an alteration of tone, from the humorous to the solemn (somehow virtue, in fiction as in life, seems to demand solemnity). What Gogol did in his much-maligned *Selected Passages from Correspondence with Friends* illustrates the dangers, for him, of such a course. The device of the digression could not accomplish the purpose either, given the necessities of fictional change that were also required.

In the result, thus, *Dead Souls* remains unfinished, essentially a fragment, a never-completed comic romantic epic.

Like most of Gogol's works, *Dead Souls* is a negative achievement rather than a positive one; that is, it is a depiction of what is not, in the attempt to generate a recognition of what is. Here, however, Gogol starts from what appears to be a low point in the opening paragraph of the book, which describes Chichikov's appearance and his arrival in the town of N.[12] Chichikov is in some ways a good deal like Khlestakov; that is, we do not know what he is, much less who he is, and we will not know until the end of Part 1, when we will find out that he has been obsessed. *Dead Souls*, Part 1, is thus a summary of Gogolian themes. It is Chichikov's lack of distinction that is immediately strongly emphasized, his basic anonymity rather than personality; he is an "insignificant" hero.

One immediately inquires if Chichikov is not meant to be a satanic figure, for is it not the devil himself who is the great acquirer of souls?[13] I do not think that this was Gogol's intention, any more than he thought of Khlestakov as satanic. Chichikov is not, after all, a seducer—what he does is simply to suggest a choice; he does not lie about the souls or the advantages that would accrue to those whose souls he is buying; he is not deceiving people in order that they may fall—they are in reality already fallen; they are already deluded, have already bartered away their freedom. Chichikov is on the whole a most amiable man who fits in anywhere, subject to others, generally speaking, rather than ruler over others. One might go so far as to say that he possesses no one; on the contrary, others attempt to possess him, in the sense that it is they who create him after the image they desire. Thus he is victim rather than master. After all, is there anyone in Part 1 to whom he seriously lies, anyone whom he hoodwinks, anyone whom he swindles? The choices made are hardly Chichikov's fault. In this, *Dead Souls* is very much like *The Inspector General,* with the difference that Chichikov is conscious of what is going on, while Khlestakov was not. He might well ask, Who is more guilty, the man who sells the money-making machine (which in this case works, since getting rid of dead serfs does bring a tax benefit), or the one who buys it? Some of the genius of Part 1 consists precisely in this difficulty of discovering who is swindling whom.

We further find that Chichikov is partially destroyed in the town of N. by the most notorious liar of the neighborhood, Nozdryov. When Chichikov leaves town, he does so because it is hopeless to remain: he may buy no more souls, but only because of what people think he may be, or who he may be, even though what they think is false. It is not because of what he really is or has really done.[14] He is not driven out because anyone finds his activity reprehensible; he must leave because of speculation, not because of perceptions of reality. Indeed, one of the remarkable things about Part 1 is everyone's lack of concern for truth; everything is based upon illusion: Manilov, that agreeable man, who has no character to set him apart, to distinguish him as a person, who in his way is a kind of "old world landowner"; Korobochka, for whom all life consists of profits and loss, who is consumed by trade, so that her mind cannot grasp anything without a balance sheet, so that she is herself a balance sheet; Nozdryov, a pathological liar who delights in the spreading of confusion (if we wish a satanic figure, perhaps we should settle on him); Sobakyevich, the "bear," to whom all men are just such beasts as himself, and who doesn't recognize any difference between life and death; the miser Plyushkin, who is so afraid of letting go of things that he has turned into a thing himself, frigid, callous, and, as a human being, dead. Each believes that he is the winner in some game that he has invented, much as Poprishchin wins by becoming king of Spain. Once again, Gogol has emphasized the overweening ego that leads to delusion, and thence to ugliness. It is not only banality, vulgarity—*poshlost'*—that is exposed; it is thingness. As many have remarked, the "dead souls" of the title refer as much to the actual personae in the book as they do to the deceased serfs that Chichikov is buying. This makes for a terrible irony in Chichikov's transaction with Sobakyevich, for Sobakyevich insists upon thinking and speaking of the serfs as though they were alive. When reminded that they are dead, he first admits it and then recovers himself with: "On the other hand, there is this to be said: What about those people who are now reckoned alive? What kind of people are they? Flies, not people" (6:103). What Sobakyevich does not recognize, because of the thingness to which he has sunk himself, is that he too is dehumanized, just as surely as is every other character in the book, that his soul is also dead. In every case, with the exceptions of Chichikov and the governor's daughter, there has been an abdication in favor of the flesh; spirit has destroyed itself in favor of matter; what might have been beautiful is ugly; instead of harmony there is the cacophony of chaos. It is thus not a living world through which Chichikov moves, but a dead one. Furthermore, Chichikov possesses the possibility of life.

Gogol's point is made doubly emphatic by his style and tone—it all *seems* so Rabelaisian (in the vulgar sense of the term) as he details food and drink, clothes and gestures, habits and features. If we look but slightly more closely, however, we discover that he does so, not in praise, but in mockery.[15] It is not good clean fun, meant to attract us, but materiality, meant to repel. In this sense he is no more giving us a portrait of reality in *Dead Souls,* Part 1, than is Dante in the *Inferno;* it is *Paradiso* that is real, just as the real world in *Orlando Furioso* is not that of Orlando mad (it is lust that made him lose his wits), but that of Orlando sane (when he returns to the battle against the infidel); just as the images on the wall of Plato's cave are a delusion, and reality is the sun. What we have is a character passing through a dream, rather than a portrait of what truly is. The question is when, and if, Chichikov will awaken.

When we look closely at Chichikov's "adventures" in Part 1, we find that they are barely adventures at all, regardless of the censor's opinion; for, other than buying dead souls, he takes no action himself. At best, like Khlestakov, he serves as a catalyst for others to expose themselves, a figure whose presence and proposals draw them out; it is only when his past life is revealed towards the end of Part 1 that we learn of Chichikov's capacity for action, which hints at his capacity for change. Only he has a future. But we do not know this until later; through a good deal of Part 1 he continues to be the undistinguished type of the opening description, although he is also the only one with whom the author shows any propensity to become intimate, for he does, as time goes on, tell us what Chichikov is thinking, so that gradually his typicality fades and his personality emerges. As this process goes on, we find that Chichikov is the one person with whom we can sometimes feel sympathy, a sympathy that is emphasized when his biography is presented.

Even earlier, however, we can wonder about Chichikov's position. For example, in Manilov's house, Chichikov, clearly the superior intellectually, follows the insipid conversation, rather than leads it; and several times he tells Manilov the truth, although Manilov obstinately refuses to believe it. When Manilov says that Chichikov is "a pleasant, educated visitor," Chichikov replies, "Why educated?" He tells Manilov that he "has neither a famous name nor even an outstanding rank," to which Manilov responds, "You have everything" (6.27). Chichikov even goes so far as to say that he is "an insignificant man and nothing more" (6:29). Manilov simply insists, regardless of what Chichikov says, that Chichikov's qualities—whatever they may be, and none of which has been displayed—are beyond compare. Manilov and his wife are more than just stupid people with pretensions to culture and intelligence. They are not only deluded about themselves, they are deluded—through their own choice, without any temptation on Chichikov's part, for they are as he finds them—about the world in which they live. They even believe that the food they serve is delicious, when it is, Gogol tells us, "foolishly and senselessly prepared" (6:26), and Chichikov eats little of it. Only once does Chichikov lie (and it isn't much of a lie), when he tells Manilov, *after* Manilov has given him the dead souls, that he has been persecuted because he always "stuck to the truth, because [his] conscious was clear, because [he] gave a hand to the helpless widow and the unfortunate orphan" (6:37). But the reader only discovers that Chichikov is giving an inaccurate portrait of himself towards the end of Part 1, and Manilov never discovers it, nor does he care to. In any event, nothing that Chichikov says has any effect on the business at hand, least of all the one lie cited above (there is a question that it is in fact a lie to Chichikov's mind), for Manilov makes everything—lie or truth—a confirmation of what he, on his own, already thinks, so that Chichikov does not at all lead him astray. One thing does *not* happen to Manilov—he is *not* swindled. He buys nothing, and by transferring the dead souls to Chichikov, he gains by saving taxes. There is, in fact, no trickery involved, unless it be that of Manilov's own refusal to admit reality into his world. This is profound persistence in delusion, through the fault of no one save Manilov himself. That he is a fool is obvious, but it is not Chichikov who has made him so.

When we turn to Korobochka, we find a woman who, while she is hospitable to Chichikov, is remarkably single-minded. Many in business are like Korobochka, Gogol tells us: "Once something is hatched in his head, there's no way you can get it out; no matter how many arguments, clear as day, you submit to him, everything bounces off him the way a rubber ball bounces off a wall" (6:53). As Chichikov points out, he is doing Korobochka a favor by taking the dead souls off her hands. He is quite right, and she realizes it—there can be a cheat only when there is a loss, but there is none here. Later she will be concerned only that she might have sold her dead souls too cheaply, that *she* might not have succeeded in cheating *him*. It is true, on the other hand, that Chichikov lies to Korobochka when he tells her that he lets out government contracts for produce. But this was a lie, Gogol tells us, "in passing, without any further thought," even though it had "an unexpected success" (6:54). As a con man, Chichikov seems to be singularly uncalculating! As Manilov believed of Chichikov what he wished, so does Korobochka believe of him what she wishes, and she promptly sets to work to make a profit, for the world consists of material exchanges. Her reality, too, is the reality of matter.[16] We have actually thus far been descending the ladder of materiality, and we will descend even further with Sobakyevich and Plyushkin;[17] but an episode intervenes, when Chichikov meets Nozdryov and Mizhuev at a tavern on his way to Sobakyevich's.

This episode could be considered to be a transition to the bestiality of Sobakyevich and the acquisitiveness of Plyushkin, for Nozdryov, who dominates it, is not only a liar, he is also a gambler, and a losing one at that.[18] At the same time, he is a vulgar celebrator of the flesh who believes that Chichikov is just such a one as himself, although Chichikov has given him no reason to think so. Chichikov plays the same role that he played before—a mirror image for a character who wants a mirror image. For Nozdryov, as for Manilov and Korobochka, Chichikov does not exist as a person; only Nozdryov's ego exists, that unreality with which Gogol has so well acquainted us by now.[19]

Nozdryov might be described as a kind of hysteric, out of touch with any reality of any kind, including his own, and certainly Gogol's. Discordance rather than harmony is his rule (if that is not a contradiction in terms).

Nozdryov, not Chichikov, is the first character we have met who is a conscious liar and cheat, although an unsuccessful one, since Chichikov discovers every one of his attempts (it is as though the dreaming Chichikov knows that he is dreaming). When he is caught, he is enraged, not because of the exposure of his dishonesty, but because of his fear that the void behind the mask will be revealed. So Nozdryov assumes another mask: ordering Chichikov to be beaten,

> the lieutenant felt a martial ardor, everything went round in his head, Suvorov floats before him, a great deed will be done by him. "Forward, lads!" he impetuously cries, never thinking that he is wrecking a careful plan for a general assault, that millions of gun muzzles are posted in the embrasures of impregnable fortress walls stretching to the clouds, that his feeble platoon will explode like fluff, and that the fatal bullet ready to slam into his crying gullet is already whistling on its way. [6:86–87]

This has no connection with any reality at all, since Chichikov, far from being an embattled enemy to whom one's courage must be displayed, is simply terrified at the thought of being beaten. The irony is that Nozdryov, who has no notion of truth, who cheats and lies for the sake of cheating and lying while accusing everyone else of lying— the irony is that it is this empty monster, this inchoate, incoherent blabbermouth who will expose Chichikov's dealings, and for no purpose. One wonders if Nozdryov knows that he is telling the truth when he makes his disclosure. Since he is incapable of distinguishing truth from falsity, probably not.

This episode stands as a central point in Part 1 because it is here that Gogol overtly states his theme of reality, truth, harmony, and beauty, for Nozdryov is as ugly as the goblins of the Little Russian tales (his capering and grinning reminds one of a goblin), and in his way he is much more frightening. The fright arises from our knowledge that he lacks any sense of value whatsoever—anything and everything may be staked, and hence all things are equivalent—live souls, dead souls, barrel organs, rubles, stallions, carriages, watches, and chains. Not only is there no distinction between matter and nonmatter, there is not even distinction among things themselves:

> At thirty-five Nozdryov was exactly the same as he had been at eighteen and twenty: a lover of carousals. Marriage did not change him at all, especially since his wife soon departed for the other world, leaving two kids who were decidedly superfluous to him. A pretty nurse minded the children, however. He could not stay home for more than a day at a time. His keen nose could spot a fair with its gatherings and balls more than ten versts away; in the twinkling of an eye he was there to quarrel and start confusion at the green table, for, like all such people, he had a passion for cards. [6:70]

This is more than just irresponsibility; it is downright destructive, for Nozdryov has as little sense of relationship as he has of value—indeed, he breaks relationships among people. In the sense of the disgust, the loathing, that he inspires, particularly in Chichikov, he, more than any other person in Part 1, is an expression of nonreality; for him falsity is a way of life, whereas in Gogol's eyes, only the true is real.[20]

From lack of distinction between ugliness and beauty, between truth and falsity, between reality and nonreality, between matter and nonmatter, we will descend to bestiality, to denial of the human essence itself. But before that happens, Chichikov, on his way to see Sobakyevich after the interlude with Nozdryov, experiences a vision of beauty:

> . . . a young sixteen-year-old girl, with golden hair very adroitly and gracefully smoothed on her little head. The pretty oval of her face was rounded like a fresh little egg, and, like it, was white with that pellucid whiteness of a fresh, just-laid one when it is held against the light in the dark-complexioned

hands of a housekeeper testing it and the rays of the beaming sun pass through it; her delicate ears were also transparent, glowing with the warm light that passed through them. The alarm in her open-held lips, in her tearful eyes—this was all so graceful in her that our hero gazed at her for some minutes. [6:90]

The contrast with Nozdryov, on the one hand, and with Sobakyevich, on the other, reemphasizes Gogol's theme; it also humanizes Chichikov, who later, when he sees the young lady at the ball, is again deeply affected:

> She seemed to resemble a kind of toy precisely chiselled out of ivory; she alone stood out white and pellucid and radiant from the dull lackluster crowd.
>   Apparently it happens in the world; apparently for a few moments in their lives even Chichikovs are changed into poets, although the word "poet" is too much. At least he felt himself like an absolutely young man, almost a Hussar. [6:169]

Although Chichikov will not physically attain the girl, still he is capable of the vision, unlike the "dull lackluster crowd."

The first meeting on the road, however, is succeeded by Sobakyevich. To light, grace, and the possibility of rebirth (the egg), there succeeds heaviness; to a figure "precisely chiselled out of ivory" succeeds one of those faces "on the finishing of which, nature has not much subtilized, has not employed fine instruments, such as files, gimlets, and so forth, but has simply hacked out straight from the shoulder: it smashed once with an axe—the nose appeared; it smashed again— the lips appeared; it dug out the eye with a large drill; and without ever planing it down, shoved it into the world, saying, 'It lives!' " (6:94–95). To what Chichikov perceived as beauty and innocence succeeds ugly matter.[21]

Everything surrounding Sobakyevich reflects his untransparent solidity (or materiality): the thick fence, the heavy beams, the oak well. Sobakyevich, uncouth, a "bear" who is always stepping on people's feet, is the very picture of ferocity waiting to be set loose. He dislikes everyone whom Chichikov mentions, the very people whom Manilov thought so fine (but Manilov seemed to think everyone fine). Education is to him a detestable thing (by "enlightenment" he means "delicacy," although he possesses none himself). Dinner is an engorgement rather than a social occasion: "There seemed to be no soul in that body at all, or if there was, it was not where it should be, and, as with immortal Koshchei, it was somewhere beyond the mountains and hidden by such a thick shell that whatever moved in its depths produced no disturbance on the surface" (6:101). When it comes to selling his dead souls, he thinks—if it can be called thinking—in entirely material terms, even more so than Korobochka. He insists upon considering the dead souls that Chichikov is offering to take off his hands as alive. By a live soul, however, he means a thing that produces a product or performs a service: the *coachman* Mikheyev, the *carpenter* Probka Stepan, the *bricklayer* Milushkin, the *shoemaker* Maxim Telyatnikov, the *trader* Yeremey Sorokoplokin. Each is defined in terms of a function performed for Sobakeyvich; each is a contribution to Sobakyevich's material well-being, rather like food. Indeed, he will later list them by function on the deed transferring them to Chichikov.

Like an animal, Sobakyevich has no sense of time, so that life and death have no meaning for him, so that the soul, as Gogol pointed out, has no reality. His bestiality is evident in his eating habits—food is meant to fill the stomach, and once having eaten, one sleeps.

Chichikov, supposedly a wily swindler, again finds it difficult to understand. He finds again that a simple matter of fact—the serfs whom Sobakyevich insists upon lauding are, after all, dead—cannot penetrate the bear's head. He finds himself beholding a dream world that the dreamer persists in regarding as real. When Sobakyevich says that many who are counted as living are no more than flies, Chichikov responds, "Yes, but they exist, and this is a dream." To which Sobakyevich vehemently retorts, "No, not a dream!" (6:103). Chichikov, embarrassed, returns to a discussion of the price to be paid. He soon perceives that any attempt to talk about the life or death of the souls is doomed to failure, although, in exasperation, he does say, "What are they really—as though this were actually something serious!" (6:104).

Chichikov does recognize what Sobakyevich is; indeed, Chichikov seems to be the only person thus far in Part 1 who is capable of perceiving reality. As Sobakyevich makes out the list of souls that he is selling, Chichikov muses to himself:

> Were you born a bear, or did a life in the wilds, sowing crops, and trouble with peasants turn you into a bear, and is that why you have become what is called a fist? But no: I think you would have been the same even if you had been fashionably

educated, even if you had entered the race and lived in Petersburg instead of in the wilds. The only difference is that here you consume half a saddle of mutton with kasha, after having snacked on a plate-sized cheese cake, while there you would eat cutlets with truffles. Here you have peasants in your power: you're in tune with them, and of course you don't hurt them, because they are yours and because it would be the worse for you; and there you would have officials at whom you would always be snapping your fingers, having grasped that they're not your serfs, or you would pillage the public purse. No, there's no straightening a man who's a fist! [6:106]

Later he thinks: "A fist, a fist! . . . and a rogue[22] in addition!" (6:107).

It should by now be borne in upon us that Chichikov is of a different order from the characters whom he meets in *Dead Souls,* Part 1. Like Don Quixote, he is a wanderer in a foreign land, but, unlike the Don, he does not change that world, although one suspects that he would like to do so. It is as though Chichikov's eyes were being opened through his "adventures" (they are really more like interviews than adventures) to a knowledge of himself. This is as much as to say that there is the beginning of an awakening in Chichikov[23] as he increasingly discovers how little a thing the ego is and as his intimations of reality and truth and beauty become more conscious.[24]

Chichikov does not yet know the depths, however. From those obsessed with things, we turn to the thing itself, Plyushkin. For the first time in Part 1, Gogol gives the reader the story of how a character got that way,[25] and one wonders if this is not meant to serve as a warning to both Chichikov and the reader of how a man can deny the humanity with which he is born, how he can deny those "clouds of glory" with which he came into the world.[26] Here materiality reaches its lowest point, beyond that of even the beast. For the beast—that is, Sobakyevich—matter, after all, served as food, in both the literal and figurative senses, while it also served as an expression of the bear himself. Now, with Plyushkin, matter exists for its own sake, as a "good" in itself, pure and untouched by human hands. Plyushkin is not just a miser who enjoys accumulation; he is more like one of the inhabitants of Dante's fourth circle, who are too obscure to be distinguished one from another. The ugliness of his world—if it can be called a world—descends to utter formlessness, like the contents of paint tubes, rather than paintings; ink stains, rather than words; cater-wauling, rather than music; rotting weeds, rather than a garden. Plyushkin values nothing, not even himself, and it is an appalling sight.

Plyushkin was not always so. Gogol tells us that "there was a time when he was only a thrifty manager. He was married, with a family, and neighbors would drive to his house to dine, to listen, and to learn management and wise economy from him" (6:117–18). The change occurred when Plyushkin's wife died; love was lost, and human rela-tionships were broken; from a thrifty manager who valued things in proper proportion and balance, he was transformed into a conserver of objects, horrified at the thought of using anything that might bring him some profit to be stored away. Of course, this might be regarded as a virtue carried to excess, a kind of dramatic example of Aristotelian vice. It can certainly be regarded as a loss of harmony, almost madness. Gogol's deliberate contrast between what was and what is informs us equally of what is real and what is not, what is beautiful and what is ugly. Proportion and balance remain Gogol's criteria—and the suspicion of a Platonic influence here grows stronger than ever.[27] The Plyushkin episode makes possibly the most powerful statement in *Dead Souls*, Part 1, of Gogol's aesthetic attitude. Indeed, Plyushkin, before his wife's death, was not much different from the landowner whom Gogol was to describe in *Selected Passages*,[28] a point that many who have castigated *Selected Passages* while praising *Dead Souls* seem to have ignored. Once balance, once concordance of elements, has been lost, Plyushkin is lost; there was a progressive deterioration until he became the thing that Chichikov finally meets:

> His face had nothing special about it; it was quite like that of many lean old men, except that his chin came very far for-ward, so that he continually had to cover it with a handkerchief in order not to drop spittle on it; his little eyes had still not lost their luster, and they skipped about under the high pro-truding eyebrows like mice when, poking their sharp snouts out of their dark holes, pricking up their ears, and batting their whiskers, they look out for a hiding tomcat or prankish boy, and suspiciously sniff the air. [6:116]

He reminds us of some of the portraits we met in the Little Russian tales. Chichikov is startled, astonished, and, finally, almost at a loss for words:

For a long time he could not devise any words in which to explain the reason for his visit. He had been on the point of expressing himself in some such spirit as, hearing of the virtue and rare qualities of [Plyushkin's] soul, he had considered it his duty personally to bring him the tribute of his respects. But he caught himself just in time, feeling that this was too much. After casting another sidelong glance at everything in the room, he felt that the words "virtue" and "rare qualities of soul" might successfully be replaced by "economy" and "order"; therefore, having transformed his speech in this way, he said that, hearing of his economy and rare administration of his estates, he considered it his duty to become acquainted and to pay his compliments in person. Of course, it might have been possible to adduce another, better reason, but no other came into his head at the time. [6:120–21]

Chichikov again seems to be the exception in Part 1, in that he consistently recognizes what is false—he knows the difference (the words he finally does use are not far from correct—Plyushkin's administration of his estate is indeed "rare") even if he has not actually found the truth for himself. He is again struck, at a loss for words, by the lack of reality of the world into which he has wandered. One can see him shaking his head and wondering if these people really exist.

Plyushkin, like his predecessors, is delighted at the thought of getting something for nothing. He, too, thinks himself wise and Chichikov a fool.[29] All the frauds and cheats upon which Gogol had so concentrated in his short stories are advanced once more, and the innocent man roves among them, wide-eyed and wondering, the sensitive man—who looks so ordinary—surrounded by ugliness. Chichikov has retained, or is rediscovering, a sense of value, unlike Plyushkin, whose possessions are important only because he possesses them, without realizing that he is equally possessed by them. It is not Chichikov who is the acquirer—as Evdokimov, for one, insists—because the dead souls that he is purchasing have a further purpose: they have value, not just as things to be collected and hoarded, to be put away whether useful or not, but for meaning, for value to be realized. In the same connection, we may note again that Chichikov has cheated no one. Even if he gets the dead souls for nothing, he is being generous, for he assumes the tax burden; he is doubly generous if he pays for them, as he usually must. No one loses by the transaction. In some distant future, some institution or individual *may* lose *if* Chichikov does not pay off the mortgages that he plans to secure with the dead souls as collateral (even here there is some question—should one pay a continual tax on what no longer exists). But if the mortages should be paid off— and given Chichikov's desire for respectability and concern with his descendants, we may assume that he will at least try to do so—not only will no one have lost, but everyone will have gained.[30] This is not to make Chichikov a spreader of sweetness and light—he makes no effort in that direction—but there is no spreading of acidity and darkness either. Chichikov may not be a reformer, but he also cannot be accused of being a corrupter. He takes things as he finds them; if anything, he is repelled by them, as he is repelled by Manilov, Korobochka, Nozdryov, Sobakyevich, and Plyushkin.

As happened so often with Gogol's fiction, *Dead Souls,* Part 1, splits into two sections of almost equal length. The first section, which carries us through chapter 6, contains Chichikov's arrival in town, his interviews with various persons, and the buying of the dead souls. In the second section, chapters 7 through 11, the action picks up as the sales are registered; a ball is given, at which Chichikov is further intrigued by the young beauty he first saw on the road; Nozdryov first tells the truth about Chichikov (without knowing that he is doing so); slanderous rumors start; Chichikov leaves town (presumably with the dead souls still registered in his name; if they have been returned to their original owners, Chichikov has certainly been cheated); and the story of Chichikov's life before he arrived in the town of N. is told. The section, and Part 1, ends with the famous troika passage and with Chichikov setting off to new adventures in Part 2.

Although this second half of Part 1 is somewhat more integrated than the first half, Gogol still shows himself to be more an episodic writer than a writer of sustained narrative, and *Dead Souls's* resemblance to the *romanzi* of the Renaissance is as strong as ever.

While the deeds of transfer are being registered, Sobakyevich gives away the fact that the souls are dead, then he quickly recovers to insist that they are alive. He deliberately lies. Curiously enough, for those who believe that Chichikov is the villain of the piece, Chichikov, although agitated that the revelation may mean that the souls will not be registered in his name, says nothing. One wonders, indeed, who is really more afraid of the disclosure, the buyer or the seller? None of the officials exhibit the slightest desire to discover the truth—and what difference, we may ask, if they did? We must again emphasize that no fraud has been committed by Chichikov. The important thing is that no one cares anyhow, and no one, aside from Chichikov, ever will. In the event, it is only appearance that will bother people, not reality.

The ball makes this particularly clear, for the ball is a microcosm of Gogol's theme. At the ball, the contrasts between falsity and truth, appearance and reality, seduction and beauty, are made manifest. The scene might have been written by Edgar Allen Poe in a mocking mood.

When Chichikov arrives at the ball, he slips, as is usual with him, into an acceptance of falsity; that is, he acts the part assigned to him of a charming millionaire who is particularly attractive to the ladies. He has not asked for the reception that he receives, but he does find it most pleasant; he is the seducee. Of course, the attitude of the town toward him is based on speculation, on what people would like to believe about him and about themselves. It is illusion that is of interest here. It is all not only superficial and banal, it is untrue. Chichikov is greeted like a movie star (if I may be permitted the anachronism) whom the guests insist upon considering in terms of his screen image rather than in terms of his actual person, and he is so seduced by the attention paid to him that he does his best to act out the part in which he has been cast. He succeeds admirably; or rather, he forgets the grasp of reality he had hitherto exhibited sufficiently to enter into the dream, discarding the face behind the mask. He has a position, he is respectable, and he enjoys it very much. This is seduction by a lie that he hasn't even constructed for himeslf, participation in other people's dreams at the will of the dreamers.

Then suddenly, "happening to raise his eyes, he stood immobile, as though struck by a blow." Before Chichikov stands the young girl whom he had met on the road, a girl whom "an artist might take as a model for a Madonna" (6:166). This beauty completely overcomes Chichikov (I do not think that the Madonna reference is accidental) and so returns him to reality that he cannot even make sensible small talk: "Chichikov was so confused that he could not utter one intelligible word and muttered the devil knows what" (6:166). The girl is taken away by her mother "while Chichikov still stood motionless, like a man who cheerfully goes out into the street for a stroll, eyes disposed to gaze upon everything, and suddenly stops motionless at the recollection that he has forgotten something. . . . So Chichikov suddenly became alien to everything going on around him" (6:167). Beauty, I would suggest, has returned Chichikov to himself, that is, to the truth, and he is not, after all, just such a one as those who had but a moment before so seduced him. He has stepped out of the dream and is now indeed alien to his surroundings.[31] All attempts to lure him back to the unreality of the ball fail. He loses the simpering grace that he had formerly exhibited, and "a kind of awkwardness appeared in all his movements" (6:169). Gogol is careful to point out that this is not a feeling of love in Chichikov. It is rather the contact with what is real and beautiful (the girl yawns at his attempts at social conversation): "she alone stood out white and pellucid and radiant from the dull lackluster crowd." Poetry has come into his life, even if to describe Chichikov as a poet, Gogol says, is "too much."

The effect is that Chichikov neglects—if he does not contemn— all the other women at the ball because of his fascination with the young lady. The final result is that they in turn find him despicable, and as they formerly attributed honorable qualities to him, they now attribute dishonorable ones, which are equally false. This is the beginning of his fall in the eyes of the town of N.,[32] which really may be taken as a compliment to Chichikov, considering the portraits that Gogol has given us of the townsfolk.

Nozdryov's drunken announcement that the souls that Chichikov has been buying are dead would have had no effect at all if Chichikov had not, because of the girl, stepped out of the dream. Indeed, it will act as no more than a first excuse to heap thoroughly undeserved calumnies upon Chichikov which will constitute the genuine reasons for making his flight from N.—he had already announced his intention of leaving and had only stayed because he was importuned—so precipitous. Again, it is Chichikov who recognizes the truth about N., even though, Gogol points out, his recognition is partially owing to the discomfiture that he had suffered at the ball. Having returned to his room after the ball, Chichikov sat in his chair, and there was something

> unpleasant, troubled, in his heart, a kind of painful emptiness remained in it. . . . What are they stupidly happy about? It's been a bad harvest year in the province, everything is expensive, and they're all for balls! . . . It's incredible for a woman to wind a thousand rubles around herself! And it's really taken from the peasants' rents, or still worse, out of our brother's conscience. It's perfectly well known why you take a bribe and act against your conscience: it's to get a shawl for your wife or lots of wide-skirted dresses . . . a ball is simply trash, it's not in the

Russian spirit, not in the Russian nature. . . . Just because a
Frenchman is as much a boy at forty as he was at fifteen, we
have to be too! No, really . . . after every ball it's exactly as
though you'd committed a sin: you don't even want to remember it. There's nothing in your head, just like after a conversation with a high society type. . . . What is it, moral or im-
moral? The devil only knows which! [6:174–75]

Such a speech, regardless of the mixed reasons for it, would be
impossible for anyone else in *Dead Souls,* Part 1, for it is only Chichikov
who has a conscience, only he to whom the moral question occurs. If
Dead Souls, Part 1, is Gogol's portrait of Hell, then Chichikov is its
almost victim, not its sovereign. I would suggest, in this connection,
that an appropriate comparison to Gogol's ball is Poe's "The Mask of
the Red Death." In both cases, the contrast between reality and appearance is emphasized, although in different ways. But Gogol's setting
is equally diseased, and is equally unaware of its disease; here, too, we
have a horror story and a tale of entrapment. Fortunately, there is an
escape for Chichikov, and he will take it while the dance is played out
behind him. There is, we may be sure, a future for him, while there
is none for those he leaves behind.

Gogol reinforces the point by the scene between the "lady agreeable
in all respects" and the "simply agreeable lady." Their first concern is
precisely with those clothes that Chichikov spoke of in his soliloquy.
From that they move on to Chichikov himself and his buying of dead
souls. The souls themselves are not of importance; the ladies are instead
interested in why he is buying them, and they decide that it is for
another, much more nefarious, purpose than his real one: it is a cover
for his elopement with the governor's daughter, the young lady who had
so captivated him at the ball that he ignored everyone else. Not only
is Chichikov slandered, so is the girl, and Nozdryov is dragged in as an
accomplice of Chichikov's. Falsity piles upon falsity, and all is taken
for truth; or rather, the ladies convince themselves—out of a sordid
spirit of resentment—that it is the truth. Before we know it, the story,
much elaborated, is all over town. Disharmony sets in as each person
worries about his own position: "They all suddenly discovered sins
in themselves that had never been. The words 'deal souls' sounded so
indefinite that they even began to wonder if these might not be an allu-
sion to bodies suddenly dead and hastily buried" (6:193). Chichikov
is investigated officially, but "all the research carried out by the officials

revealed that they did not know exactly what Chichikov was, but that he certainly had to be something" (6:196). Speculation is piled upon speculation, confusion upon confusion, as they try to find a personality for Chichikov (at no point does anyone ask Chichikov himself why he is buying dead souls, whether he is a counterfeiter, whether he is a robber in disguise, whether he is Captain Kopeikin, whether he is Napoleon escaped from St. Helena; furthermore, those from whom he bought his deal souls continue to insist, for their own purposes, that he is a fine fellow). All the investigations get nowhere, so they decide to ask, of all people, Nozdryov. Says Gogol: "These officials were very strange people, but so are those of other vocations: they knew very well that Nozdryov was a liar, that not one word of his was to be trusted, not even in the most trifling matter, but it was precisely to him that they resorted. Just try to cope with mankind!" (6:207). Nozdryov happily confuses things even further by confidently recounting that: Chichikov had bought an enormous number of dead souls from him, Nozdryov; Chichikov was a spy; Nozdryov had gone to school with Chichikov, where Chichikov had been a notorious tattletale; Chichikov was indeed a counterfeiter; Chichikov was planning to elope with the governor's daughter, aided by Nozdryov (entirely fictitious details of the elopement are given). In answer to a question about Napoleon, Nozdryov "talked such nonsense that it not only had no resemblance to truth [*pravda*], it simply had no resemblance to anything at all, so that the officials moved away from him sighing. . . . The officials were in a worse position than before, and the end of it was that they could in no way learn what Chichikov was" (6:209). Gogol's description of the public prosecutor's reaction makes the chaotic state of the town perfectly clear:

> All this gossip, opinions, and rumors for some reason affected the public prosecutor most of all. They affected him so much that when he went home he began to think, and suddenly, for no reason, as they say, he died. Whether it was a stroke or something else that hit him, as soon as he sat down, he banged down from the chair onto his back. As is the custom, they wrung their hands and cried out, "Oh, my God!" sent for the doctor to bleed him, but saw that the public prosecutor was only a soulless body. Only then did they in condolence recognize that the deceased had indeed had a soul, although in his modesty he had never shown it. At the same

time, the phenomenon of death is just as terrifying in a little man as it is in a great one: one who had walked not too long ago, moved, played whist, signed various papers, and whose thick eyebrows and blinking eye had so often been seen among the officials, now lay on a table; his left eye did not blink at all, but one eyebrow was still raised in a kind of questioning expression. What the deceased was asking, why he died or why he lived, God alone knows. [6:209–10]

There is little room for wonder about how the public prosecutor's unknown question will be answered. Any doubt that the "dead souls" of the title refer to the inhabitants of N. as well as to the serfs that Chichikov is buying should also be dispelled by this paragraph. Discord, ugliness, unreality have lain like a pall over the town; the "red death" was in their midst, and they will all succumb to it. Not only did his fellow citizens not recognize the public prosecutor's soul, he did not admit it, "in his modesy," himself. Nor, it is safe to say, do the others recognize their souls either. This amounts to a refusal to admit, which becomes a willful denial of the truth, so that the dream becomes a nightmare. "What is truth?" asked Pilate, "And did not stay for an answer" (John 18:38).

But, we are told, "Chichikov knew absolutely nothing of all this" (6:211). Indeed, he wanders about the town unable "to decide whether he had gone out of his mind or the officials had lost their brains, whether all this was a dream or whether a waking stupidity, more vivid than any dream, had been brewed" (6:213). When Nozdryov comes to see Chichikov and informs him of the falsities with which he is surrounded, adding a few for good measure, "Chichikov rubbed his eyes several times, in an attempt to convince himself that he was not hearing all this in a dream" (6:214–15). This is the point at which Chichikov, after some difficulties, leaves town, being stopped for a few moments by the public prosecutor's funeral, whose path crosses his. He thinks to himself: "Nevertheless, it's a good thing to meet a funeral; they say it means good luck if you meet a funeral" (6:220). There immediately follows an apostrophe to Russia.[33]

With this funeral the town of N. is laid to rest. It is indeed a sign of good fortune for Chichikov, because it means his escape from the nightmare, his escape from death. Never again will N. and its inhabitants be mentioned by Gogol or thought of by Chichikov. In reality, it was dead from the very beginning, and if it had a soul, it certainly did its utmost to keep it hidden, though hardly "out of modesty." If all that Gogol had in mind was a satiric portrait of corruption, *Dead Souls,* Part 1, might have ended here—with certain changes of emphasis throughout, to be sure. This would be comparable to having *Orlando Furioso* stop with canto 39 and Orlando's recovery of his wits. But there is more to be said; the tale is not yet over, for there is still a victory to be won. Reality had to be asserted, not just negatively implied; matter must be succeeded by spirit, ugliness by beauty.

Thus Gogol turns, as though starting upon a new path, to a discussion of Chichikov's character and origins, in preparation for that new world into which Gogol wished to launch him, a world that we can guess was meant to be portrayed in *Dead Souls,* Part 2 (and possibly Part 3). We will see, Gogol tells us, "how the business will further advance, what successes and failures will come to the hero, how he will resolve and overcome more difficult obstacles, how colossal images will be displayed, how the secret levers of the broad tale will move, its horizon further expand, and it all take on a majestic lyrical flow" (6:241).[34] As Gogol has indicated before, and as the troika passage at the end of Part 1 also indicates, the subject is in fact a much broader one than the adventures of Pavel Ivanovich Chichikov. This is also emphasized in the recounting of his life. He is indeed but a "fellow passing by," as a relation described him at his birth (6:224). And Gogol establishes him as a stranger to the world from the very beginning, with neither friends nor, shortly, parents. His father's last advice is that money "is the most reliable thing in the world. A comrade or friend will swindle you and be first to betray you in misfortune [Chichikov certainly found *that* out], but a kopek will never betray, no matter what misfortune you may find. You may do anything and break through anything in the world with a kopek" (6:225). Much of Chichikov's life thereafter consisted of attempts to follow his father's advice, although "it cannot be said that our hero's nature was so bleak and hard and his feelings so dulled that he knew neither pity nor compassion; he would even have liked to help, if it did not involve a significant sum, if he did not have to disturb those monies he had determined not to disturb" (6:228). Gogol carefully points out, however, that it is not money for its own sake that interests Chichikov, unlike most of those we met in *Dead Souls,* Part 1. It is always a means to an end, never an end in itself. The end is always "decent, seemly, decorous,"[35] involved with comfort, material possessions, descendants, and a respectable position in the world, it is true, but there is something else behind it all. "Whatever bespoke wealth and contentment produced an impression on him that he could not comprehend himself" (6:228). Another way of putting it is to say that Chichikov himself is unable to define some obscure yearning within him, some hidden awareness of a higher order than that of the banal vulgarity with which he is surrounded, symbolized by "wealth and contentment." He is ambitious to attain a kind of harmony, and he thinks that following his father's advice is the way to get there. Of course, he is wrong, but that is the lesson he must learn. At the same time, Gogol constantly stresses Chichikov's difference from his surroundings, despite his ability to adapt to them when need be. He never, however, confuses the mask that he often finds it convenient to wear with reality—not because he knows *what* reality is, but simply, inwardly, because he knows *that* it is. He never takes appearance, his own or anyone else's, for truth. Method, not end, is the problem.

It is most interesting that, although Chichikov's schemes (which consisted of following custom, but putting custom to better use than most) often came close to success, at the last moment something always happened to ruin him, and he had to start over. His position is set forth by himself:

"Why me? Why should misfortune come down upon me? Who misses opportunities in his duties these days—everybody grabs. I've never made anyone unhappy: I haven't stolen from widows, I haven't ruined anyone, I've taken advantage of abundance, I've taken where anyone would take; if I hadn't taken advantage, others would have taken advantage. Why do others prosper, and why must I die like a worm? What am I now? What am I fit for? With what eyes could I look into the eyes of a respectable father of a family? How can I not feel pangs of conscience, knowing that I burden the earth to no end, and what will my children say? They will say, 'Father is a swine, he hasn't left us a fortune!'" [6:238]

The answer is that misfortune dogs Chichikov because he is taking the wrong approach—he is bound to fail until he realizes that it is the inward path that he must take if he is to reach his goal, instead of the outward one; until he actualizes his intimations; until he comprehends that a mask is as capable of deceiving the wearer as it is the audience.

Thus Chichikov with a past is no longer the mere catalyst that he was for a good deal of Part 1. The biography Gogol supplies us with gives him much greater distinction than he had previously, both as an individual and as a symbol. He certainly can no longer be regarded as an unimportant person. It would appear, by the time we get to the troika passage, that Chichikov had changed in Gogol's mind and that Gogol may have thought that he was taking on the qualities of an embodiment of the nation; that is, that he was becoming a real epic hero.[36] The biography and the troika passage (this is not the first time, as we know, that Gogol marks an important event in Chichikov's career with a carriage, although this is the first time that the carriage is positively identified with Russia) indicate a definite shift in point of view, in tone, and in concentration, something that does not happen in Ariosto—or in any of the other *romanzi* writers, for that matter. That a serious romance could be written had of course been shown by Spenser (whom Gogol probably did not know), when he promised to "overgoe Ariosto," and by Tasso. But those were complete conceptions from the beginning; they did not involve the kind of change that Gogol was proposing in midstream. What Gogol originally had, or was given, was an *idea,* no more—the idea of a man who had conceived the project of buying dead souls that were still on the census rolls in the hope of mortgaging them later on and using the money that he had borrowed with this strange collateral in order to make a fortune. It was immediately obvious that this setup would give the author an opportunity to travel around the country and to survey the state of the nation. In this conception the central character would serve as a kind of observation post. It was not long, however, before the necessity to make this central character stand in contrast to his surroundings was borne in upon the author. This meant, as time went on, that he, rather than his interlocutors, became the central focus, and along with him, further possibilities opened up, and Gogol perceived that he might well have a *romanzo* hero on his hands. But Chichikov continued to grow, and by the end of Part 1, by which time the necessity for positive rather than negative expression became clear, he began to look more and more like an epic hero. Humor, the prime mode of Part 1, is not easily—if it is at all—adaptable to such expression. A real Chichikov was taking the place of the anonymous negation who had appeared at the beginning, and now positive exemplars had to be placed before him so that there could be genuine interaction and so that a genuine reformation could be accomplished.[37] Ariosto's device of madness and recovery from it, which had provided a framework, could no longer be used (Chichikov had often expressed his bewilderment at the "dream," a variation of Orlando's insanity, that he found himself in) simply because of the growth in Chichikov; a repetition of the device would have meant retrogression rather than progression. Furthermore, the giving up of madness meant a change, to Gogol, from the humorous to the serious (there is little humor, we note, in chapter 11). It was now the turn of either *Gerusalemme Liberata* or *La Divina Commedia*. But this turn from *Orlando Furioso* proved to be an insuperable artistic problem. The only possibility would have been to end *Dead Souls* earlier and then write a completely different work instead of attempting a continuation.

As he recognized Chichikov's value as a symbol, however, Gogol found himself at a loss. Chichikov simply could not be given up (even if Gogol had wanted to, it is doubtful that his public would have allowed him to). On the other hand, the "majestic lyrical flow," the Dantesque style that he had thought possible and that he had promised in at least two of the digressions in chapter 11, did not seem to fit with the artistic form with which he had started. As Chichikov's biography indicates, form and content were no longer suited to each other, the harmonious whole that artistic composition required (he was aware of the failure of a different method in *The Inspector General,* a failure so far as the audience's comprehension was concerned) could no longer be achieved; at least one point that he was trying to make—the realization or the embodiment of beauty—could not be accomplished. Thus Part 2 had to be burned, and *Selected Passages* would remain.

6
The Digressions of
Dead Souls, Part 1

Unlike many of his critics, Gogol thought that the digressions of *Dead Souls*, Part 1, formed an integral part of his poem. Actually, the word digressions, although I will use it, is a misnomer: these are comments, increasingly lyrical, which are carefully interwoven with the actions and characters; they are footnotes, if you will, that serve as a way for Gogol to inform his audience that his fiction, fantastic as it may appear, has real meaning, that the tale is a statement about reality, that it is neither a divertissement nor simple social criticism. He had of course indulged in digressions before, but never had they shown the integrated sequence that we find here. Indeed, they display as much development as does the fiction itself.[1]

The digressions start with remarks, in chapter 2, on the place of "low" characters in a work of this sort, and end with an almost mystical statement about Russia in chapter 11. Even in the former case, however, Gogol lets us know what his subject is to be:

> The author is deeply ashamed of having so long occupied his readers with people of a low class, knowing by experience how reluctant they are to meet the low estates. Such is the Russian: a powerful passion to put on airs with someone whose rank is a bit higher than his own, a nodding acquaintance with a count or a prince for him is better than any close friendly relations. The author is even fearful for his hero, who is only a collegiate councillor. Perhaps court councillors will make his acquaintance, but those who have already stolen up to the rank of general, God knows, perhaps they will cast one of those scornful glances that a man proudly casts at anything that licks his boots, or, still worse, perhaps pass by

with an inattention murderous to the author. But however deplorable either may be, we must return to the hero. [6:20–21]

The book, we are told, is not necessarily to be a "pleasant" one. Its subject, furthermore, is not to be restricted. In accordance with the principles laid down in "A Textbook of Literature for Russian Youth," a new word will here be uttered. The ultimate subject is Russia, and Gogol's address is to the Russian. This is not to say that in his character portraits Gogol wishes always to remain on the typical level, for "all these gentlemen . . . who seem so very much alike—still if you look closely, you will see many of the most elusive peculiarities; these gentlemen are terribly difficult to portray" (6:23–24).[2] This warning about the subject matter was meant to make the reader aware that Gogol was not just another social satirist aiming at a reform—or overthrow—of the system. The aim was a far broader one, still not completely revealed, and Gogol was to make it explicit only gradually. The earlier digressions are all in a more or less playful mood, cajolements rather than exhortations, tinged with a certain sarcasm as he moves, for example, to an attack on egoism and pretension in chapter 3: "It must be said that if we in Russia have not kept up with foreigners in anything else, we have far surpassed them in our ability to handle ourselves" (6:51) by adopting different personalities according to the circumstances in which the Russian finds himself and the people he is talking to (the remark is made apropos Chichikov's chameleonlike ability to make himself agreeable no matter what the company surrounding him). It is jocular, but the "we in Russia" enlarges the scope to include the character and meaning of the entire country. The vast majority of the digressions that take Russia for their subject will be closely connected with Chichikov (and the digressions will become increasingly serious, the jocular tone will be gradually dropped, until, in chapter 11, nothing of it will remain), a point, I think, of particular significance, since it is connected with the changing character of Chichikov himself, his movement towards becoming the epic hero.

One could collect the digressions under various headings, such as "The Russian Landscape," "The Art of Character Drawing," "Women's Love of Gossip," "The Uses of Language," and so on and so forth. This would be to separate them from the poem, however, and to destroy their meaning,[3] which arises—as it must if *Dead Souls* is an artistic work—out of their context and sequence as well as out of what is specifically said in them. Their greater frequency as the poem advances is an indication of this. They sweep, in chapter 11, when the end of Part 1 is approaching, to a crescendo as they become increasingly lyrical.

I do not think that any of this was deliberately planned; that is, I do not think Gogol had fully worked out the details of his project beforehand beyond the ideas, first, of a novel and, then, of a comic romance. The project grew, however, according to the dictation of the material that Gogol had chosen, which increasingly and more obviously expressed his own convictions—not because of manipulation on his part, but because, feeling as he did, being a subjective rather than an objective writer, he could not keep those convictions out, even if he had wanted to. The convictions were what many critics found difficult to accept, so that, more to justify themselves than genuinely to evaluate Gogol, the expedient of finding change in him was brought into play. If we look seriously at these digressions, however, we find that no such change in fact occurred.

The point is emphasized towards the end of chapter 3, when Gogol has for a moment decided to turn away from Korobochka, lest, he says, "the gay in a flash turn into the mournful, if you remain immobile before it too long, and then God knows what will come into your head." It is too early to adopt a solemn tone, and Gogol advises jocularity. Still, he wonders, attempting to plant a seed in the reader's mind: "Is there indeed such a great abyss separating her from her sisters? . . . Why amid unthinking, gay, careless moments does another magical current, of its own accord, rush past?" (6:58). Gogol's reference is to two things: what he hopes his own art is accomplishing—that is, striking the reader at a deeper level of sensibility than the obvious, and rather crass, social one, evoking a further and more general meaning than is immediately apparent on the page; he is also reading a lesson by asking the reader to be aware of the magical innate current that points to a truth more profound than the one that the reader assumes in superficial observation of the world in which he lives. Thus early are we made aware of the difference between matter and reality. This is paralleled by the contrast in the fiction itself between dream and truth. That "magical current," we note, rushes past "of its own accord,"[4] subject neither to the processes of rational consciousness nor to the ordinary concerns of make-a-living lives. The truth, the "intimations of immortality," those "clouds of glory," remain pure within us and capable, when recognized, of returning us to reality: "The laugh has still not completely vanished from your face, but . . . you are already different from what you were, and your face is already lit by a different light" (6:58). It is this light that gives the possibility of resurrection.

Two chapters later, after the Nozdryov episode and after a digression at the beginning of chapter 5 on the wonders of middle-class digestion, Chichikov meets the young lady, and the "magical current" flows once more:

> Everywhere, wherever it may be in life, among its callous, roughly poor and dirty-moldy lower orders, or among its monotonously cold and boringly tidy upper classes, if only once on his way, a man will meet a phenomenon unlike any that he has hitherto happened to see, which, if only once, will awaken a feeling in him unlike those it has been decreed for him to feel all his life. Everywhere, through whatever sorrows out of which our life is plaited, a splended joy flashes gaily past, just as sometimes a splended carriage with a golden harness, picturesque horses, and windows glittering with brightness suddenly, unexpectedly, scuds past some seedy poor hamlet that has seen nothing but rural carts.[5] [6:90]

Exactly what this light is we are not told (although it does remind one of the light that appeared on Mount Tabor), but we do know that neither Chichikov nor anyone else—particularly the reader—is hopelessly lost so long as he is capable of recognizing it. Despite corruption, swindlers, cheats, glorifiers of matter, closed minds, liars and deceivers, this life is not a vale of tears, no matter how "sad" our Russia may be. Even in the most grubby surroundings, beauty exists, and there is an inner impulse which yearns for its actualization, its embodiment. What is fictionally described in *Dead Souls*, in other words, is meant as a contrast with reality rather than as a portrait of it. The real world remains the world created by God.[6]

Unfortunately, Chichikov, like most of us, has been deceived by the ways of matter; he has spent so long in illusion's grasp that it is exceedingly difficult for him to escape from it. For

> if some twenty-year-old youth had then found himself in Chichikov's place . . . God! what would not have been awakened, would not have been stirred, would not have begun to

speak in him! Long would he have, insensible, stood unmoving, his eyes unthinkingly fastened far off, his road forgotten, and all the reprimands awaiting him and the scoldings for his delay, himself, his employment, the world, and whatever may be in the world—all forgotten. [6:92]

The remarks are aimed as much at us as they are at Chichikov, and one is reminded of Gogol's specific teaching essays, most of them written before he began work on *Dead Souls,* in particular "On the Teaching of Universal History" (1832), "Thoughts on Geography" (1829), and "A Textbook of Literature for Russian Youth" (sometime between 1831 and 1842).[7] All are addressed to the young. Gogol clearly thought, in anticipation of Tolstoy, that it was overconcern with the world, with material things, that put men off the track, that, as Wordsworth put it,

> The world is too much with us; late and soon,
> Getting and spending, we lay waste our powers;
> Little we see in Nature that is ours;
> We have given our hearts away, a sordid boon!

No more than Wordsworth, however, is Gogol referring to the "noble savage"; nor is he an early species of *narodnik,* despite the slavophilic strain we may discern in him.[8] It is, rather, the possibility that as we go on, growing into habit, our true nature—our God-given humanity and knowledge—may be abandoned, as the old-world landowners abandoned theirs. Chichikov himself stands in grave danger of such abandonment, but since there is "a little bit of Chichikov in each of us," so do we, which is the reason that so many of the digressions become exhibitions of Gogol in his teaching role, his "service" role, his role as prophet and seer. Just as much of *Selected Passages from Correspondence with Friends* displayed the mission that Gogol was devoted to and that impelled him to his work, so do these digressions and articles.

The youthful theme is followed up by Gogol in the long digression that opens chapter 6, the middle chapter of the book. In this chapter, Chichikov meets Plyushkin, whose early background is related; he also makes the last of his purchases. It is here, furthermore, that the connection between digression and fictional content is perhaps best exemplified, that Gogol's claim that the digressions form an integral part of the total design is best borne out. Plyushkin's youth becomes an example for Chichikov, a statement of balance and proportion for Gogol, and a revelation of proper relations for the reader.[9]

The problem, Gogol tells us, is that with age one becomes jaded (he was at most thirty-two when this passage was written), that habit replaces perception, that we begin to wear dark glasses, seeing "through a glass darkly," as Milton put it, instead of purely. "Oh, my youth!" Gogol says, "Oh, my freshness!" (6:111), remembering the enthusiasm with which he had set out on his quest for beauty. What he has in mind, I think, is the process of mechanization, of dehumanization that takes place as we become engulfed by material concerns—the turning of a man into a thing—which occurs, going a step further than Wordsworth, *because* "we lay waste our powers." This waste is what Gogol wishes to call to the reader's attention, first through the lyrical statement of the digression, then through the fiction of the Plyushkin episode, with a later return to digression.[10] The personal lyrical quality of the opening digression accomplishes a double purpose: it avoids preaching, so that the reader does not feel personally attacked; and it makes Gogol himself one who has wasted, with the implication that the hope contained in the very fact that he is aware of his situation is also available to the reader, if the reader should also accept awareness.[11] The point is reemphasized in two later, nonpersonal digressions that are even clearer than the ones we have mentioned; it is a part of Gogol's technique to increase intensity as he goes along. When Plyushkin is reminded of his youth and the friendships he had at school,

> a kind of warm ray suddenly glided over that wooden face, expressing not feeling but a kind of pale reflection of feeling, a phenomenon like the unexpected appearance on the surface of the water of someone who has been drowned, giving rise to a joyous shout in the crowd clustered on the shore. [But] . . . that appearance was the last. All is blank and the surface of the unanswering element now abated is still more terrible and empty than before. [6:126]

Plyushkin has died, but he need not have, and his death should warn us all, Chichikov included.

The last of the digressions in the chapter clinches the point and makes complete the movement from the personal, with which the chapter opened, to the general:

Can one change so? Does this resemble truth?[12] It all resembles truth; it can all happen to a man. Today's fiery youth would recoil in horror if you should show him his portrait in old age. Take with you on your way, as you emerge from gentle youthful years to stern embittering manhood, take with you all human motions; do not leave them on the road, for you will not rouse them later! Dread and terrible future old age is before you, and it will give nothing back! The grave is more merciful than it; on the grave is written: "Here is a man interred"—but you will read nothing on the cold, insensitive features of inhuman old age. [6:127]

Finally, having carefully prepared his audience to receive his statement, the author launches forth into a direct appeal, concluding his sermon. I would suggest that the entire chapter, including the digressions, should be viewed as a continuous rhetorical exercise, so that the story of Plyushkin becomes a kind of parable, which the digressions explain. It is a sermon in the grand style. As for the digressions themselves, however, they start with a personal lyrical evocation by the author, speaking in the first person singular, proceed to a mid point between author and audience, indicating that the opening lyric has wider application, and conclude, rather subtly, with a direct statement to the reader himself. I say "rather subtly" because the last passage cited above starts with an impersonal "you" ("if you should show"), proceeds to a second person plural imperative ("take with you," which is repeated by "take with you"—literally, "do not leave behind"), thence to a second person plural with a future verb ("you will not rouse"), and ends with the directness of a second person singular ("you will read nothing").[13] In these passages, especially in the last, Gogol also stresses his themes of the human and nonhuman, reality and nonreality, beauty and ugliness. He ends, after all, with the grave and something even worse than the grave, "inhuman old age."[14] After this—once he believes that his themes are well set in the reader's mind, through both the fiction and the digressions—Gogol can move to greater concentration upon, and development of, his hero, Chichikov.

Chapter 7, like chapter 6, opens with a digression, one indicating that Gogol intends to take a new direction. This digression, which not only opens the chapter but also the second section of Part 1, returns to the digressions that we found in chapter 2,[15] but far more seriously, for Gogol again finds reason—and at greater length this time—to explain, or justify, the kinds of characters he has chosen and the kind of book he is writing. His characters, he agrees, do not display "the lofty virtue of man"; his portion is rather to depict "all the terrible, staggering slime of trivialities enmeshing our lives, all the depths of cold, fragmented, everyday characters with whom our earthly, sometimes bitter and tedious road swarms." This does not mean, however, that what he is depicting, he is depicting for its own sake, that he is a gloomy writer deprived of heart and soul. Even at this point in Part 1 he is after something other than the "slime" that he mentions himself: "The contemporary critic does not recognize that much spiritual depth is needed in order to illumine a picture taken from contemptible life and to elevate it to a pearl of creation" (6:133–34). It is the "spiritual depth" that Gogol wishes to be recognized, the elevation that is important. He seems to be terribly afraid that he will be regarded simply as a vulgar realist, or, in Belinsky's language, as a "naturalist," and for this reason be dismissed as a "lower" species of writer. If he is a "realist," however, he is, he thinks, a realist in "a higher sense," as Dostoevsky was later to say of himself. *Dead Souls,* in Gogol's opinion, is first and foremost a work of art; and the aim of art, the aspiration of the artist, as he said elsewhere, is beauty. If a simple depiction of triviality, vulgarity, banality (*poshlost'*) constituted his book, then he would indeed be a "lower" writer. But there is something more, and some day this will be clear, although that day is still distant: "Still far off is the time when in another stream an awesome blizzard of inspiration will arise from a head then enveloped in holy terror and brilliance, and the majestic thunder of different speeches will be read in confused trembling" (6:135). Gogol is referring to a stylistic difference, not to one of content or aim, to that "majestic lyrical flow" he was to mention towards the end of chapter 11. The eventual formal shift was already, in chapter 7, before his eyes, although he had not yet realized he would not be able to accomplish it successfully. What is remarkable, although it may well have been based on previous experience, was Gogol's anticipation of critical reaction, not that it would be negative—there he was wrong—but how it would classify him. I think that he was warning his readers—and the critics—that style is only a means to an end, never an end in itself. He wished to leave a legacy to more than just Russian literature, for he was bearing witness, he felt, to truth, to *pravda.*

The subject of appearance and reality, implied in most of the digressions that we have cited, is continued in several that succeed, in those chapters where Gogol moves away from the specific, although perhaps "typical," persons that we find in the first six chapters and onto a more general plan.[16] So in chapter 8 we are given a general description of the ladies of the town of N.: "Our portion is only a couple of words about their outward appearance and superficial qualities" (6:158). It is as though Gogol were already embarking on a new work, or at least adopting a different point of view, reminding the reader, through his restraint, that there really are further depths: "If one were to delve more deeply, then of course many other things would be revealed; but it is very dangerous to delve deeply into a lady's heart. So, limiting ourselves to the superficial, we will continue" (6:159). This is that preparatory manner that Gogol adopts when he has something more serious in mind, when he is returning to the central question of the difference between illusion and reality. He makes us aware of this when he tells us that "the ladies of the town of N. were what is called presentable" (6:158). The focus of his tale is shifting from the emphasis upon deception and disharmony, which has characterized *Dead Souls* thus far, to a concern with the depiction of truth. The ladies are mocked, but not just for the sake of mockery. The presentation of the superficial is there to emphasize that it *is* superficial, and hence not real. We are to expect something else.

Several other digressions, of the same general sort and couched in the same general terms, follow and continue through chapter 9. These digressions, when taken in the context of the fictional content, must be concerned with the superficial, for *overt* falsity has become Gogol's subject. These are puppets, not persons, of artificial conventions who act and react entirely in terms of those conventions. They are things, and as such must be depersonalized. After all, it is because of falsity that Chichikov will have to leave town; his downfall is as conventional and artificial as the ladies are.[17] There is only one relief from fakery in chapters 8 and 9: the scene when Chichikov sees the young girl at the ball, which is accompanied by a short passage that is half digression and half simile. Chichikov, we are told, stood like a man on the street who has forgotten something,

> and nothing can be stupider than such a man: in a flash the carefree expression flies from his face; he tries to recall what he has forgotten—a handkerchief? But there is a handkerchief in his pocket. Money? But there is also money in his pocket.

It seems he has everything with him, but still a kind of mysterious spirit whispers in his ear that he has forgotten something. And then he looks perplexed and vaguely at the crowd moving before him, at the flying carriages, at the shakos and guns of a regiment passing by, at signboards—and he sees nothing clearly.[18] [6:167]

We have already discussed this passage in another context.[19] Not only does it highlight a contrast between Chichikov and his surroundings; it also increases the intensity of the work as a whole, bringing us ever closer to the core of Gogol's subject: the falcon is returning to the falconer as the sequence of the digressions interweaves with the sequence of the fiction itself. Gogol was still, despite the practical division into two parts (a normal procedure for him) in control of the totality, although it seemed to be leading him in directions he had not anticipated. We are increasingly involved, in digression as in fiction, with the fantasy of human refusal to be human. It is neither mere grotesquery nor the mere impulse of a romantic that engages Gogol, valid in their own terms as these categories may be. If there is intrusion of the unreal upon the real, it is a result of man's giving up his own reality rather than of his being overwhelmed by the power of deception, by the ladies' more-than-stupidity, their willful unwilling of themselves so that they imprison themselves in illusion. Gogol was as much convinced as was Dostoevsky after him that the powers of darkness can gain a victory only when we refuse to exercise our freedom. How else, indeed, could we fall victim to deception, how else be swindled?

The digressions also point out the unnaturalness, in the deepest sense, of these creatures, an unnaturalness that the reader may well share with them and that he must recover from if his salvation is to be achieved. They are no different, we are told, from "we brothers, an intelligent people,[20] as we call ourselves, [who] act the same, and our learned arguments are the evidence" (6:188). At fault are the adoption of foreign ways, of false ways; the refusal of natural knowledge (the stirrings within Chichikov at the sight of the girl); and the insistence upon irrelevancies.[21] The ladies are most profoundly beside the point. The same conclusion is reached in the digressions in these chapters that deal with the use of French instead of Russian in polite conversation. The very artificiality of the practice indicates an alienation of the person from truth.[22] At the same time, Gogol, like Pushkin before him in the famous passage concerning Tatyana's letter to Eugene in *Eugene Onegin,* is attempting to justify his practice of using what appears to be the common language in *Dead Souls*.[23] This is, Gogol tells us specifically, "this his Russian poem" (6:183).

The ladies have thus provided Gogol with an opportunity to serve several purposes: a means to forward the plot (what little plot there is in *Dead Souls*); a reiteration of a theme; and an excuse to emphasize his art in nationalistic terms.

With chapter 10, Gogol's tone becomes increasingly and overtly serious as the epic conception comes to the fore and he begins to zero in on what was perhaps the second-closest subject to his heart (the first being Orthodox Christianity)—Russia. Chichikov was becoming a symbol of Russia itself, but he had not started out that way, so that now the digressions had to take on the task of elucidating the author's attitude towards his native land, in preparation for this new hero. This direction is continued until the climax is reached in the troika passage, that last digression, which I believe was meant to set the stage for Part 2. Unfortunately, Gogol had a problem in that he was still not entirely sure of the precise line to take. The digressions, therefore, show more his yearning to understand Russia than his settled convictions as to what Russia is. Gogol was apparently puzzled by what seemed to be the double nature of his country and countrymen—in this, he was already anticipating Dostoevsky's struggle with the same problem. In the first of the digressions in chapter 10, for example, he puzzles over the contradiction between the Russian's anarchic tendencies and his authoritarian needs: "In general, we somehow have not been made for representative assemblies. In all our gatherings, from peasant meetings of the mir[24] to every possible learned and other committee, if there is not one head ruling it all, an awful mess occurs" (6:198). He goes on to say that the Russian is incapable of abstract considerations and decisions (does this mean that the Russian is different from the West European?), although he proves himself quite apt when he has to deal with individuals on a personal basis. On the other hand, this does not imply a readiness for concrete action: "The aim may be fine, but it never has an issue. Perhaps this is because we are immediately satisfied at the very beginning and already think it has all been done" (6:198). Gogol is asking, in his "Russian poem," what it means to be a Russian. What is it that makes him what he is? Are the apparent contradictions reconcilable? Is there some principle of harmony and truth, or better, is there a reality that may make him whole? That is, are these contradictions really real?

We already know what Gogol's answer will be. He begins his reply in a digression on the Russian tendency to see things in apocalyptic terms,[25] superstitious as these terms may sometimes be. For the inhabitants of N., the religious framework is of course debased: they neither understand it nor act in accord with it; for them it is more a habit of mind than a commitment of soul. For the first time in *Dead Souls*, Part 1, Christ enters Gogol's work, although in a negative way—that is, the townsfolk think that Chichikov may be Napoleon escaped from St. Helena, and in the popular mind, Naploeon, the invader who was defeated by Holy Russia, is the Antichrist. In this digression (6:207) Gogol quickly points out that this notion was a part of the mysticism of his day and that the inhabitants of N. quickly recovered from it; they rapidly returned to practical considerations (leaving the implication that perhaps they would have been better off if they had stuck with the Apocalypse). But Gogol's digression leaves another thought: that the Antichrist is not Napoleon does not mean that the Antichrist does not exist; it just means that the town of N. does not recognize him. In this sense, these "dead souls" are refusing truth, not because they dimiss Chichikov as Antichrist (they are right there, but for the wrong reason), but because they dismiss *Revelations* itself. Instead of looking inside themselves, where the Antichrist really lives, where the truth may really be found, the officials turn to a questioning of Nozdryov. From superstition, emphasized in the digression, they turn to the liar, from one deception to another. As Gogol says, this all shows "what kind of creature man is: he is wise, intelligent, and sensible in everything that concerns others, but not in what concerns himself" (6:209).

Again Gogol uses a digression to drive his point home:

> Many delusions have visited the world. . . . what distorted, blind, narrow impassable roads carrying one far astray has humanity chosen in its yearning for eternal truth, while the straight way was always open before it, like the way leading to the magnificent temple appointed to be the tsar's mansion. It is the broadest and most splendid of ways, lit by the sun by day and illumined by fires at night, but people stream past it in blind ignorance. And how many times, even when directed by an understanding sent from Heaven, have they started

aside and been deflected, have amid day's brightness found themselves anew in an impassable maze, anew have loosed a blinding fog into one another's eyes, and dragging themselves after marsh fires, have reached the abyss, and then in terror asked one another: "Where is the way out? Where is the road?" The current generation now sees everything clearly, wonders at the distortions, and laughs at the follies of its ancestors, not seeing that that chronicle is outlined with heavenly fire, that every letter in it cries out, that from everywhere a piercing finger is fixed upon it, upon it, the current generation; but the current generation laughs and self-sufficiently, proudly, begins a series of new distortions, at which its descendants will also laugh. [6:210-11]

Finally, Gogol makes his overt statement—the truth exists, not hidden in obscure writings and not to be discovered by tortuous reasonings,[26] not to be sought without, but revealed within, and revealed, further, in the history of mankind, in his chronicles. In this connection, one is reminded of the essays on history that Gogol had written in the early 1830s and had published in *Arabesques* in 1835, particularly "On the Teaching of Universal History," which tells us of the "paths of Providence" that are everywhere in the world (8:27). As he approached the end of Part 1, Gogol was increasingly overwhelmed by his vision and his mission. There is almost a sense of urgency in those passages that immediately precede the biography of Chichikov. Foremost is the task of Chichikov's transformation into a hero who will be capable of carrying the epic burden. Like the mad Orlando, Chichikov is one who has gone astray and must be returned to the true path. Through delusion and distortion[27]—by turning away from reality and making ugly—Russia, with which Chichikov is becoming more and more identified, has put itself in danger. The proper path, the way of Providence, however, is clear, waiting for Chichikov to follow it.

The metaphor of the road, or path, is soon connected with Chichikov's carriage and with the Russian land. The carriage, after having been stopped for a time by the public prosecutor's funeral (a symbol that can be taken to reemphasize the entire story of Chichikov's relationship to the unreal quality of the town, a summary of Gogol's attitude), finally reaches open country, and Gogol embarks on a lyrical evocation of Russia (obviously, the town of N. was meant to be a diversion from truth rather than a portrait of it).

Like most of *Dead Souls,* this passage was written while Gogol was living in Rome. It is one of the longest digressions in Part 1, interrupted only by a few lines when a government troika passes Chichikov's carriage going in the opposite direction, which may in itself have some significance. We start with a contrast, if not to say paradox: "Rus! Rus![28] I see you, from my wonderful, beautiful distance, I see you" (6:221).[29] Russia, or "Rus," is poor, incoherent, and shelterless, uncheered by either nature or art, towns, palaces, trees, or ivy; it has no waterfalls, no precipices, no mountains, no silvery clear skies.[30] All this is in contrast to Italy, Gogol's second home, where physical beauty reigns, in nature as in art. For the first time we are being told that when Gogol speaks of beauty, of the beauty to which he aspires, he is speaking of neither sunsets nor human creations, *as such.* At best, they may point to beauty, but they are not beauty itself. Beauty, as neither Hanz Kuechelgarten nor Piskaryov realized, is not a matter of the physical realm. Its actualization, therefore, lies in the spirit, not in the flesh; the quest is of the soul, not of the body. We note that when Gogol asks what "inscrutable, secret power" draws him to Rus, the answer comes in the musical terms of Rus's melancholy song, which calls and sobs and seizes the heart, a harmony, melancholy though it may be, whose meaning transcends the senses.

Music, particularly the song, had long intrigued Gogol. At least two of his early essays had been concerned with music's peculiar powers. In "Sculpture, Painting, and Music," written eleven years before the publication of *Dead Souls,* Part 1, he says: "To our youthful and senile century [God] granted mighty music, in order swiftly to turn us to Him. But if music should indeed abandon us, what then will happen to our world?" (8:13). Music, it appears, was the especially Christian form, rather than sensual sculpture and painting; it was thus the highest of forms. In addition, natural music, the song, was something especially native to the inhabitants of Rus. In "On Little Russian Songs" (1833) Gogol wrote of the songs of Little Russia (ancient "Rus") as embodying a "faith . . . as innocent, as touching, as chaste as an infant's chaste soul. They appeal to God, as children do to a father," and "His artless image becomes sublime in them by virtue of their simplicity" (8:94). Gogol also informs us, passing beyond Little Russia, that songs of this kind are sung all the length of Russia, from the Arctic Circle to the Caspian Sea; they are expressive of a yearning after beauty and truth that is especially Russian.

It is thus peculiarly fitting that in *Dead Souls,* Gogol hears a song from his native land, a kind of music of the spheres, which demands that he fulfill his mission. Furthermore, the song arises from the people (*narod*) and the land (*zemlya*), not the world (*svyet*) and the state (*gosudarstvo*). The song is of Rus, and much is within it foretold: "Is it not here, is it not within you, that limitless thought will be born, since you yourself are without end? Is not here a hero's place, since here he may expand and spread? . . . Oh, what a gleaming, wonderful prospect unknown to earth! Rus!" (6:221). Is it, one asks, Chichikov whom Gogol now sees as the prophet of "limitless thought" and the "hero" expanding? Perhaps, for perhaps Gogol now considers himself the successor to Pushkin as the poet of Russia, the one called upon to express the essence of the people and the land. Certainly, *Dead Souls* is no longer the poem on which Gogol had embarked in 1835. Hanz Kuechelgarten is on the way home, not disillusioned but with a revitalized vision of reality. I would suggest that Gogol took very seriously the Chronicle legend that ancient Kiev, Rus, had been converted to Orthodoxy because of the beauty—as well as truth—of the Orthodox service. It was to this beauty that he wished to return.

That the quest had assumed additional importance to Gogol is symbolically represented in the continuation of the digression: "How strange, alluring, uplifting, and marvellous is this word: the road! How wonderful is the road itself!" (6:221). We return to the path that Gogol had spoken of earlier, with the difference, however, that Gogol now felt that his search had meaning in itself. He tells us of the sights to be seen, by day and by night, and of the sense of warmth and security that the traveler feels: "God! how good you sometimes are, long, long road! How many times, perishing, drowning, have I caught at you, and every time you magnanimously bore me up and saved me! And how many wonderful projects, poetic dreams, have you given rise to, how many amazing impressions have I experienced!" (6:222).

So personal does this digression become that Gogol has to shake his head and remember that there is also a fictional hero on the road: "Even our friend Chichikov at the time was aware of dreams that were not at all prosaic." Chichikov is acquiring lineaments completely unsuspected when the tale began so long before. The comic hero is no longer a subject for laughter; he, like Gogol, has become a traveler responding to a call, even if he does not hear the call so clearly as his creator sitting beside him in the carriage. A most extraordinary and unexpected thing has happened. Gogol's subject, which from one point of view had always been Russia, was beginning to be personified in the fantastically unsuccessful swindler Chichikov, who fails because the swindle is alien to him, whether he knows it or not: it is an importation from foreign, secular lands, an ugly construction of that apostate world beyond Russia's western borders.

The digressive introduction to Chichikov's biography indicates where the road will lead. Although Gogol cannot take a virtuous man for his hero, yet, he says:

> Perhaps in this tale other, hitherto unplucked strings [again a musical image] may be sensed, the countless riches of the Russian soul may appear, a man gifted with divine powers [the "hero" that Gogol had mentioned earlier] may come forth, or a wonderful Russian girl, such as is found nowhere else in the world, with all the marvelous beauty of the feminine soul, all magnanimous aspiration and selflessness. All the virtuous people of other races will seem dead beside them, as a book is dead beside the living word! Russian movements will arise . . . , and they will see that what only glided through the nature of other peoples has made a profound impression on Russian nature. [6:223]

One cannot help wondering if Gogol planned eventually to transfer Annunziata to Russian soil, there to marry the epic hero from whom, mythically, the Russian race will descend. Was Chichikov, hitherto a mad Orlando, to be transmuted into a kind of Gofreddic Aeneas? The ending of Part 1 indicates that Gogol was at least toying with the possibility of such a transformation. So far as we know, of course, that transformation did not take place, and we can only speculate on what was contained in the versions of Part 2 that Gogol burned. Perhaps, instead of transforming Chichikov, he planned to substitute another hero for him—there are some indications of this in the four apparently consecutive chapters of Part 2 that have survived. But whatever Gogol's first intentions may have been, Chichikov's biography and the first digression that follows upon it do provide a kind of summary of what had come to be Gogol's main conscious theme. Chichikov, we are told, is a man who is not so very different really from other men, a man who had, in his choice of alien means, been deflected from his proper goal, although he may yet return to the right path. It is even possible that "the passion that drew him on did not come from himself and in his cold existence was imprisoned something that would prostrate a man in the dust and on his knees before the wisdom of heaven. It is still a secret why this image has been represented in the poem now appearing to the world" (6:242). It is thus not reformation that Gogol has in mind so much as awakening and return. That Chichikov has a symbolic character connecting him with Russia is also pointed out, for "which of you, full of Christian humility, not openly but silently, alone, at a moment of lonely colloquy with himself, will not inwardly probe his soul with this painful question: 'Is there not in me some part of Chichikov?'" (6:258). If we take these remarks in context, remembering what Gogol had said only three pages earlier, we discover that they are far from satirical. They are addressed, further, not to the world at large, but to the Russian, as many other references in the digression indicate. The Russian, although he knows the way, has strayed, and he must return to the proper path, which lies within him, as Chichikov will discover. This is where the truth to be acknowledged lies. The Russian is quoted as possibly saying: "'What will foreigners say? Is it really so wonderful to hear a nasty opinion of yourself? Do they really think it doesn't hurt? Do they really think we're not patriots?' I admit I cannot find an answer to such wise remarks, especially the one concerning the opinion of foreigners" (6:243). It seems to me that here the thrust, to use that much-abused word, of Gogol's attitude— and purpose—is apparent. His poem is not meant to degrade the Russian, not even, despite the laughter, to laugh at him. It is to rescue him. That Chichikov had been seduced by the glitter of gold is correct, but this is not the real Russian way, and the Russian has hidden within him the knowledge that this material road is an alien one. "What will foreigners say?" Perhaps that is where the fault, the deception, lies. Perhaps Chichikov is a failure simply because of his Russian soul, his inner knowledge that the town of N. belongs to a different world from his.

The last digression of Part 1, the end of this volume, has Chichikov rushing onwards in his troika. The land across which he speeds is Russian; his vehicle itself is peculiarly Russian, made by a "smart Yaroslav peasant"; and the coachman wears "no German boots" (6:247). This troika itself, Gogol has already told us, is "a bird," and the horses, he informs us later (6:247), "hear a familiar song" and "harmoniously" strain their chests. Finally, "the bell breaks out—a wonderful pealing;

the air, torn to bits, resounds and builds with the wind; all flies past, all that is on earth; and other peoples and states, looking askance, stand aside and cede the road to her" (6:247).

In this last paragraph, Gogol brings together the two images he has used increasingly, but separately, as the tempo of Part 1 increased: the song and the road; harmony, or beauty, and truth. And they are brought together in connection with the figure whom the troika is bearing, Chichikov.[31] Here, at last, the symbols are united and Gogol's subjects made one.

It is this final digression that makes Part 1 a whole, bringing together fiction, earlier digressions, and symbols. Unfortunately, however, although a whole had been formed, it was an introduction, not a conclusion. The problem that now faced Gogol was how to proceed from here. Part 1 ends with an Orlando who is far from mad (and Chichikov's biography in fact points out how sane he is), an Orlando who is ready, in his troika, to go forth to battle with the heathen. For Ariosto this had been no difficulty at all, because he had not taken either Orlando or the heathen seriously. But Gogol was committed as Ariosto had never been; it was now the crusader Tasso whom he found more congenial, for his aim was indeed to liberate Jerusalem. The problem was enormous: how to shift from *Orlando Furioso* to *Gerusalemma Liberata?* how to make Orlando into Gofreddo? Another possibility, of course, was open—*La Divina Commedia,* which posed equally enormous problems, both theological (Gogol had no Aquinas, much less Augustine, to rely on) and practical (he had neither cosmic geography nor well-established allegorical tradition to guide him). On the other hand, there was always *Pilgrim's Progress,* but Part 1 of *Dead Souls* had already been written with a central character who, while he might be considered a pilgrim, was aimed more at reality than he was at ethics; he was also a pilgrim on his way back, rather than on the way forward. So far as we know, these problems were never solved to Gogol's satisfaction. Instead he published *Selected Passages from Correspondence with Friends,* much of which may be regarded as a series of digressions for a never-completed work of fiction. One wonders if Chichikov was not to turn into the celebrant on Easter Sunday and if the essay of that title was not to close Gogol's work.

7

Dead Souls, Part 2

What we have of *Dead Souls,* Part 2, is more a group of fragments than it is a connected whole, giving rise to the suspicion, which we have already expressed, that, no matter what the author's intentions may have been originally, he was finding it next to impossible to fulfill them. Certainly, continuity from Part I (assuming that we do have the beginning of Part 2) is lacking, as though Chichikov's troika had either stalled or broken down entirely. Perhaps Gogol discovered himself caught between what he wanted to do and what his public wanted. His own desires, for all the reasons we have given, were hard enough to accomplish without the pressure to produce a sequel in the same vein as Part 1. Compromise was equally difficult, although that seems to be the path he chose, so far as we can judge from the fragments that we have. Unfortunately, compromise was but a way to ensure failure, as Gogol quickly realized. Whether or not the burnings were a result of the failure of compromise, whether he finally gave it up and attempted to follow his own vision, we do not know. All that we do know for certain is that, if he was not totally frustrated, he was at least convinced finally that success was beyond his grasp.[1]

A glance at the history of Part 2 (Part 3 was probably never even begun) illustrates Gogol's problems. We know that he was at least thinking of Part 2 even before the final revisions of Part 1 had been completed.[2] By August 1842, under pressure from both friends and critics to continue and troubled by this pressure because of the questions posed by the new path that he wished to take, Gogol wrote to S. T. Aksakov that "the full meaning of the lyrical hints can only be elucidated when the last part is published" (*P*, 117). That very elucidation was the difficulty, even though he was fully persuaded of the value of his position. Beauty and truth, perfection indeed, was his ultimate subject, but, he says in the first paragraph of Part 2, "What is to be done if the writer's character is such that he has fallen ill of his own imperfection?" (7:7). I would suggest that it is not only moral imperfection that Gogol had in mind here; of equal import, if not of greater import, was what he perceived as his own *artistic* imperfection, as a person and as a writer. Actualization of beauty had, to him, both aspects, and neither could be accomplished without the other. It was not that his artistic powers were failing, that he had "burned himself out," but that the goal was of a different order from those powers—means and ends could not meet. As the latter portions of Part 1 indicate, he was identifying himself with his work. Several times in Part 1 he had spoken of lyricism, and he spoke of it again in his letter to Aksakov. In "A Textbook of Literature for Russian Youth" he defined the lyric, or rather lyrical poetry, as follows:

> Lyrical poetry is a portrait, a reflection and a mirror of the loftiest movements of the poet's soul, notes necessary to him, the biography of his ecstasies. It is, from the loftiest to the lowest of its kinds, nothing other than an account of the poet's own sensations. Whether he thunders in an ode, sings in a song, plains in an elegy, or narrates in a ballad, everywhere the poet is expressing the personal secrets of his own soul. In short, it is the pure personality of the poet himself and pure truth [*pravda*]. A lie in lyrical poetry is perilous, for the inflation will expose it: the moment someone who has the flair of a poet hears it, he will call him a liar wearing the mask of a poet. It is vast and comprises the entire internal biography of a man. [8:472–73]

The lyric, self-expression, had been Gogol's ambition at the very beginning of his career, and we know that he returned to it in some of the digressions at the end of Part 1 and at the time of his first attempts at Part 2. Even before beginning Part 2 he had evidently realized that Gofreddo was impossible, and he had resolved upon a shift to the lyrical mode, which meant—as both the first paragraph of Part 2 and "A Textbook" indicate—a shift to himself. The epic went the way of compromise. Rather than write a totally new work, Gogol went backwards, abandoning the line of development that had been followed from Virgil to Dante to Milton (and including Ariosto himself), a line that James Joyce was later to make much of; he proposed to replace the objective by the subjective. This shift in form was even more drastic than Gogol's first impulse to change from the comic style to the epic itself, and just as doomed, as he discovered. The task was not only beyond his powers; I suggest that it would be beyond anyone's powers. Perhaps the proper course would have been to turn away from *Dead Souls* entirely—this he later also tried to do. Unfortunately, he used the wrong form again, at least so far as the public was concerned—namely, *Selected Passages.*

In any event, Gogol did try to go on, but was decidedly dissatisfied, for in November 1843, eighteen months after the publication of Part 1, he burned just about all he had thus far written of Part 2, deciding to start anew. This he did, although the work proceeded slowly. By April 1845 he had reversed himself, and the following July he again burned everything that he had written of the second version of Part 2. This was not a total abandonment, however; he meant, rather, to redo the work, and probably thoroughly to revise Part 1 at the same time, so that an overall wholeness could be achieved. By the end of 1847, after the almost totally negative reception of *Selected Passages,* he put the continuation aside entirely in favor of accomplishing his long-felt desire to visit the Holy Land. He returned to Russia in the spring of 1848, never to leave it again. During the last four years of his life, Gogol continued to work on *Dead Souls,* and he worked fairly regularly through 1849. By August of 1849, two chapters were finished and given to Shevyryov; in January 1850 he showed the same chapters, revised, to Aksakov. Work was dropped, then taken up again in the winter of 1850/51. It seems to have gone rather slowly, then increased in tempo during the spring and summer, during which time he frequently read finished or almost finished chapters to various friends. In July 1851 he asked Pletnyov to get ready for the publication of the whole of Part 2. By the fall it seems fairly certain that he had eleven chapters— a perfect match to Part 1, and thus probably the whole—ready. By November he was thinking of a complete revision. Then, on the night of 11/12 February 1852, he burned the entire manuscript, for the third time, and died ten days later.

Whatever was written of *Dead Souls* between 1846 and 1851, thus, was known only to some friends to whom Gogol had read what he wrote in these years. What we now have are either fragments written before the first burning of 1845 or later first drafts found by Shevyryov among Gogol's papers. The first four chapters are usually dated as being of 1841 or 1842; the other fragment, sometimes called chapter 5, is probably earlier; some think it belongs to 1840 or 1841. Indeed, some even think that the so-called chapter 5 belongs to Part 3 rather than to Part 2.[3]

What has come down to us is interesting, not for its intrinsic merit (since we do not have the whole, judgment of merit is next to impossible for us; the only person who knew the entire work and could judge it was Gogol himself, and he decided against it), but for its clarification of matters raised in one way or another by Part 1. In other words, it serves largely the same function as *Selected Passages,* in this sense.

Most immediately obvious in Part 2 is that Gogol has moved his story out of town and into the countryside.[4] Furthermore, approximately two-thirds of chapter 1 will pass before Chichikov enters on scene. We start instead with a description of the life and character of the landowner Andrei Ivanovich Tyentyetnikov, "a young thirty-three-year-old master, a collegiate secretary, an unmarried man" (7:9).[5] In many ways Tyentyetnikov is anticipatory of Ivan Goncharov's character Oblomov in the novel of that name, which was begun in the late 1840s, about the time that Gogol and Goncharov met in 1848. There is no reason to believe, however, that Goncharov took his character directly from Gogol, although that the latter had some influence on the former seems a reasonable proposition. "Andrei Ivanovich's existence was neither good nor bad—it was simply a waste. Since there are not a few people in the world who waste their lives away, why should not Tyentyetnikov waste his away?" (7:9). The account of his day is the story of nothing done; like Oblomov, he can barely get out of bed. But as he did with Plyushkin and Chichikov, Gogol tells us how Tyentyetnikov got that way: intelligence and education made superfluous by a world that had no place for them. There is nothing at all amusing in his story, nothing to make the reader laugh as he did in Part 1. It is, rather, the story of a serious man who wishes to do serious things and is constantly hindered by formalities, by rigid artificial relationships. The city, where Tyentyetnikov had spent some time in the service, was the alien environment that did much to destroy his ambitions to use his talent and brains.

One is immediately sent back to the essay that Gogol had written not too many years before, "St. Petersburg Notes of 1836," which amounts to an excoriation of St. Petersburg as a foreign city, an artificial construction divorced from the real Russian character, a city built for and inhabited by aliens to Russia. Indeed, all through his life the only city Gogol seems to have found congenial was Rome. He appears to have felt that the urban environment—even the small-town urban environment—was destructive of the soul, for the city was the habitat of officials and merchants, those who reduce people to paper and those who deal in material things. St. Petersburg was the worst of all, the most completely false; the point is made not only in "Petersburg Notes of 1836" but in every one of the Petersburg tales as well. Here the lie has become a mode of life (or death), and reality is utterly lost, for Petersburg is the very exemplar of foreign intrusion into Russia. In contrast was the land (Gogol's happiest descriptions, his most lyrical evocations, are of the Russian landscape), where the real, the true, and the beautiful were to be found, where God's work was to be done.

So Tyentyetnikov concluded when he decided to give up the service and return to his estates. A "sophisticate" who had learned much of theory, Tyentyetnikov aimed to put his estates in order and to direct his peasants in a humanitarian way so that his land would become a model of owner-peasant cooperation and efficiency,[6] all in accordance with the principles of political economy that he had studied. But despite all his efforts, his schemes based on abstract considerations go awry: somehow Tyentyetnikov's land does not produce, while the land that the peasants cultivate for themselves flourishes. As Gogol puts it, the peasants "soon understood that, although the master was a lively sort of chap and desirous of undertaking much, he did not yet know how, he somehow talked too correctly and intricately, so that peasant learning could not grasp it. The result was that, while master and peasant did not completely misunderstand each other, they simply did not sing together, were not adapted to raise one and the same note" (7:19–20). The point is a familiar one to readers of romantic literature in general and of nineteenth-century Russian literature in particular. Tyentyetnikov, because of his artificial education and because of the time that he has spent in the artificial capital, has lost contact with his country; communication has been cut, and harmony has been destroyed; the problem now is how to reestablish that harmony.[7] But Tyentyetnikov was so frustrated that "finally he entirely stopped going to see to work being done, completely threw up administering justice, stayed indoors and even ceased to accept reports from his steward" (7:22). He is now totally apathetic, incapable of making a decision and acting upon it—a complete Oblomov.

Tyentyetnikov was almost roused from his lethargy by his love for a young lady who was visiting a neighbor, but an insult by the girl's father sent him back to his dressing gown. This is the sort of man Tyentyetnikov is, and this is the situation that he finds himself in when a visitor arrives at his house—Pavel Ivanovich Chichikov.

Chichikov is older, we are told, than he was when last we saw him, and somewhat shabbier. He still travels in his troika, but evidently his road has not been an easy one, and his destination is as unsettled as ever. His ability to make himself agreeable, however, is greater, and he makes a fine impression upon Tyentyetnikov,[8] into whose home he soon moves, and he immediately seems to be the bringer of life, searcher after dead souls though he may have been: "A transformation occurred in the house. Half of it, hitherto in a state of blindness, . . . suddenly recovered its sight and was lit up" (7:28). Instead of the mere catalyst that we found in much of Part 1, Chichikov is now active, and positively active at that; instead of simply adapting himself to situations and people as he finds them, he now sets things in motion, at least so far as Tyentyetnikov is concerned. He makes a positive contribution in that he does much to arrange a reconciliation between Tyentyetnikov and his beloved, a young lady who is reminiscent of the governor's daughter of Part 1: "If a transparent picture, illumined by a lamp from behind, had suddenly blazed in a dark room, it would not have been so startling as this statuette, radiant with life, that had appeared as though expressly to light up the room. It seemed that a ray of sunlight flew into the room with her, suddenly illuminating the ceiling, the cornice, and the room's dark corners" (7:40). It is as though Annunziata had once again appeared. This is at least the fourth time that Gogol has used this symbol: the essay "Woman," the fragment "Rome," and Part 1 of Dead Souls are the previous three. Once again it is time to mention medieval and Renaissance backgrounds that Gogol may well have drawn upon. I would suggest that this symbol—whose ultimate derivation is Platonic, which developed through Venus cults and the courts of love, which culminated in the dolce stil nuovo of Dante and his circle, and which was passed on through Petrarch and Platonists like Ficino of the fifteenth century to the poets of the Renaissance in Italy, France, and England (Ariosto is only one such poet in sixteenth-century Italy— one could also mention Michelangelo; France had its Heroët, Scève, Bellay, and Ronsard; England had its Sidney, Spenser, and Donne, not to mention Shakespeare; Spain had its Cervantes)—was the one that

Gogol, attempting to give himself an artistic tradition as well as a Russian one, had in mind. It was a symbol that encompassed the Virgin Mary; Venus; Astraea; Helen of Troy; Queen Elizabeth, for Donne (the *Anniversary Poems*) and Spenser (Gloriana of *The Faerie Queene*); for the successors of Dante, Beatrice; as for the successors of Petrarch, a successor himself, it was Laura. She was also, of course, employed by Renaissance painters—Botticelli, for example. At the same time she could be used as a symbol of pure art, an ultimate revelation, an Annunziata, sent to the poet by God in order to bring the poet—and through his inspiration, all mankind—to beauty, to truth, to goodness—to perfection, to divinity itself. Translated into Russian terms, she becomes an icon.

It stretches credulity to ask one to believe that Gogol—with his interest in medieval history and with his knowledge of both Dante and at least some of the writers and painters of the High Renaissance, much of it probably gained during his sojourns in Rome—was unaware of this tradition. It was not, I would suggest, a mere romantic idealization of woman which arose because of Gogol's own sexual difficulties; it was, rather, a genuine attempt to use, for purposes of his own quest for beauty as well as for purposes of Russian nationalism, a well-recognized and long-hallowed symbol. As Beatrice did for Dante, so "woman," the governor's daughter, Annunziata, and Tyentyetnikov's lady show, for Gogol, the possibility of salvation, not in themselves, but because through love they lead to ultimate harmony and reconciliation. They are conduits, so to speak, through which man may rise to ultimate reality. Now we find that it is Chichikov who pours oil on troubled waters; it is he who arranges a reconciliation between Tyentyetnikov and the girl, Ulinka, who is pictured, in all her attitudes as well as in her appearance (although she is not quite plump enough for Chichikov's taste), as just about perfect in virtue, as all her predecessors were, because, given their function, they had to be. Gogol, who is constantly aware of the role of this feminine figure, over and over again uses tricks of light to describe Ulinka—not because she is deceptive but because reality transcends the material. He wishes to indicate the truth that supersedes physical sight, the beauty that is to be seen by the inner eye, rather than the appearance that is available to the outer one.

Like the road and the three-horse carriage, this feminine image has been repeated throughout Gogol's work. It differs from the road and the troika, however, in that it is the image of a goal to be attained; a reality that depends at least partially upon us for actualization; something to be quested after, as Spenser's knights quest, rather than an object passively to be received. After all, Beatrice did not come to Dante until canto 30 of *Purgatorio,* after Dante had been purified. So, for Gogol, "Rome" remains unfinished, Chichikov does not get the governor's daughter, and although Chichikov arranges a reconciliation between Tyentyetnikov and Ulinka, they are never brought together before our eyes, and that part of the story, at least so far as the fragments are concerned, is uncompleted.[9] Also, Chichikov himself continues to yearn for happiness with "a good woman": "a fresh, white-faced wench, perhaps even of the merchant class, while at the same time formed and educated like a noblewoman—so that she would understand music, although music was not the chief thing, but why, if it is so accepted, why go against social opinion?" This is coupled in his mind with the idea of settling down and running an estate as it ought to be run, finding the beauty and peace of a harmonious life on the land. If he can accomplish this, then "he would not have passed through the land like a kind of shadow or specter, he would not be ashamed before the fatherland" (7:31). Chichikov's quest, like Gogol's, is still not finished, nor does he yet, despite his impulses, fully understand it.

The concentration upon the land, the peasantry, and the landowner, and the proper relationships among them, continues through the remainder of these four chapters, which read really more like an essay on how harmony is to be attained than they do like a piece of fiction. It is, perhaps, an interlude of rest for Chichikov on his travels, a period of evaluation. This soon changes, however, as Gogol attempts to "accentuate the positive." Tyentyetnikov is left with hope,[10] and truth is shown to Chichikov. The comic epic begins to take on aspects of the classical epic journey, although Gogol remains ambivalent in his handling of the material. Chichikov is even supplied with a companion for his travels, one with whom he may leave the cave, Platon Mikhailovich Platonov,[11] who "was an Achilles and Paris at once: a shapely build, picturesque stature, freshness—it was all brought together in him. A pleasant smile with a light expression of irony, as it were, strengthened his beauty. But, despite all this, there was a certain lack of liveliness and a somnolence in him. Neither passions nor sorrows nor shocks had put any wrinkles on his virginal, fresh face to enliven it" (7:51).

It is this innocent classical figure whom Chichikov invites to travel with him, thinking that, if he is lucky, he will be able to stick Platonov with all their expenses. This indicates a curious kind of uncertainty in Chichikov's character in Part 2: on the one hand, he brings light to Tyentyetnikov's house and attempts to improve Tyentyetnikov's relationship with Ulinka—both praiseworthy activities; on the other hand, he plans to cheat Platonov. It is as though Gogol could not quite manage to fit Chichikov in with what he wanted to do. Chichikov apparently realizes his ambitions and undergoes a reformation when he legitimately buys land, under the influence of Platonov's brother-in-law, Skudronzhoglo, a representative of the really proper Russian landowner who is devoted to his estates and to those who work them. Skudronzhoglo describes Chichikov's new position to him and defines the values that he should adopt:

> You have peasants so that you may protect them in their peasant way of life. What is that way of life? What is the peasant's occupation? Tilling the soil. So you do your best for him to be a good tiller of the soil. Is that clear? There are clever people who say, "He must be raised from this state. He leads too simple and gross a life: he must become acquainted with objects of luxury." It's not enough that, thanks to this luxury, they have themselves become milksops and not people, and have picked up the devil knows what diseases, and that there is not an eighteen-year-old boy who has not tried out everything, so that he's toothless and bald—they now want to infect the peasants. Thank God one healthy estate is still left that is unacquainted with these fancies! For this we should simply thank God. Yes, for me, tillers of the soil are the most honorable of all. God grant that all be tillers of the soil!
> . . . Experience has shown that the purest morals are those of a man of the agricultural calling. Where tilling the soil is the basis of social life, there is abundance and prosperity; there is neither poverty nor luxury, but there is prosperity. . . . First think of making every one of your peasants wealthy. Then you yourself will be wealthy, without factories, without mills, without foolish ventures. [7:69–70]

This statement of Skudronzhoglo's comes close to an enunciation of Gogol's creed, to be even more specifically declared in "To a Russian Landowner." The ideas of Western civilization are the infections; they are at fault, and Russia must return to its roots, while exorcizing the demons from abroad. Although Skudronzhoglo's remarks on the subject may be regarded as the clearest made in Part 2, all of the first four fragments add up to a tract on estate management, an exhortation on the subjects of peace, harmony, and the establishment of a Garden of Eden, a garden that existed in the old Russia—in Rus—and that has, among some, been lost because of the new, false ideas of Western commercialism and libertarianism. Gogol's medieval studies have not been lost, for his view of the social structure is very close to the concept of mutual obligation that supposedly existed in the West before the rise of the bourgeoisie. In the literal meaning of the term, Gogol is a reactionary, as opposed to liberalism as were his potential opponents of the far Left, in the name, like them, of harmonious relationships that assure the well-being of all. For both sides the guilty party is the bourgeois liberal; it is he who brings chaos and fosters false values. For Gogol, what is needed is a return to the Russian way of life, which involves a reawakening of the old spirit. The point is made three times by Platonov's brother Vasily. The first occurs when Vasily tells Platon that Platon is the victim of a "spiritual lethargy" (7:93). The other two occur in remarks to Chichikov: "Fashion is not a decree for us, and Petersburg is not a church"; and "custom for me is a sacred thing" (7:93). These observations come very close to the end of chapter 4 as we have it: they are followed by a hiatus after a few more lines and a short fragment that constitutes a complete change of scene as Chichikov meets Lyenitsyn, a rogue, with the implication that Chichikov is going to take up a swindling career in a much more serious way.

There has already been a serious break in Part 2, however, in that, while Chichikov has become acquainted with—and has even cultivated —good things, while he has acquired genuine land and live serfs, while he has considered proper management and peace, his character seems to have shifted in the opposite direction. While in Part 1 the governor's daughter was Chichikov's vision, now Ulinka is Tyentyetnikov's love, and Chichikov finds her a little too plump for his taste anyhow. In addition, he actively and consciously lies as he pursues his affairs, telling General Betrishchev, for example, an involved tale about a nonexistent uncle in order to get the general to give him some dead souls.[12] This kind of deliberate, elaborate falsification for a calculated purpose was not indulged in by Chichikov in Part 1. If he is our "old friend" when he finally appears in the first fragment, he at best bears a resemblance to the Chichikov of the beginning of Part 1, certainly not to the Chichikov at the close of Part 1. He seems to have developed—or rather degenerated—in contrast to his surroundings rather than in accordance with them. The influence that they should have upon him—and for which Part 1 prepared us—simply does not take place. In addition, the symbol that seemed to be growing in the latter portions of Part 1 new reverses direction, so that Chichikov is no longer even an attractive rogue, capable of being saved, much less the germ of an epic hero. Instead, he has become simply nasty.

It is possible, of course, that Gogol was thinking of a change of heroes, that Patonov, perhaps, was to take over and become the Gofreddo who would conquer the infidel. Certainly he has the potential. But if Gogol allowed such a development, what would happen to the unity of the work as a whole? On the other hand, if he went back to the style and tone of Part 1, what more was there to be said, why should there be a continuation at all? In either case, the problem of Chichikov's regeneration remained before Gogol, and it was insoluble without a complete change of form, which in itself would have meant (and, I suggest, did mean) an artistic failure.

At the same time, Gogol was faced with other problems: he was convinced that, much as Part I had been praised (Gogol was always highly sensitive to criticism), it had also been misunderstood; it now, therefore, had to be clarified (the four fragments appear to be aimed largely in this direction). Also of importance was the constant pressure to produce a continuation that, to Gogol at least, would be largely repetitious. To give in to this pressure would be only to compound the misunderstanding. How could these difficulties be resolved so that he could fulfill the grand design—or rather, conception—of a work in three parts which would form a harmonious whole, a proportioned, balanced poem that in its very form would indicate that beauty which he thought the goal of every genuine artist? To Gogol, *Dead Souls* was unfinished. Part 1 in his mind was only Part 1, much as *Inferno* is only a part of the whole that is *The Divine Comedy*. If the first four chapters we have were really intended to be the beginning of Part 2, then they seem to me to constitute a false start, and Gogol's dissatisfaction with his work was probably well grounded. The comic epic was turning counterproductive; transition to the epic was doomed to artistic disunity; the lyric—as Gogol understood the lyric—was equally, now, out of place. The only solution available was the nonfiction of *Selected*

Passages, whose public failure sent Gogol back to try once more, and burn once more.

Whether what we have said applies equally to the second and third versions of Part 2 we cannot, of course, know; but I, for one, am inclined to go along with Gogol's judgment. I do not think that the burnings were wanton, fanatic destructions committed in moments of aberration; more probably, they were considered critical judgments which were made on the basis of the work in hand (we do have evidence that Gogol retained his critical abilities to the end). The tragedy is that Gogol did not leave—or was not allowed to leave—Part 1 as it was and that he did not go on to write a completely new work of fiction to embody his vision. For some reason, however—perhaps the very strength of his convictions coupled with his unease with the critical reception of his poem—he forced himself to continue. (We may also recall Gogol's problems when *The Inspector General* was produced.) Finally, in February 1852, he resigned himself to what he regarded as his failure and destroyed not only his work, but himself.

8
The Artist

For many years Gogol's style has fascinated analysts of Russian literature, and there is no doubt that Gogol himself paid meticulous attention to the subject in his work. To enter into a minute discussion of style in an exploration such as this, however, would seem to be out of place, involving, as it would, a constant shifting back and forth between two dissimilar languages. As is well known, translation may capture spirit, may communicate letter, may be faithful to the images and sequences of thought of the original; but style—that is, the ways in which the language itself is employed—is something else again.[1] Detailed analysis would thus be little to the point here. On the other hand, some general remarks on the subject may prove useful as an introduction to this chapter as a whole.

It was perhaps fortunate for Gogol that he was born and brought up in the Ukraine rather than in Great Russia and that he did not receive a formal advanced education. The two together meant—at a time when the Russian literary language was still in a state of development,[2] and when there was still much debate and uncertainty about prose, particularly prose fiction—that he could avoid being locked into any of the schools that usually spring up at such a time. In his prose in particular, Gogol had a wealth of barely tapped sources to draw upon, which he felt free to use and to combine, and on the basis of which he could invent according to his need.[3] Many of these sources, perhaps because of his nationalistic feelings, were common expressions—he often praises the Russian peasant's ability to turn a phrase—everyday images, similes, and metaphors. This is one reason that some of the contemporary critics called him coarse, ungrammatical, even incomprehensible. He also delighted in wordplay, puns, and simple sound for its own sake.[4] All this, plus his use of illogical detail, makes it extremely difficult to translate Gogol, as difficult as it is to translate Pushkin's exactitude.

With all his contributions to Russian prose, however, Gogol seems to have thought of himself primarily as a poet, even though we have only one example of a formal poetic attempt on his part, "Hanz Kuechelgarten." The final description of *Dead Souls* in large type as a POEM was neither a practical joke (although Gogol was very fond of practical jokes) nor mere pretension. He saw poetry, I believe, as something more than consistently arranged rhythmic patterns (which he was, incidentally, quite adept at employing in his prose when he felt it necessary), and assuredly more than stanzaic divisions and rhyming lines, all of which marked the usual poetic productions of his time. In fact, most of his acknowledgedly acute critical work was devoted to discussions of the poetic mode.[5] Poetry, for him, was a matter of aesthetic attitude rather than of simple technique, and the poet was one who employed language to express and communicate things of a different order from that of ordinary empirical data. In "A Textbook of Literature for Russian Youth," the one place I am aware of where Gogol defined the different kinds of literature, he wrote:

> There are two languages for literature, two garments for words, two very distinct kinds of expression: one is highly elevated, harmonious throughout; it is not only a vivid, pictorial representation of every thought, but it amplifies the power of expression by the most marvelous combinations of sounds and most vividly reproduces the life of everything being expressed—a kind within the reach of few, and reached by those few only in moments of a deeply moved, sincere, emotional mood, called the poetic, lofty, human language, or, as all peoples call it, the language of the gods; the other, a simple one that does not seek too vivid images, picturesqueness of expression, or agreeable combinations of sounds, is given over to the natural sequence of its thoughts in the calmest disposition of spirit, a kind of which everyone is capable—the prosaic kind. [8:471]

Gogol is always aware, he says, that either may slip over into the territory of the other, and "sometimes poetry can condescend almost to the simplicity of the prosaic and prose rise to the grandeur of the poetic." We note that it is *sound* primarily that makes the difference, and harmonious sound at that. The point is to bring something alive, while prose merely communicates. Thus, poetic language is not only expository and allusive, it is also musical, not only, or just, because it is rhythmic, but because it has an effect upon the ear. One would suppose that a man who was born deaf could never, therefore, read poetry, any more than he could hear music.

Gogol thought of himself—and a careful analysis of his work I think will bear him out—as one who belonged primarily to the first category, although he also at times joined the second. One suspects, indeed, that his mention of "majestic lyrical flow" in *Dead Souls* was meant to define himself and his work in this way. As a "formal poet"— that is, as one who employed recognized forms in a recognized way— he had been a failure: "Hanz Kuechelgarten" is mediocre by any standard, including Gogol's. While he may at first have attempted to destroy all copies of the "poem" because of adverse critical reaction, I suggest that his own aesthetic convictions would have led him to the same conclusion eventually anyhow.[6] The technical form that he had adopted was too confining for a genius who felt the possibilities of language as he did. In this he was, perhaps instinctively, too advanced for his day.[7] This very use of language was what puzzled so many of his contemporaries, leading some to reject him and others, the majority, to call him, first, a "naturalist" and then a "realist," mistaken as those categories now obviously are. He was doing something new, so far as the Russian language was concerned, and he was aware of it; this is why he made remark after remark about the picturesqueness of Russian speech (again we note an interest in sound, *speech,* in what is heard by the ear rather than what is read by the eye, in tone rather than in rhythmic or metrical structure). That he thought of language in such terms is made clear by his repeated and emphatic use of such words as "sound" and "resound," by his frequent references to birds, and by his mentions and employment of Russian songs in his fiction.[8] Considered in this way, he was exactly what he thought he was—a lyric poet, a singer expressing the movements of his own soul. I would suggest that he was, in this, remarkably akin to both Rabelais and Thomas Wolfe, attuned to the pure flow of word sound for its own effectual sake. Sometimes sound overrides grammar, syntax, and logical sequence, making Gogol's thought, as thought, very difficult to decipher; translations usually make the mistake of straightening him out too much, sacrificing ear to mind. Biely was right, in other words, when he called Gogol "volcanic," perhaps the most apt description of his style. It is a sensual effect that his eruptions achieve, however, not a mental one.

Gogol's position in the development of Russian prose thus stands in much the same relation as Rabelais's position in the development of French prose—that of the innovator who, while accomplishing great things himself, showed possibilities for later practitioners in the medium. It is thus with Gogol, rather than with Pushkin, that modern Russian literature begins (contemporary Russian literature, we remember, began with a revolt against Pushkin).

This does not mean that Gogol was in favor of composition of gibberish in the fashion of some of the Futurist experiments of the 1920s. He also had a strong yearning for form, as we know, for form was a human way to point to that eternal harmony which was the expression of beauty itself, beauty that he thought was both the inspiration and the goal of every artist. Hence his great admiration for Pushkin, who, despite the artistic differences between them, he thought had attained harmony in his work.[9]

Gogol's prime motivation as an artist, thus, was aesthetic, as V. V. Zenkovsky has pointed out.[10] This does not mean, however, that Gogol thought of himself as a creator of beauty; rather, his task was to reveal beauty, if he could. Like Michelangelo, he saw the artist as one who broke through enveloping material and disclosed the beautiful form that lay within. Even descriptions of the ugly, uses of the grotesque, and the employment of laughter have this aim, for they are the cuttings away of imprisoning material that are meant to inform the reader of material's deceptive character and turn him towards the beautiful by a negative reaction of revulsion. To Gogol, however, this "solution" was at best a poor one: drawn by the aesthetic though he was, the beautiful remained indescribable, beyond the bounds of actual embodiment. He could do no more than indicate it by portraying its opposite, which contrasted with the language employed and with the form of the artistic work, the latter of which would be a balanced "fitting-together" of the various parts so that a "whole" would be fashioned in which nothing essential was omitted and nothing superfluous included. In general terms, of course, this bears some resemblances to the classical view of art, and Gogol did indeed have an appreciation for the classical. When considered in conjunction with his language and his episodic manner, however, it makes him, as an artist, more closely akin to the men of the sixteenth and early seventeeth centuries in the West, as I have tried to indicate.

Gogol's greatest difficulty, perhaps because of the state of literature in Russia in his time and its lack of a grand tradition on which to base itself, was precisely that he was an episodic writer rather than one capable of composing on a large scale—a composer of études rather than symphonies (one returns to the category of the lyric)—despite his somewhat grandiose ambitions. A survey of the body of his work will, I think, bear this out. He completed not one long, sustained narrative work of fiction (remembering that *Dead Souls* was, in Gogol's view, unfinished), not one long work of nonfiction (despite his youthful plans to write many-volume histories), and only one full-length play. This episodic quality did not mean, however, that unity escaped him. As G. A. Gukovsky puts it in his *Realizm Gogolya* (Moscow and Leningrad: Khudozhestvennoi literatury, 1959, p. 26):

> Gogol's striving to perform cycles, to overcome separation in his works, was so strong that it could sweep beyond the limits of an individual artistic work and form an unexpected and extremely rare unity out of the collection *Arabesques,* which weaves articles, sketches, monologues, and stories together into the community of a system that is not only artistic, but methodological and, in general, ideological.

This is another way of saying, and quite correctly, I believe, that Gogol's technique is more that of variations on a theme than it is of thematic development. Hence what I call his episodic quality. Hence, also, what he regarded as the formal failure of *Dead Souls,* which was, he said, even greater than his critics had realized.[11] Gogol still thought, in 1843, as he continued work on Part 2, that the problems would be overcome when the rest of the poem was published and Part 1 was revised. For once, the variations on a theme did not seem sufficient, and he thought it proper to attempt thematic development, which led to the formal failure.

So far as *Evenings on a Farm near Dikanka* is concerned, a certain kind of unity was achieved in each volume, as I tried to show in chapter 1. The unity of the first volume, however, is not the result of anything that is necessary and inherent to the work; it is instead a consequence of the summary contained in the last story, "The Lost Letter," which ties together everything that preceded it in terms of theme and meaning, but *not* in terms of structure. Neither this story, nor any particular story, *had* to be *there*. So far as structure is concerned, the work remains episodic; "The Lost Letter" is not a conclusion, merely an ending. What unity we have, thus, is artificial, imposed; an organic whole is not formed, and the stories are held together by a teacher repeating the lesson in outline so that his students may pass the examination. Gogol already had his vision, his goal, but he did not yet know how to reach that goal.[12] This was an artist on the way, one who was learning fast, but not yet one who had achieved.

Gogol's reaction to his problem was twofold: the second volume of *Evenings on a Farm near Dikanka* and a definitive turn to the teaching profession, which latter entailed, in addition, the writing of essays on a variety of topics, all of which, including even "Thoughts on Geography," were based on Gogol's vision of the reality of the harmonious beauty of the universe.

The first fictional attempt had worked, but, as we have said, it was artificial, and it was unsatisfactory to a Gogol who had taken on Hanz Kuechelgarten's quest. His position, despite his wide reading and his particular acquaintance with many of the German romantics—philosophers, critics, poets, and writers of fiction, all of whose influence may be discerned in his work of this period and later—was the difficult one of an innovator who finds it necessary to make his own form rather than that of an innovator who is revolting against, or trying to give a new direction to, an already established tradition. From the very beginning, the problem was not what, but how. The what, he felt, had been given, as it is mysteriously given to a prophet and seer. (I do not mean to question the importance of influences and climate here; this is rather a question of what Gogol seemed to feel, as indicated by his essays and letters as well as by his fiction. While he did doubt his own moral purity, he never doubted the vision that was guiding him, any more than he doubted God, which amounts to the same thing.)

The second volume of *Evenings on a Farm near Dikanka* also attempted to solve the formal how.[13] Its success was greater than that of volume 1, but it was still not entire. Now Gogol tried to achieve unity, or wholeness, through tone, contrast, and pairing. The first and fourth stories—the outside group, "Christmas Eve" and "A Bewitched Place"—form a tonal pair (both are humorous devil tales) surrounding the thematically paired but contrasting stories "A Terrible Vengeance" and "Ivan Fyodorovich Shponka and His Aunt" ("A Terrible Vengeance"

is a straight horror story, and "Ivan Fyodorovich" has horror under-
lying it and ends with a nightmare) and constitute a contrast with them.
Variation on a theme (the outside stories are only tonally in contrast
with the inner ones) is here consciously and deliberately used, while
the entire set is intended to constitute a whole. The unity, however,
although more varied in its parts than that of volume 1, still does not
demonstrate, as a form, the harmony at which Gogol was aiming. The
stories remain separate units which need not be read together. Again,
what unity there is, is thematic rather than structural (as we know,
many of the stories in both volumes were in fact published separately
as self-contained tales; and Rudy Panko is a collector and observer, not
even a commentator, much less a participant, so that, while the device
of the overseeing narrator might be used as a necessary and unifying
element who may even become the center of attention—as Babel demon-
strated in *Red Cavalry*—Gogol did not so employ it). Since the unity
and harmony are arranged after the fact, as it were, this is not the art
that conceals art, but the art that reveals it. Even in some of the individual stories there are splits or shifts in the narrative flow, as, for
example, in "A Terrible Vengeance," where the change occurs as Gogol
tries to explain what has happened in the main body of the tale, and in
"A May Night, or The Drowned Maiden," where he seems to have
allowed his episodic tendencies and thematic interests to overcome his
concern with overall form.

Mirgorod does not improve the situation materially,[14] although
the first, second, and third stories—"Old World Landowners," "Taras
Bulba," and "The Tale of How Ivan Ivanovich Quarreled with Ivan
Nikiforovich"—each maintains a unity within itself. In fact, it might
be said that the first succeeds better than any other of Gogol's stories
in the use of the narrator as the unifying element both thematically and
structurally. There is still, however, no overall form to bring the entire
book together. Again, there is little reason other than the thematic one
for considering these tales as a group.

Of course, the Little Russian tales are still those of a man who is
feeling his way, a man who has much to learn about his craft, innovator though he be, before he can achieve his goal. Gogol had intuitively
grasped his basic subject, but the problem of its embodiment, its formal
demonstration, continued to plague him. When he turned to a new
setting, St. Petersburg, the problem was compounded, because the city
deeply revolted him and because there was no possibility of his using

a lyrical evocation of a countryside of beauty as relief. To him, St. Petersburg, far from being the "Venice of the North," was the epitome of ugliness itself—an alien, fog-enveloped, deceptive, and corruptive world that was an excrescence of the antithesis of what Gogol believed to be the truth, a truth that he wished to indicate in his work. It was here, however, that he finally realized his artistic method—contrast, but not between one story and another (he had tried some of this in the volumes of Little Russian tales) or obvious contrasts within the stories themselves (this he had also experimented with).[15] The contrast is much more subtle, more in the style of Greek tragedy. In most of the Petersburg tales it consists of a contrast between what is delineated in the story itself, what is depicted on the page, and what the audience knows, or what Gogol hopes the audience knows.[16] It is not simply a matter of conflicting events and beliefs within each story or between one story and another; here we find truth and falsity, beauty and ugliness, assigned to both the observer and the participant. The former does not identify with the latter; he is instead raised to a greater consciousness of his difference from and superiority to him. What is put before the audience, in the Petersburg tales, in *The Inspector General,* and in *Dead Souls* (with qualifications in those cases where the participant is allowed a glimpse of reality) is the false and the ugly, so that the audience, remaining outside the work and secure in its position, may be raised to a greater overt awareness of its inner knowledge of the true and the beautiful. The knowledge is always presumed to be in the possession of the audience at the start, but lacking in the persons who inhabit the stories. That is why we know, for example, that Chartkov, Poprishchin, Kovalyov, and Akaky Akakyevich are all wrong. When someone inside the story does have an intimation of truth (as in "Nevsky Prospekt" and "The Portrait"), he does not see its full implications and, indeed, rejects it, so overwhelmed is he by habit and material. At best, we pity him, wishing that he could understand things as we do, but aware that he cannot. Our knowledge thus always stands in direct contrast to his, and we can put down the work with precisely that raised consciousness of reality that Gogol wished to achieve for us.

Perhaps Gogol's most successful use of this method is in *The Inspector General* (although one might also point to "The Diary of a Madman" for an example, even if the passage at the end, where Poprishchin calls upon his mother, may be regarded as a flaw). That we have entered a false world is clear at the very beginning of the play, and this falsity immediately appeals to our knowledge of its opposite, thus imposing an awareness upon us at the outset. Our inner world is in direct contrast with the artificial world that is presented on stage, and we cannot take the latter seriously as a portrayal of reality. This is not to say that the stage world does not exist; on the contrary, we know from the beginning that it does, but we are also forced to recognize that existence and truth are not synonymous terms (that is, what is true necessarily exists, but what exists is not necessarily true). As commonly occurs in comedy, we feel superior to the presentation because we know where the truth lies, while the persons whom we are shown do not; our existence is real, in other words, whereas theirs is not. The untruth portrayed by those on stage in fact brings us to a higher consciousness of its opposite. Their discord produces our harmony; their ugliness, our perception of beauty.

Gogol's use of contrast has a further dimension, however, one that is artistically more subtle. Instead of making form and content one, instead of having one reflect the other, which is the normal literary method,[17] Gogol deliberately sets up a clash between them. Action and character are always consistent both in themselves and in relation with each other. Furthermore, the action describes a complete circle, so that formally the play is a whole, harmonious in all its parts, with nothing to be added or subtracted. It is beautiful, thus, as a mathematical formula is beautiful;[18] that is, it is formally beautiful. Nowhere do we find any inconsistency or contradiction; nothing is out of place to mar the cohesiveness of the whole. When we come to content, however, we are confronted with the exact opposite: stupidity, lying, discord, refusal to recognize one's own truth (much less the truth of others), and a spiritual and moral ugliness that is totally unrelieved in the course of the play. There is no hint of concern on the part of any person that he may be pursuing the wrong path; no one within the play, that is, perceives, even fleetingly, that beauty which we in the audience perceive through the form. Each of the characters displays only a deep-rooted interest in himself (a false self) as a separate and selfish ego whose overriding ambition is the furtherance of his own material, social, or sexual fortunes. What concerted activity there is—as, for example, the plots of the Mayor and the officials—is in the nature of a temporary alliance among individuals, each of whom is attempting to pursue what he mistakenly conceives to be his own advantage, rather than the movement of a whole, acting in concord. Within the play, that is, in content, we have divisiveness rather than harmony, separation rather than one-ness; and this is in direct contrast with the formal unity.

The satisfaction that the audience feels with the play is thus a result of the formal cohesiveness—*that* is where the truth lies, and we recognize this, which in itself is the "message" that Gogol wished to convey, and certainly Gogol was a "message" artist, devoted to beauty itself. From this point of view, he goes beyond mere satire, beyond a mere call for social or moral reform, beyond, that is, mere "realism"; he rises to a statement of faith that is finally made clear in the last scene, which closes the formal circle while emphasizing the parodic nature of the content, thus reinforcing the clash and driving his point home.

It was primarily when Gogol tried to be explicit about his message that he ran into formal trouble, as he did, for example, in his use of digressions both in *Dead Souls* and in his plans for the continuation of that work and as he did in his essays on social and religious topics. Most critics give the impression that they wish these writings did not exist, not because Gogol had no right to digress or because he had no right to express opinions in poetic passages and discursive prose, but because of what he attempted to say in these passages, which often contradicts the critical stance. For Gogol, however, these excursions were necessary, because he thought that his work, especially *The Inspector General,* had not been understood, that his art, in other words, had failed. The service that he wished to perform remained always of greater importance than mere literary success: art, for him, had purpose, and the artist's purpose at that; if the purpose was not achieved, then it was incumbent upon the artist to tell the public at least what it was. (Of course, I be-lieve that Gogol *was* artistically successful, despite his own doubts.) This is not to say, however, that Gogol thereupon changed his basic artistic method. On the contrary: the contrast between beauty/truth and ugliness/falsity—which is sometimes implied and sometimes, as in certain passages of *Dead Souls,* explicit—remained. We can see it in almost every piece of fiction that he wrote: sometimes, as in *The Inspector General* and "The Tale of How Ivan Ivanovich Quarreled with Ivan Nikiforovich," the contrast is between form and content; more usually it is between fictional portrayal and the audience's knowledge, the false and the true. The clash between form and content, while it is the more ingenious and more subtle, also proved the more difficult to grasp for a Russian audience that increasingly insisted upon "social command," failing to understand that meaning could be contained in form itself, while content, in the sense I have been using it, could merely be an illustration of the reverse side of the coin.[19] Gogol was an experimenter who was doing something that no one had done before and few have done since. In addition, the call in nineteenth-century Russia, as in the Soviet Union, was for a literature—an art—of action, devoted, not to beauty, but at least to social renovation. The decline in the popularity of poetry from the 1830s until the last decade of the century is an indication of this. Thus, Gogol's prime concern—the quest that was the cause of his work and the resolution of which was the goal of his work— was precisely that element that was ignored by even so discerning a literary practitioner as Turgenev.

Curiously enough, despite all the tales, despite the plays, and despite *Dead Souls* itself, Gogol's impulse seems to have been lyric rather than narrative, as I have tried to suggest. Few of his works, a notable one of which is "The Overcoat," have plots or develop situations and characters in the way that we have come to expect of narrative; we usually wind up right back where we started. In most cases we are instead faced with set situations and with characters that exhibit little change, as though time and happenings within it were deceptive constructions of minds that have been beguiled. In this, Gogol is very different from writers like Turgenev and Tolstoy, on the one hand, and from Kafka, who bears many resemblances to Gogol in other respects, on the other. Gogol is a static writer rather than a dynamic one like Dostoevsky. When he does attempt to relate an intimately connected story that involves change, as in "The Portrait" and "Nevsky Prospekt," the narrative splits, and the tale's effect depends upon a deliberately inserted lyrical passage—the final paragraph of "Nevsky Prospekt," for example.[20] The concluding note does not bring the story to a denouement, solving problems raised in it; it is instead a personal expression of the author's feelings about his ultimate subject, which has little to do with the central characters in the story or what happens to them. We are told what Gogol, not Piskaryov or Pigorov, feels about St. Petersburg—namely, that it is a lie.

These personal lyrical expressions pervade Gogol's work, from "Hanz Kuechelgarten" onwards. These "poems" extend from the evocation of melancholy at the end of "The Fair at Sorochintsy" through the nature passages that we find sprinkling all the Little Russian stories, the descriptions of Nevsky Prospekt in the story of that name, the statements on passion for gold in "The Portrait," and the personal excursion that begins "The Overcoat," right down to the troika passage at the end of *Dead Souls,* Part 1, not to mention the lyricism that informs such essays as "Boris Godunov," "Woman," "Life," "1834," and much of *Selected Passages from Correspondence with Friends,* particularly the last article in that volume, "Easter Sunday." These expressions are in the nature of prose poems, meant primarily to focus attention on Gogol's own feelings and knowledge.[21] They are, furthermore, excellent examples of what he himself described as lyric poetry in "A Textbook of Literature for Russian Youth":

> Lyric poetry is a portrait, a reflection and a mirror of the loftiest movements of the poet's soul, . . . the biography of his ecstasies. It is, from the loftiest to the lowest of its kinds, nothing other than an account of the poet's own sensations. . . . In short, it is the pure personality of the poet himself and pure truth. [8:472]

Gogol had written earlier in the same essay:

> The source of poetry is beauty. The sight of beauty arouses an impulse in a man to praise it, to versify, and to sing. To praise with such words that others may feel the beauty lauded by him. The poet is only one who is more capable than others of feeling the beauty of creation. The need to share his feelings inflames him and turns him into a poet. [8:472]

We remember that Chichikov, at the sight of the young girl, almost turned into a poet.[22]

Gogol's lyricism, I would suggest, best expresses his attitude and his aim. It makes most immediately obvious his revulsion at ugliness and his attraction to beauty, which latter he always couples with the true and the real. As an artist, he saw his prime task to be a revelation of this truth that he had been vouchsafed as an individual, not different from others, but more highly "gifted" than others.[23] The lyricism, thus, was essential to Gogol's art, for in the lyric the artist was also practicing his function as teacher and prophet, the one to whom a more highly integrated vision of ultimate reality had been given and whose duty it was to bring that vision to consciousness in others by the process of sharing. This was the "service" that Gogol wished to perform, a service to which his art became increasingly devoted as his career progressed, and this was a groundwork for his lyrical declarations.

To the same end, this most serious of writers used the device of laughter, which is in fact but a variation on the method of contrast,[24] as are his employments of exaggeration and the grotesque.[25] Gogol's laughter follows the pattern of a device that is employed to inspire rejection on the part of the audience by appealing to previously possessed but unexpressed knowledge, a device to bring about a conscious acknowledgment of reality, in other words. Rarely (most often by using the feminine symbol, or in a lyrical passage) does Gogol pretend that he is depicting things the way they really are, that page or stage is serious. The point is normally the exact opposite, and the laughter arises out of the preposterous proposition that anyone would take these scenes as portrayals of truth. Over and over again the comedy results from the refusal of persons within the presentation to perceive reality; that is, out of a contrast between the awareness of the audience and the lack of awareness of those within the story, out of a species of incongruity to which only the audience is privy.[26] This is using irony for comic effect.[27]

Our laughter thus arises out of a deliberately emphasized sense of superiority and security, for we dwell in reality, we know where the truth lies, we have an aesthetic sense, while the objects of our laughter do not. For this reason, many of the Little Russian devils, Ivan Fyodorovich Shponka, Ivan Ivanovich and Ivan Nikiforovich, Kovalyov, Ikharev, almost all the characters in *The Inspector General,* and all the persons we meet in *Dead Souls* (although only rarely Chichikov himself, who, because of his intimations of truth, verges on tragedy; and never the governor's daughter) are figures of fun. It is their incredible insistence upon remaining ignorant that does them in. We not only know better; we are made conscious that we know better. It is, in this sense, laughter at idiocy, at what exists but what is not in any meaningful way alive.

Comedy is thus employed by Gogol to accomplish the same effect as the horror in some of the Little Russian stories. He himself seems to have been quite well aware of this, for he sometimes went so far as to conjoin the two elements in a single tale, as in "Nevsky Prospekt," "Diary of a Madman," "The Overcoat," and even in *Dead Souls* itself. The most obvious instance is the first of these. The part of the story that concerns the painter Piskaryov is told seriously and almost sympathetically, to wind up in gruesomeness and revulsion with the young man's suicide and funeral:

> He locked himself in his room and admitted no one; he asked for nothing. Four days passed, and his locked room was not opened once; finally a week went by, and the room was still

locked. People pounded on the door, began calling him, but there was no answer at all; finally, they broke down the door and found his lifeless corpse with its throat cut. A blood-stained razor was lying on the floor. His arm convulsively flung out and his terribly distorted expression might lead one to conclude that his hand had been unsure and that he had been tormented a long time before his sinful soul left his body.

So he perished, a sacrifice to a mad passion, poor quiet, shy, modest, childishly ingenuous Piskaryov, who had a spark of talent that might in time have blazed broad and clear. No one wept over him; no one was seen beside his lifeless corpse except the usual figure of the local policeman and the indifferent mien of the coroner. His coffin was quietly conveyed to Okhta, without even religious rites; only a sentry following it wept, and that because he had drunk one bottle of vodka too many. [3:33]

Set beside this the last scene in which Pirogov appears (keeping in mind that both Piskaryov and Pirogov have been deceived in their amatory attachments):

But all this ended rather strangely: on his way he went into a cafe, ate two puff pastries, read something in the *Northern Bee,* and went out in a less angry state. Besides, a rather pleasant, cool evening induced him to stroll a bit along Nevsky Prospekt; by nine o'clock he had calmed down and discovered that it wouldn't be a good thing to trouble the general on a Sunday, besides he had undoubtedly been called away somewhere; so he set out for an evening at the home of one of the directors of the control board, where there was a very pleasant gathering of officials and officers. There he spent a pleasurable evening and so distinguished himself in the mazurka that he delighted not only the ladies but their escorts. [3:45]

For Pirogov it doesn't matter, but for Piskaryov it does; hence the humor associated with the former and the horror associated with the latter. There is really little difference in the situations of the two, however: each has taken the false for the true and has fallen because of his error; both have missed the point. The one evokes horror, on the other hand, because we too might fall into the trap (it is not so easy to see through the fog of Nevsky Prospekt), while the other evokes humor because we are sure of ourselves (thus far we would certainly always be able to see). A warning is succeeded by reassurance; we are taken out of a situation that we have every right to fear, because of the difficulties to be faced when we seek to actualize truth (one wonders how much Piskaryov represents a spiritual self-portrait of Gogol himself), and we are relieved by a situation that reinforces our prior intuition and our superiority (Pirogov has no inkling of that innate knowledge of which Gogol has made us aware). In other words, we have been shifted from possible identification to an objective view, a technique often used in the classic Greek theater when a comedy succeeded to a tragedy, both of which were by the same author and both on the same theme.[28]

"The Diary of a Madman" and "The Overcoat" follow much the same pattern, but more subtly, more gradually, and with a reversal of direction; that is, the alternative approaches are not clearly delineated by a character and story break; rather, one, humor, leads into the other, horror. In neither case does Gogol aim at any identification at all; we are drawn to look further into ourselves; our consciousness of reality is heightened more and more by the meaning that is given to laughter, an effect that is achieved by this movement into a world that can never be ours, one that is completely foreign to our intuition of the truth and therefore unreal. The real joke and the shock is that comedy and horror are twins,[29] that laughter at the end is cut off, that in "The Dairy of a Madman" the last line should be funny but instead is terrifying.

"The Diary of a Madman" begins on a comic note. It is October 2, and "an extraordinary adventure occurred today" (3:193). Two pages later, having been kept in suspense but knowing that the adventure, whatever it is, will be both fantastic and probably somewhat "nutty," we discover that Poprishchin (who is still unnamed, who is only a kind of disembodied "I") has overhead a conversation between two dogs, which we are immediately told, in a reinforcement of the fantasy, was not really surprising at all: "later, when I considered it properly, my astonishment ceased. Indeed, a great number of similar instances have occurred" (3:195). Astonishment returns, however, when one dog speaks of writing letters. The joke is an extremely old one, on the same pattern as that of the talking horse in the bar. That the point of the joke is the naïve foolishness of a participant who takes the adventure seriously gives rise to our amusement: we know better. The humorous tone continues through the regular time sequence of Poprishchin's entries in his diary, that is, from October 3 through December 8. Then, as the time sequence is disrupted (the next entry is dated "2,000, April

23"), the comic gives way to pity as Poprishchin loses touch not only with the world around him but with himself: we had not expected the joke to have such serious consequences. Finally, both humor and pity disappear entirely, and there is an increasing descent into horror until we reach the concluding lines:

> Is that my mother sitting at the window? Dear mother, save your poor son! Let but one tear fall on your sick boy's head! See how they torture him! Clasp the poor little orphan to your breast! He has no place in the world! They are persecuting him! Dear mother, pity your poor little baby! . . . Do you know that the Dey of Algiers has a boil under his nose? [3:214]

There is incongruity here, increased by the speaker's use of the third person instead of the first (he had previously employed the first person, so one wonders if he has any personality, of any kind, left at all), but there is nothing in the least amusing. Instead of the Dey of Algiers being a figure of fun, the context makes the image a sign of Proprishchin's nightmare, and we recoil from his unreal, discordant world. We have descended to an ugliness (the picture of the boil which is associated, because of the preceding lines, with this new, third-person Poprishchin) that produces only revulsion. Can we read the story again and laugh without fear? It is the very discordance of the humor, its "madness," that produces the horror.

"The Overcoat" follows much the same pattern, although the emphasis varies. Again we start on a comic note, with the long passage on the naming of Akaky Akakyevich and the appropriateness of his family name—Bashmachkin—the reader can feel secure that this tale will be funny, that he will be regaled by a story about the butt of everyone's joke. The comic tone continues until Akaky Akakyevich becomes obsessed with his new overcoat (there is a touch of madness about such single-minded attachment that gives us a certain unease). Gogol then manipulates the reader's reactions in masterful fashion: sympathy for the hero, coupled with outrage at the treatment accorded him by others (hence the view of Akaky Akakyevich as the poor oppressed "little man"), followed by a sense of emptiness, although not loss, at the loneliness of Akaky's death as we are told the circumstances of his passing:

Vanished and stolen away was a creature defended by no one, of interest to no one, who had not even attracted the attention of a naturalist (who wouldn't let the chance to stick an ordinary fly on a pin and look at it under a microscope go); a creature who had humbly borne the gibes of the office and for no special reason had gone to his grave, but who nevertheless, even though at the very end of his life, had fleetingly been visited by a radiant guest in the form of an overcoat, for a moment enlivening his poor life, one on whom unbearable misfortune then fell, as it has fallen upon the sovereigns and masters of this world. [3:169]

But Gogol is not satisfied—the reader might rest with the "little man" interpretation:

Who could imagine that this was not all there was to Akaky Akakyevich, that he was fated to live on sensationally for a few days after his death, as though in recompense for his life having been unnoticed by anyone? But so it happened, and our poor story unexpectedly acquires a fantastic ending. [3:169]

We are then treated to a corpse that, while it terrifies the inhabitants of St. Petersburg, has no frightening effect upon the reader. Now, indeed, terror within the story provokes laughter from the observer. Gogol has in effect combined the two elements in such a way as to bring all normal (that is, material) perceptions of reality into question. Laughter and horror, the comic and the nightmarish, have become so intimately connected in the concluding passages of this story as to constitute almost a species of "black humor," whose essence is precisely this calling into question of values that we habitually hold in the material world. The very end of the tale, it seems to me, does this calling into question by making us unsure of all that we have previously thought. A policeman has seen a ghost, presumably that of Akaky Akakyevich (although when referring to the dead Akaky Akakyevich, Gogol uses the word "corpse" rather than "ghost"), and

he followed it in the darkness until finally the ghost suddenly glanced back and, stopping, asked, "You want something?" and showed such a fist as you won't find among living men. The policeman said, "Nothing," and turned back immediately. The ghost, however, was much taller, wore enormous moustaches, and, having directed its steps, it seemed, to Obukhov

Bridge, was completely hidden by the darkness of the night.
[3:174]

Deceptive St. Petersburg is clearly with us once more, the city that
had already served Gogol as a symbol of falsity in the Petersburg tales.
The last passage does have a certain element of humor in it, but perhaps
we may trick ourselves by that very humor, if we are not extremely
careful.[30]

This combination of methods—from the overt contrast of "Nevsky
Prospekt" through the gradual descent of "The Diary of a Madman"
to the intertwining of "The Overcoat"—reached its finest expression in
Dead Souls in the doubling between the explicit (the comic) and the
implicit (the horror), while at the same time there is an attempt to
portray the true and the real (the beautiful), which last is absent in the
other stories. What is funny in *Dead Souls*—the delineations of various
character types, the activities that these types engage in, the outlandish
similes, the illogical sequences, and so forth—is also terrifying. The
very opening description of Chichikov may serve as an example of the
combination: He was "not a handsome man, but not of bad appearance either, neither too fat nor too thin; he couldn't be called old; on
the other hand, he wasn't particularly young. His entry into town made
absolutely no noise at all and was not accompanied by anything special"
(6:7). This seemingly light, rather vague, and offhand tone will continue for some time. The author obviously does not wish us to approach
this poem in a "high," or even a solemn, frame of mind: the story is
not going to be heroic, nor will it be, at least on the surface, tragic.
However, the language of this opening also stresses the negative quality
of what is to come: the first paragraph, from which the above quotation
is taken, consists of twenty-three lines; the first nine of these contain
ten negatives as well as one "rather," which detracts from the beauty
of Chichikov's carriage rather than adds to it, one "but," and one
"however." The rest of the first paragraph, consisting of fourteen more
lines, contains four more negatives and one "on the other hand." In
twenty-three lines, thus, we have fourteen negatives and four quasi-
negatives. This is a very large proportion indeed, and it has the effect
of informing us that we are to be confronted with what is not, rather
than with what is; with the void; with horror. But this horror will be
below the surface of the overtly humorous tone. It is a horror that is
the essential quality of the vulgarity, the ugliness, the banality, the

emptiness (the *poshlost'*) whose portrayal Gogol so emphasized as his special talent in "Four Letters to Divers Persons Apropos Dead Souls" (*SP*, 96–110). Over and over again, particularly in the second of the four letters (dated 1843 by Gogol), Gogol speaks of the emptiness that is to be met in Russia, of "soulless objects[s] in [Russia's] empty spaces" (*SP*, 101), of "things missing in Russia" (*SP*, 102), in short, of what should be there but is not.[31] Then, in the third letter, also dated 1843, he speaks of *poshlost'* itself, telling his readers that, although his "heroes are not at all villains," still

> the banality of all of them frightened my readers. What fright-ened them is that my heroes follow one after the other, one more banal than the other, that there is not one consoling scene, that there is nowhere for the poor reader to rest and take a breath, and, after having read the whole book, it seems exactly as though he were emerging from some stifling cellar into God's light. . . . The Russian is more frightened of his insignificance than of all his vices and shortcomings. . . . Whoever is strongly disgusted at his insignificance probably has everything opposite to insignificance.
>
> . . . I saw what something whose spring is the soul and is a spiritual truth means, how frightening a sight it can be to a man when he is presented with shadows, and how much more threatening is *the absence of light.* [*SP*, 103–5]

I would suggest that in these passages Gogol defined the essence of his art in its highest development, particularly as it worked in *Dead Souls.* Superficially, the work is a comic one, at times farcical (the Alphonse-Gaston act performed by Manilov and Chichikov; the over-turning of Chichikov's carriage by his drunken coachman, Selifan; the feather bed on which Chichikov sleeps at Korobochka's house; Sobakye-vich at his table), giving rise to belly laughter; at times satirical (the registration of the souls that Chichikov has bought, the description of the ladies at the ball, the conversation between the lady-agreeable-in-all-respects and the simply-agreeable-lady), provoking chuckles and a feel-ing of well-being in the reader; at times simply amusing (the account of Madame Manilov's education, the conversation among the towns-people about what Chichikov is going to do with the souls he has pur-chased, the cleverness of Chichikov's responses to whomever he meets). Combined with this, however, is that negation which Gogol adum-brated in the opening paragraph and which pervades the entire poem.

This negation, further, defines the vulgarity, ugliness, banality, emptiness —the *poshlost'*; it gives rise both to the fright—to the horror of which Gogol speaks—and to the laughter experienced by the reader. Instead of contrast between comedy and horror, instead of descent from comedy to horror, instead of intertwining comedy and horror, Gogol in *Dead Souls* brings the two together in such a way as to make the one simply an aspect of the other.[32] What he has done in *Dead Souls,* in other words, is to fuse the two ancient Greek modes (modes also employed by the Grand Guignol) to form an artistic whole. At the same time that we laugh because we know better, we are frightened because of the discordancy and "thingness" that we are confronted with, and that in turn raises our consciousness of the real, the true, the beautiful (we are certain that the feelings aroused in Chichikov by the governor's daughter are right, symbolic though she may be).

Although, thus, Gogol did not solve the formal problem posed to him by *Dead Souls,* he did attain to, and he did practice incomparably well, an artistic method that few before the twentieth century have attempted, much less accomplished.[33]

9

The Christian

As V. V. Zenkovsky points out, "in general, Gogol never experienced religious doubts—there were periods of quiescence of religious feeling, but no doubt regarding the truth and power of Christianity." Zenkovsky, however, has a tendency to separate Gogol's aesthetic concerns, his aesthetic "world view," from his religiosity. For Zenkovsky, the aesthetic period, "which began in 1836 and ended around 1840, lasted until the religious break. The second period began at this time,"[1] and presumably continued for the remainder of Gogol's life.[2] Thus, like Gippius and many others, Zenkovsky clings to the theory of a "religious crisis" in Gogol's career. From this point of view, Gogol's quest for beauty and his quest for God are two different things, to be considered apart from each other, despite the acknowledgment that the faith was always strong in him.

That Gogol became more explicit about religion in his later years, particularly in his letters and in *Selected Passages from Correspondence with Friends,* there is no question; that he was seeking to explain himself while convinced of his own spiritual, hence moral and artistic, unworthiness, there is also no question. But that this meant a break, a crisis, and a "new path" is something else again. His very desire to reissue those articles that he had published in *Arabesques* in 1835, along with a second edition of *Selected Passages* (which no one other than Gogol wanted), seems to me to indicate that at least he was not aware of any break. He was personally convinced, regardless of what his contemporaries might have thought,[3] that he was being perfectly consistent, that he was but being more outspoken, because of what he had always regarded as the misunderstanding of his fictional work. For him, the concentration that we find in his later writings is part of an attempt to clarify the vision that he had pursued in his fiction, for to Gogol the aesthetic and the religious were not separate categories; they were in reality one—the Kingdom of God was the Kingdom of Beauty.[4]

Gogol's religious attitude was, in this sense, in accord with the Russian Orthodox legend, reported in *The Primary Chronicle,* of the conversion of ancient Kiev to Christianity. The envoys of Grand Duke Vladimir returned from the mission to Byzantium on which Vladimir had sent them and reported:

> The Greeks led us to the edifices where they worship their God, and we knew not whether we were in heaven or on earth. For on earth there is no such splendor or such beauty, and we were at a loss how to describe it. We know only that God dwells there among men, and their service is fairer than the ceremonies of other nations. For we cannot forget that beauty. Every man, after tasting something sweet, is afterward unwilling to accept that which is bitter, and therefore we cannot dwell longer here.[5]

Like Vladimir's emissaries, Gogol also found it impossible to "dwell longer here." That beauty of which the *Chronicle* speaks may not be actually here on earth, but it is real nevertheless, and one may stand in its presence—that is, in the presence of God. This is not to say, on the other hand, that Gogol was attracted to some other, some mystical, reality outside human experience, to "pie in the sky"; for him, this reality, even while different from the "factual" environment upon which men often mistakenly concentrate their attention, was possible to him who perceived truly. Furthermore, this reality can be actualized; false "fact" can be overcome, in the sense that the pristine purity of God's creation, the world at which God looked and saw that it was good, is already here and needs but a shift in perspective for man to live in it. Gogol never doubted the true existence of this God-created world; he searched for it throughout much of his career; his was the Christianity of Transfiguration.

Gogol's religious outlook was, of course, conservative (Florovsky calls it "archaic"), in the sense that he had no intention of upsetting, much less reversing, accepted views and in the sense that he based himself, in common with Orthodox tradition—despite the strong influence of German romanticism[6]—on the *Gospel According to Saint John.* For him, Christ is the great reconciler of all, the ultimate paradox within Whom all things are united, the ultimate actualization of harmony.

What applied to the artist also applied to the man of religion: what was good was that which accomplished peace; what was bad was that which brought about discord. It is in these terms that Christ and Satan could be defined, and in these terms that Gogol made his distinction, as his stories show. Contrary to Merezhkovsky, the two did not, for Gogol, represent two principles, the spirit and the flesh,[7] which were engaged in a war for man's soul, despite a certain superficial appearance of such a conflict. It is not a battle between principles that is the problem, but affirmation or rejection of truth. The lie cannot be a principle; even for a hypocrite it is only useful in action, and hypocrites are rare in Gogol's work.

On the surface, that is, if we think Gogol believed that the ugliness he portrayed was a representation of reality, the division appears quite plausible, and it can be supported on the basis of Gogol's fiction. However, such a division in itself goes against Gogol's view of reality as a whole. Indeed, it amounts to accusing him of the Manichean heresy, which is as repugnant to Orthodoxy as it is to Roman Catholicism (even if Augustine is not a saint in the Orthodox Church). As I have tried to indicate, Gogol saw the world in a different way—in common with most of those of a Christian religious persuasion, he did not see it as a battleground between opposing forces, existent as evil may have been, but as a unity that is unfortunately too often unacknowledged. Materiality is not a principle in itself; it is rather a denial of principle that results from a loss of perception of reality, which itself is the consequence of deception by the *Gospel According to Acquisition*. While it is a matter of fact, it is not real; like St. Petersburg, it is a lie; and surely the lie cannot be taken as an affirmation of a truth opposed to truth. As for Dostoevsky, so for Gogol, Satan was the "Prince of Lies," and thus a "not," not an "is": the refuser of truth who cannot, despite all his efforts, negate it, for the reason that truth is indestructible, no matter how assiduously it may be denied—the law of gravity cannot be repealed, even if some other theory may subsume it.[8] Satan is at best the Goethean spirit that constantly denies (that spirit also, though always desiring evil, always works good. One might legitimately wonder if Gogol was not, through the negative portrayals in his fiction, consciously attempting to accomplish the same end that Mephistopheles, against his desires, also accomplished). The devils, goblins, witches, and reincarnations of the Little Russian stories; the fog, madness, deception, frivolity, and obssessions of the Petersburg stories; the parodic quality of *The Inspector General;* and the grubby materiality of *Dead Souls,* Part 1—all seem to be concentrated upon this same end. The very anonymity that Evdokimov speaks of as the special characteristic of evil in Gogol's work reinforces our argument rather than detracts from it, for the anonymous man (Akaky Akakyevich, Kovalyov, Khlestakov, and, in Evdokimov's opinion, although not in mine, Chichikov) is one who has lost his soul because he can no longer see his soul, he is a seducee of artificiality, of the false, accepting the temptations offered Christ in the desert rather than affirming their opposite.[9] But it is the affirmation that Gogol desires—if a Mephistopheles at all, he was a Mephistopheles whose portrayals were aimed at the exorcism of monsters whose ugly horror he knew and whose falsity he wished to destroy, whose cacophony threatened salvation.

It is on the general grounds outlined above that Gogol's aesthetic and religious convictions became one—the ultimate aesthetic creation, the alpha and omega of beauty was precisely the Trinity, the ultimately harmonious creator of itself as well as of the universe.

The articles and essays that Gogol wrote in the course of his career emphasize that the harmony he so often speaks of overtly or implies is good, in a religious as well as in an artistic sense, and that discord is evil. In this connection, we may note that Gogol had a tendency to end his articles, of whatever date and on whatever subject, on a religious note. Thus, in "Sculpture, Painting, and Music" (1831) we learn that music, the highest of the arts, was given by God in order to bring man to Him (8:13). "On the Middle Ages" speaks throughout of the religious impulse and concludes with the Gothic cathedral as an expression of that impulse (8:25). "Life" (1831) ends with all the civilizations of the ancient world bowing down to Him Who was born in the manger (8:84). The great value of Pushkin's *Boris Godunov* (1831) lies in the "tear of reconciliation [that trembles] in the blurred eyes of the criminal restored" (8:152). And "1834" calls upon his genius, that "deity inaccessible on earth," to bless his labors (9:16). "Petersburg Notes of 1836" ends with Lent and, symbolically, the Resurrection. Certainly, "An Author's Confession" (1847) is permeated by Gogol's concern with God and with his own desire artistically to serve Him. One cannot escape the conclusion that Gogol from beginning to end was religiously committed, and that his commitment did not change, although it may have grown in intensity, in the sense that he grew increasingly conscious of it and began to express it in his later years more overtly, out of disappointment, perhaps, that his audience had so consistently refused to acknowledge its presence in his writings.[10]

Biographers and critics of Gogol have sometimes stated that his God was one of hellfire and damnation, that Gogol had been imbued by his mother with fear of the awful punishments that await sinners in the afterlife, and that he lived in such dread of these horrors, as though he belonged to some extreme evangelical sect convinced of the all-pervasiveness of sin, that he became a religious fanatic, indeed, a madman.[11] Although there is some evidence to support this view, it does not seem to me that a reading of Gogol's works, both fiction and nonfiction, in the context in which he meant them to be read, supports it sufficiently for it to be accepted without serious question. Gogol was no more a "gloomy Russian" than was Dostoevsky, simply because of his concentration upon beauty and harmony. While the Apocalypse is present in his writings, he is more interested in chapters 21–22 than in chapters 13–18. He may have had to become "better," as he put it; but it is Heaven that beckoned, not Hell, as the essays emphasize.[12] Thus, the Resurrection and the Transfiguration, the two most important feasts of Russian Orthodoxy, are what lie in the background and what Gogol attaches himself to, not Calvary. This means that for Gogol, as for Dostoevsky, the living Christ is central, not the dead Jesus. He overcomes evil, as the *Revelation of St. John the Divine* foretold, and through Him, man may overcome evil, precisely because in Him is all, in Him is the universal harmony that reconciles all; He is the very exemplar of beauty itself. This is as much the point of "Life," written in 1831, as it is of "An Author's Confession," written in 1847; and these two dates just about encompass Gogol's entire creative career. While he most often spoke of evil in his later essays and letters when he was worried about his ability to accomplish the task that he had devoted himself to, and while he often attempted to depict the nature of evil, the negative, in his fiction, Gogol remained an optimist, for to be pessimistic would come perilously close to denying Christianity as he understood it. Harmony and beauty—Christ—were realities to be attained; and Gogol believed, until almost the end of his life, they were capable of at least approximation. There were two media through which man could work towards this goal, art and soul, with the former acting as a spur to the latter. Thus the artist, while devoted to beauty, was of necessity devoted to God; nonreligious art would be a contradiction in terms.

The most overt and clearest statements of Gogol's religious position as such are contained in two late essays, "Easter Sunday," which is the culminating article of *Selected Passages from Correspondence with Friends,* and *Meditations on the Divine Liturgy,* which had been completed by 1847 but which was not published during Gogol's lifetime. In both cases, Gogol emphasized the centrality of Christ and the reality of unity and harmony as being basic to Christianity itself. In common with many other Russians of his time, he regarded this position as fundamental to his tradition.[13] The first paragraph of "Easter Sunday" reads as follows:

> The Russian has a special interest in the celebration of Easter. He feels it more vividly if he should happen to be in a foreign land. Seeing how everywhere in other countries this day is almost indistinguishable from other days—business is as usual, life is normal, there is a humdrum expression on people's faces—he feels melancholy and cannot help turning to Russia. It seems to him that there this day is somehow celebrated better, and a man is more joyful and better than on other days and his life is somehow different, not normal. It suddenly appears to him—that portentous midnight, that universal sound of bells, as though the whole earth had fused into one ringing, that exclamation "Christ is risen!" which on this day replaces all other greetings, that kiss given only among us—and he is almost ready to exclaim: "Only in Russia is this day celebrated as it ought to be celebrated." [*SP,* 250]

We note that here again, when writing on this most serious of subjects, Gogol uses sound, in this case "universal" sound, to exemplify his meaning.

The Resurrection, further, while a historical event, is not merely historical, nor, on the other hand, is it merely a promise of some future salvation. It involves the immediate oneness of all mankind, if not of all creation, in love:

> . . . the ties binding us [to our brother] are stronger than the earthly blood of our kin: we are related to him through our perfect Heavenly Father, who is many times closer to us than our earthly father; on this day we are in His actual family, in His very house. This day is that holy day on which all human-

ity, to the last one, celebrates its holy, heavenly brotherhood, from which not one man is excluded. [*SP*, 251]

To Gogol, this love and union, this bringing together in harmony, is real; it is neither an intellectual concept nor a fanciful fiction; it is the vital experience of man's life, into which he willingly enters, knowing beforehand that it is true. Falsity and unreality, thus, lie in putting distance between oneself and Christ, as do ugliness and discord; they lie in the acceptance of the temptations in the desert, all of which are material. Since Christ is always here, since at least on Easter "we are in His actual family," the Kingdom of God can be made manifest in this world; we need not wait for death to reach a consciousness of perfection and to live in it.[14] This, it seems to me, is optimism of the highest order, a denial of the Grand Inquisitor's argument that is even stronger than Father Zosima's, although it is based ultimately on the same convictions as the Elder's.

If *Selected Passages* as a whole outlines discursively what Gogol intended to do in Parts 2 and 3 of *Dead Souls,* some of which is implied in Part 1 and some of which is stated in the fragments of Part 2 that we have, then "Easter Sunday" appears to be the statement of Gogol's final conclusion, the end at which all his work was aiming. It requires little imagination to see Chichikov (or Platonov) developing into the Russian of the passages from "Easter Sunday" that we have cited, the man who has wandered among alien peoples and ideas and finally comes back home. On this score, it seems possible that Hanz Kuechelgarten was not really disillusioned at all, that he was merely returning to the land where truth and beauty really resided. This is precisely what happened also to the Italian prince of "Rome," who discovered Annunziata in his native city, not in the streets of Paris from which she had been symbolically exiled. The daughter of Chichikov's governor and Tyentyetnikov's love were also, we note, native.

The religious reality and the beauty at which Gogol was aiming are further stressed in *Meditations on the Divine Liturgy,* which is, once again, anything but a radical work. On the contrary: it is still known and used by the Orthodox Church (and not only the Russian Orthodox Church) for the instruction of the faithful. The *Meditations* consist of a kind of guided tour through the Liturgy, with Gogol's comments and emphases interspersed throughout. Certainly, he is convinced, and tries to convince us, that in the Liturgy we are confronted with a reality and a beauty which we may make our own (that is, which we may experience) and which are both true and existent in the absolute sense:

> "Everyone of you can ascend the seraphic heights, if only you want to do so," as St. John Chrysostom has said. "Only recall and gather in your memory all the most beautiful things that you have seen on earth and which have delighted you, and reflect that all these things were so lovely only because they were a reflection of the great heavenly beauty, only the gleaming hem of the mere mantle of God, and of itself your soul will be transported to the Bosom and Source of eternal beauty and will sing the song of triumph, casting itself down with the Seraphim before the eternal throne of the Most High." [ML, 40]

The same point is made in one of Gogol's comments on the Lord's Prayer: "By the words: **But deliver us from the evil one,** we pray for the joy of Heaven. For as soon as the evil one leaves us, at once joy enters our soul and though on earth it is as though we were in Heaven" (ML, 48).[15] (The closeness of Gogol's comments to remarks in the *Chronicle* is striking, although we cannot of course know whether he intended the connection.) After all, Gogol reminds his reader, the Office of Preparation ends with the priest's exclamation: "Blessed is the Kingdom of the Father and of the Son and of the Holy Spirit, always, now and ever, and to the ages of ages" (ML, 18). Truth and beauty are not relative terms, dependent upon empirical judgments; they were and are and will be, regardless of factual deceptions like St. Petersburg.

The evidence can only lead to the conclusion that Gogol's religion, unlike that of, say, Tolstoy, remained always firmly rooted in the beliefs and practices of his particular ritualistic church, with its emphasis on the beautiful nature of the Divine.

Thus the question of whether Gogol's religion formed a part of—or, rather, was coincident with—his art, as I have insisted, or whether they are, as some commentators believe, two separate realms that have little to do with each other, must be answered, on the ground alone of his concern with beauty, in the affirmative: art and religion were always one for him. The charge that in his later years Gogol gave up art for religion must be rejected as missing the point.[16]

What we are suggesting, in the final analysis, is that Gogol's view of reality was iconographic, in the sense that he saw the truth in much the same way that a painter of icons does, and he attempted to apply

many of the same principles to his literary production. As Georges
Florovsky puts it:

> An icon-painter should be guided . . . primarily by his religious
> insight, in which "another world" of realities is disclosed to
> him, and the immediate world of his environment appears as
> "trans-parent" and "trans-figured." [Icons are not] simply
> illustrations of religious ideas. Nor are they supposed to be an
> expression of the personal "imagination" of the painter or of
> his individual convictions. The painter's hand, his craft, must
> appear in the icon, and it will determine its artistic quality.
> But the painter's mind must be faithfully subordinate to the
> catholic mind of the Church. . . . the "themes," or the "struc-
> ture" of the Icons are given by the faith. There is no room
> for "new findings" (*nearon epheurema*) or "invention," in this
> field. Yet artists are sovereignly free and must be "creative" in
> their own field, in the field of "art." . . . Faith and art belong
> together.
>
> Thus, the icon-painting as an art is different from all
> other kinds of painting. It is opposed to all kinds of "natural-
> ism," which misses the dimension of mystical depth, and moves
> on the surface of sensual empiricism. It differs from the
> "imaginative" art, which reveals just "impressions" of indi-
> vidual onlookers or embodies their "phantasies" or ideals. It
> differs from the "symbolic" art which endeavours to invent
> suggestive "images" which would allegorically remind one of
> the "unfathomable" and "indescribable." What is actually
> "indescribable" should never be present on the Icons. . . .
> The original name of this craft was *zographia,* a description
> of life, of actual life in the context of our visible world, and
> under its conditions. Only this world is seen in its depth,
> in its fulness, in the fulness of its potentialities, and not
> in its occasional and accidental shapes and forms. And
> the vision of the empirical is enlarged and deepened by the
> insight of faith, which does not deny "appearances," but com-
> prehends them in the context of "integral" being of things.[17]

I would suggest that the principles adumbrated by Florovsky un-
derlie much of Gogol's literary production; they are most immediately
and obviously at work, to the reader although not always to characters
in the stories, in passages of "Nevsky Prospekt," "The Portrait,"
"Rome," and *Dead Souls,* while they are strongly implied in other tales.
Sometimes the character makes a mistake and clings too stubbornly to

the physical representation, as Piskaryov does in "Nevsky Prospekt"; he jumps to the wrong conclusion about what is behind the image, that is, he asks, incorrectly, for material embodiment, turning icon into idol. For example, when he first visits the house of the girl he sees in the street, he is terribly disappointed, for it is a place

> where man has sacrilegiously trampled on and laughed at everything pure and sacred, everything that beautifies life, where woman, the beauty of the world, the crown of creation, has been turned into some strange, ambiguous creature, where she is deprived of everything feminine along with purity of soul and loathsomely appropriates masculine tricks and insolence and ceases to be that weak, that lovely creature so different from us. [3:21]

Gogol leaves the reader in no doubt about the connection between the pure and the sacred and beauty; indeed the persecution of beauty, the perversion of it, is a sacrilegious act. Piskaryov, although unaware of it, joins in the sacrilege. His difficulty is his lack of faith, his misapprehension of what an icon is. Since what he expected is not what he got, he attempted to change the fact, thinking that in fact is truth. What he did was to make an idol out of an icon; he was lost when fact turned out not to be divine after all (as the man of faith makes icons, so Satan makes idols):

> Really, never does pity so powerfully possess us as when we see beauty touched by the putrid breath of depravity. Ugliness may unite with it, but beauty, tender beauty . . . in our thoughts it may merge only with chastity and purity. The beauty who had so entranced poor Piskaryov was really a miraculous, an extraordinary phenomenon. Her residence in this filthy environment seemed even more extraordinary. All her features were so purely formed, the entire expression of her lovely face was marked by such nobility that it was impossible to think that depravity had spread its terrible claws over her. . . . but alas! by some terrible willful act of the hellish spirit who thirsts to destroy the harmony of life, she had been cast into this abyss to the accompaniment of loud laughter. [3:22]

(An icon does not have to be in a church to be sacred. It retains its sacred character regardless of its environment.) It is the shock of confrontation with the actuality of this devil-made idol, in whose making he himself collaborated, that destroys Piskaryov; he perceives an empirical datum rather than reality; with the loss of beauty is lost "the harmony of life." Instead of meeting Christ the reconciler, Whom he should have sought, Piskaryov encounters Satan the sower of discord, the only possible result to one who does not see the difference between what God has created (the beauty) and what Satan has twisted (the depravity), the difference between the icon and the idol.[18]

"The Portrait" also makes use of the idol; this time even more obviously, since it is one we can all recognize immediately—the idol of gold.[19] As in "Nevsky Prospekt," the idol is satanic, leading not to the true world of eternity and beauty, but to the false world of time and ugliness, the world of matter. So far does Chartkov succumb to this world that at the end he buys works of real beauty, icons in the broadest sense, only to destroy them, and, Gogol says, "It was as if an enraged heaven had expressly sent this terrible scourge into the world out of a desire to take away all its harmony" (3:115).

The falsity, the nonartistic quality, of the portrait, is pointed out by the very man who painted it: "This was not a creation of art, and therefore the feelings that invaded everyone at the sight of it, rebellious feelings, are not the feelings of the artist, for the artist breaths peace into unease" (3:136); that is, the true artist is an iconographer, as this painter, in contrast with Chartkov, has become.

"The Portrait" is the only one of Gogol's stories that makes use of the icon and the idol in this overt way. Usually it is Gogol himself, rather than a character in the story, who is the iconographer, [20] as he is in those passages we have cited that have to do with love (Piskaryov was not in love; rather, he was fascinated by a possibility of satisfying his ego; he was closer to Henry Higgins than to Dante). In each case the character who is confronted with the icon, in particular Chichikov and the Roman prince, has a sense of being brought in touch with a reality that transcends his material surroundings (hence "Annunziata"). From the point of view of art, this reality may be regarded as beauty; from the point of view of religion, it may be regarded as the Kingdom of God. Further, in each case, including that of Tyentyetnikov, the character has an intimation that a greater value may attach to himself, that he may gain personality rather than lose it, within the universe, in harmony with creation, than as a being pursuing his own material or (as in the instance of the Roman prince) intellectual ends. The isolated ego is shown to be meaningless in the face of the ultimate; he has meaning only in relation to it. Thus recognition and acknowledgment of truth will bring about the individual's salvation. Chichikov in his troika has a future before him, in other words; no one else in *Dead Souls,* Part 1, has. Their idols can only bring about their annihilation.

These icons are items for the contemplation and veneration of the characters within the stories, as well as of the reader; they are meant to emphasize the goal, the "thrust," of the tales themselves. Thus Gogol tells us that the painter who became a monk in "The Portrait" chose the Nativity as his subject, and he describes the painting as follows:

> The feeling of divine humility and mildness on the face of the Immaculate Mother inclining over the Babe, the profound intellect in the eyes of the divine Babe, as though they were clearly seeing something far off, the exultant silence of the Kings, struck by the divine miracle, prostrating themselves at His feet, and finally, the holy, ineffable stillness pervading the whole picture—all this was presented in such concordant strength and potent beauty that the impression was magical. All the fraternity fell to its knees before the new icon, and the profoundly affected prior pronounced: "No, it is impossible for a man to produce such a picture with the aid of human art alone: the holy supreme power guided your brush, and the blessing of heaven rested upon your labor."[21] [3:134]

What applied to painting applied equally to literature for Gogol, and his most successful use of the method, his truest icon, occurs in *The Inspector General*; indeed, *The Inspector General is* an icon, when considered from the point of view of its form.[22] It is in the form of that play that the artistic and religious impulses combine, and in Gogol's quest for beauty is exhibited his quest for God. His failure as an iconographer, his failure in form as he saw it, was what distressed him about *Dead Souls.* Perhaps this is what he meant when he talked about becoming "better." For Gogol, however, harmonic form is not a self-subsistent creation in itself (few Russians have believed in *ars gratia artis*), but a way to reveal the reality that had been disclosed to him, accomplishing such a result that "the immediate world of his environment appears as 'trans-parent' and 'trans-figured' "[23] to his audience as well as to himself. This is not to say that this other world is but an abstract construction; on the contrary, if we are brought to see it and then act in it (passages of *Dead Souls,* Part 2, and some of the essays in *Selected Passages* adumbrate the action to be taken), it is infinitely more meaningful than the false, material, and hence idolic world of *poshlost'* and corruption. When Gogol displays idols, he does so, not to convince us that they are real, but so that we may taste and compare. In back of his mind was the Transfiguration, as reported in the *Gospel According to St. Matthew* 17:1-7:

> And after six days Jesus taketh Peter, James, and John his brother, and bringeth them up into an high mountain apart, and was transfigured before them: and his face did shine as the sun, and his raiment was white as the light. And, behold, there appeared unto them Moses and Elias talking with him. Then answered Peter, and said unto Jesus, Lord, it is good for us to be here: if thou wilt, let us make here three tabernacles; one for thee, and one for Moses, and one for Elias. While he yet spake, behold, a bright cloud overshadowed them: and behold a voice out of the cloud, which said, This is my beloved Son, in whom I am well pleased; hear ye him. And when the disciples heard it, they fell on their face, and were sore afraid. And Jesus came and touched them, and said, Arise, and be not afraid.

Of course, this all implies that Gogol did consider change necessary, but it was the change of awakening rather than of reform, change in a Christian sense (as he understood Christianity) rather than a social one; that is, his concern was with the soul: "and be not afraid." From this would flow a reordering of the relations among men in brotherhood; beauty would be attained, and man would return to his original iconographic nature, the image of God.

It follows from this that moral precepts (much has been made by various commentators of what they consider Gogol's moral stress) are not ends in themselves (that would make them idols).[24] The advice that he gives in many places of *Selected Passages,* which is so repugnant to readers, is aimed much more at the attainment of Christian harmony than at a Gogolian display of maxims of conduct for their own sakes. In accordance with his view of Christ as the reconciler of all things, human behavior, to be Christian, must be aimed at harmony, just as a genuinely artistic work must be. Man, too, can be a work of art—as the Renaissance also believed, although in a different way. This is the "brotherhood" that Gogol speaks of in "Easter Sunday," while "Woman in the World" tells of the automatic effect of "sublime beauty, the pure fascination of a special innocence . . . in which [a] tender soul shines forth to everyone" (*SP*, 16), so that "it seems to the souls of those listening . . . that they are joyously talking with angels about the heavenly childhood of man" (*SP*, 18). In essay after essay he emphasizes the reality of this heavenly light that redeems, so that, like certain of Dostoevsky's heroes, Chichikov too may one day arise a "new man" (such, indeed, seems to have been Gogol's intention). The moral regeneration of man, in other words, is pointed to in the Transfiguration (Jesus talks with Moses and Elias) and is accomplished in the Resurrection; that is, the Christian enters into the reality of "ages of ages."

It is worth noting in this connection, that after his earliest stories, Gogol did not subject his audience to clever characters, to hypocrites, so that the humor does not arise from the same manipulations as it does in, say Jonson or Molière; nor do we have one sane and, generally speaking, "moral" person, be he character or narrator—as we do, for example, in Rabelais and Swift—who serves to point up the madness of the others. We have no Pantagruel or Father John set off against Panurge; no Mosca against Volpone; no Madame Jourdain against Monsieur Jourdain; no King of the Brobdingnagians against Gulliver. In a more tragic context, we do not even have a Fool to play opposite Lear. It is, in Gogol, self-trickery or self-negation that the humor comes from, an incongruity whose root is self-deception, which is never clear to anyone in the story and usually, indeed, is unperceived by the character who is its victim, but is always clear to the audience, which remembers its "heavenly childhood." Unlike the vast majority of comic writers, Gogol does not appeal to reason, to intelligent sanity as such. His appeal, rather—in what one might regard as his religious naïveté—is to inward knowledge. In this sense, for Gogol, the ultimate joke is on Satan, and it is God who laughs, and Gogol's statement that his "business is *the soul and the durable things in life*" (*SP*, 110) should be taken quite seriously.

10
The Russian

That Russian nationalism grew as a transplant from German soil, much as California grapes replaced those that died in the French vineyards, there is no doubt.[1] Nevertheless, French wine (when not adulterated) is French, not American, although it is exported back to America, as the Russian idea was exported back to Germany at the end of the nineteenth century. In the same way, Gogol, despite the influences of such German theorists and practitioners as Herder, Schiller, and E. T. A. Hoffmann, and equally despite his attachment to some of the writers of the High Middle Ages and Renaissance (Dante, Ariosto, Tasso, Cervantes), despite his long sojourns in Rome and the possible imbibing of some Roman Catholic theological ideas—despite all this, and more, Gogol remained peculiarly Russian, in both fiction and nonfiction, and the reader immediately recognizes him as such. This is largely owing to many of the attitudes and concerns we have discussed in the preceding pages. In fact, it would be surprising, rather than otherwise, if we found his view of Russia radically different from his views of art and religion; that is, if we found him proceeding from a different base in this particular area, as though, when he turned to Russia, he gave up unity for diversity.

Like many Russians of the nineteenth century, especially the earlier part, Gogol, born and raised in the Ukraine, was deeply concerned with the problem of his "roots," for he was a citizen of a comparatively new country without the long ideological tradition that for the West had begun in the ancient world. Western notions of legality, for example, whether it be Anglo-Saxon or Romanist, were lacking in Russia. She had also had only a few hundred years of religious unity with Byzantium before the onslaught of the Tatars—in comparison, the West had at least twelve hundred years of religious unity before the Reformation. Gogol resolved the problems, both of his Ukrainianism and of ideology, by taking a position very much like that of the superpatriotic immigrant, the convert, *plus royal que le roi,* more Catholic than the pope.[2] After all, when he was growing up, he had two choices, culturally speaking, before him: to take the path that some of his fellows like Taras Shevchenko were taking, that of Ukrainian nationalism, in an attempt to revive what they considered to be an ancient and separate civilization,[3] or that of Russianism, which later in the nineteenth century became Slavicism.[4] It is doubtful, however, that the choice was really a serious one for Gogol, since both his Little Russian tales and his essays on Little Russian topics invariably concentrate upon the past rather than upon a living present, while his stories and essays on Russian topics invariably emphasize the contemporary. The Ukraine, which many have claimed he knew but poorly,[5] did not possess the vital reality that he found in Russia itself. In fact, the Ukraine seemed to possess something of the foreign for Gogol, something culturally alien, so that the Little Russian tales have something exotic about them, indicating a somewhat anthropological interest.[6]

We also know that Gogol thought of St. Petersburg as foreign, not because it belonged to a past that—no matter how exotic—was dead, but because it was an alien intrusion upon the truth, in this case an intrusion of the West and of Western values (the same could also have been said, although Gogol did not do so, about the Ukraine, since the Polish and Roman Catholic influences had been strong there from at least the sixteenth century onwards). St. Petersburg was a mechanizer and deceiver, permeated by an ugliness and a fog of unreality that were at odds with the goodness and truth—and beauty[7]—represented by the real Russia, by the Russian whole.

None of this attitude towards and belief in Russia was a matter of rational analysis on Gogol's part; he was not a historian, at least not in the contemporary sense of the term. It was rather a matter of intuitive, one might say naïve, conviction, grounded neither in politics nor philosophy, nor in moral system, but in feeling, and in artistic feeling at that. He did not concern himself with theological argument or with precise definitions, for example, of the attributes of God, or with wonderings, à la Dostoevsky, about the existence of God to begin with. Distinctions and arguments of that kind—like political distinctions and arguments—were foreign both to his native intuition and to Russian reality as he perceived it. The reality, he felt, was given and should not be disputed. Much of his creative career may thus be regarded as a battle against those who were in revolt against what had been received, what he "knew." From this point of view, Gogol might be described as a naïve Russophile who believed that, in form and substance, Russia was a holy and appointed messenger, a nation and a people, a *narod*, anointed by the Lord; that is, Russia was the third—and last—Rome.

Although many of his contemporaries, particularly those of a Western orientation, considered Gogol's work to be an attack on the established system in Russia, nowhere, in either his fiction or his essays, do we find a criticism of Russian institutions. Indeed, if anything, he defended those institutions, while attacking what he regarded as non-Russian deceptions, as I have tried to point out. When he does find something wrong, and he often does, it is with unperceiving persons, never the whole. As he says in "Four Letters to Divers Persons Apropos *Dead Souls*":

> In Russia, now, it is possible to make oneself a hero at every step. Every rank and place demands heroism. Each of us has so disgraced the holiness of his rank and position (all positions are holy) that heroic powers are necessary to lift them to their legitimate height. I perceive that great vocation which is not now possible for any other people, which is possible for the Russians alone, because before them alone is there such scope and their soul alone is acquainted with heroism. [*SP*, 102]

In impulse, at least, this is an artistic statement, for it is an insistence upon the necessity for practice to accord with professed faith; in other words, Gogol desires unity of form and content, a unity on the personal or individual level that he believed already existed on the national level ("all positions are holy," and "each of us has disgraced the holiness"). This is not novelty that Gogol believes he is proposing, simply actualization. Persons lost themselves, and they betrayed the truth, not because there was anything inherently wrong with Russian form as such, but because they did not see it, they had been blinded by material and ego, had been confused, and in their confusion had fallen prey to alien deceiving influences, had chosen to worship the idol rather than to venerate the icon, had opted for St. Petersburg over Moscow.

Dead Souls, a "Russian" poem, may be regarded as a statement of this position, for Chichikov's difficulty—and it is a difficulty that proved insurmountable for Manilov, Korobochka, Nozdryov, Sobakyevich, and Plyushkin—is that he has been seduced by non-Russian values, the contemporary, capitalist, individualistic, and thus chaotic values of the West. This does not imply, on the other hand, that Gogol favored socialist values; to him they were equally Western and equally pernicious. Such a dichotomy was false in his terms, since both capitalism and socialism sprang from the same general world view, while Russia's view was different, of another genus. Only when Chichikov would reject those values in favor of his Russian soul would he be saved. His, after all, is the harmonious troika at the end of Part 1, rushing no one knows whither. But, as we know, the "whither" was to be revealed in the succeeding volumes of *Dead Souls*—there the real Russia would be announced, and the truth and beauty of its soul would shine forth in its pristine purity, through the figure, possibly, of this same Chichikov, who would at last find his "roots."

The basic problem, as Gogol saw it, was that truth, reality, was all too often replaced by divisiveness and discord. The theme is not only artistic and religious; it is also national. Over and over again, Gogol stresses the need for expression in and of wholeness, which is not, for him, a rationally conceived idea nor a mystic ideal end, but an intuitively perceived reality, even though he never defines that reality precisely. As early as his essay "A Few Words on Pushkin," which appeared in 1832, the same year in which he published the second volume of *Evenings on a Farm near Dikanka,* Gogol was stressing what he thought of as Russian reality. "From the very first," Gogol says, Pushkin "was national, because genuine nationality consists not in a description of a *sarafan,* but in the spirit itself of the people. A poet can be national even when he describes a completely foreign world, but looks at it with the eyes of his national elements, with the eyes of a whole people, when he feels and speaks so that it seems to his compatriots that they themselves are feeling and speaking" (8:51). The previous year his short essay on *Boris Godunov* had emphasized the reconciling power (a Russian trait, in Gogol's opinion) of Pushkin's art, its ability to bring together what had seemed to be disparate (8:151). The points of these two essays were themselves to be reconciled, in another context, in "Easter Sunday" sixteen years later, when Gogol wrote, first, that "this day is that holy day on which all humanity . . . celebrates its holy, heavenly brotherhood" (*SP*, 251), and then that the feeling of brotherhood is peculiar to Russia, and "it is by basing ourselves on this that it is possible to say that the celebration of the Resurrection of Christ is celebrated among us before among others. My soul says this to me firmly; this is not a thought invented in my brain" (*SP*, 259).[8] Gogol's soul had always said this to him; never had it been a matter of the brain. In this sense of feeling, of conviction, not only that there are such things as a "Russian soul" and a "Russian way of life," but that to be genuinely a Russian is in some absolute sense good and beautiful and produces goodness and beauty, Gogol is naïve.

One immediately asks if Gogol's position makes him a Slavophile. I do not think so, despite his closeness to the Slavophile Aksakov family and despite some superficial resemblances to some Slavophile ideas. First, the Slavophiles were thinkers, philosophers, one may say, who were capable of rational thought and analysis, even though they rejected these modes as a basis for Russian culture; they did not depend upon intuitive vision. They also were willing to recognize—and often proclaimed—that Russian institutions, in particular, serfdom, left a good deal to be desired (it is too often forgotten that the Slavophiles were as unpopular with the Tsarist regime as were their Westernizing opponents). Gogol's attitude, on the other hand, led him to a defense of the social and political organization in Russia, even of the autocracy, that shocked many of the Slavophiles.[9] When Gogol said that Russia was holy, he really meant it, blindly and confidently. He was quite sincere, despite the opinions of both Aksakov and Belinsky. As I think Gogol's work shows, he was utterly convinced—without recourse to factual data and without recourse to argument or analysis—not only that the depository of ultimate truth on earth was Russia, but that he had been appointed to proclaim that truth, even if, like Moses, he did not always consider himself sufficiently purified for his mission. His task, the "service" he had discovered that would enable him to fulfill the parable of the talents, was to remind his audience of its heritage, to return those who had been corrupted, by accident or design, and who had betrayed their real tradition, to the real Russian way. Thus we find that the characters of both *The Inspector General* and *Dead Souls*, as well as many in the Little Russian stories and most of those in the Petersburg tales—Akaky Akakyevich, Chartkov, Poprishchin—are alienated persons, rootless and egoistic individuals who are outside reality, victims of the portrait, in whose souls dwells unease. Their alienation, however—unlike the alienation that we find in many twentieth-century novels, in both Russia and the West—is not meant to enlist our sympathy, for it is they who are in error, not the institutions. They do not understand the world; it is not the world that does not understand them. It is they who, for one reason or another (usually the pernicious influence of Western antivalues), in one way or another, have divorced themselves from true Russian brotherhood, and thus from Christ. And Gogol in the long run felt that to deny Russia was to deny Christ. He saw no contradictions whatsoever between Russian institutions, as such, and the faith. Indeed, these institutions, from serfdom to autocracy, were themselves a part of that faith and could have arisen only on Russian soil. If one should ask *why* they could have arisen only there, the answer is, because they *are* there. Russia was indeed the third Rome, and that was justification enough. In a way, Gogol anticipated Dostoevsky by casting Russia, this chosen land, in the role of Job. It is Job's remark to God, "Do Thou ask and I will answer," that forms the pattern; it is not the reasonings of Eliphaz, Bildad, and Zophar, and certainly not the sophistries of that bumptious young man Elihu. At the same time, the image of Don Quixote seems to have stood before him as the very embodiment of national truth. The Knight of the Melancholy Countenance and the perfect and upright man of whose story Father Zosima was to say, "the passing earthly show and the eternal verity are brought together in it,"[10] combine to form the image both of Gogol himself, as missionary and possible martyr, and of the "Russian soul," which bears the truth within itself despite the vicissitudes of the passing show, which is only a show, a mask.

Two of Gogol's early essays may be used as examples to clarify Gogol's attitude: "Al-Mamoun," written in 1834, and "On Little Russian Songs," written in 1833. In both cases, Gogol, somewhat in the style of the later populists, places his emphasis upon the people, the *narod,* as the vital element in both civilization and culture. The former essay, "Al-Mamoun," attempts to pinpoint the reasons for the disintegration, as Gogol sees it, of the orderly empire that Al-Mamoun had inherited from Haroun-al-Rashid. That Al-Mamoun was a highly intelligent and cultured man, Gogol quite agrees; but in Gogol's view, he was also divorced from the soul of his nation. "He died," Gogol writes, "without having understood his people and without having been understood by his people. . . . He proved to have been a sovereign who, despite all his desires for good, despite all his gentleness of heart, despite his selflessness and extraordinary passion for learning, was, incidentally and unwittingly, one of the mainsprings that accelerated the fall of the state" (8:81). As in his artistic and religious comments, Gogol is invoking the principle of harmony and unity, of wholeness. As Rousseau might have said, the nation is one body, with a will of its own to which the monarch must be attuned and in harmony with which he must act. If the monarch is alien to his people, divisiveness will spread, and the state will fall apart.

If one should ask the further question of how and why the separation between ruler and ruled came about in the unified state that Haroun-al-Rashid had left him, the answer lies in Al-Mamoun's well-meaning but grossly mistaken introduction of foreign ideas and forms. Discord could not help but result. He brought "an alien Greek world into his state," we are told, and "Baghdad was converted into a republic of divers branches of knowledge and opinion" (8:79). In effect, he made an attempt to change his nation against the very will and nature of the nation itself, an attempt that, despite the excellence of Al-Mamoun's motives and despite the quality of his abstract enlightenment, could bring only confusion, discord, and disintegration. Al-Mamoun, Gogol believes, "overlooked a great truth: that culture is derived from the people itself, that an alien enlightenment should be borrowed only insofar as it can help natural progress, but that a people should develop out of its own national elements" (8:79).

One wonders if this short essay was not meant, unconsciously perhaps, as a parable and a warning to the Russia of Gogol's own day. A few substitutions would make it so: the state of Al-Mamoun is the state of Russia after Peter the Great; the "alien Greek world," a world of reason and science, is Western Europe; Al-Mamoun himself is symbolic of those Westernizers who wished Russia, in the name of progress and enlightenment, to adopt Western culture, to the eternal ruin, Gogol would say, of the Russian nation itself. Read in this way, the piece becomes, not just an historical exercise, but a Russophile statement, whether Gogol consciously meant it to be read that way or not, and one may certainly suspect that he did. The conclusion here, as in Gogol's fiction, is that Russia must not follow the blandishments of the West, the temptations in and of the desert, but must cling to its own revealed truth, the truth of the Chosen People as a harmonious whole following the right path. Job's sufferings are not to be relieved by adopting the ways of the rational world.

The ostensible subject of Gogol's earlier essay "On Little Russian Songs" is, of course, the Ukraine. In general terms, however, it may well be regarded as an overall statement of his position, his feeling, in regard to the people, the nation. Again Gogol emphasizes the people as a whole, as a body with its own soul, distinct from any individuals who may be components of that body. Folk songs furnish a means to comprehend that soul. "I will not enlarge on the importance of the people's songs," Gogol writes, "they are the people's history, vivid, bright, full of color, of reality, revealing the people's entire life" (8:90). What he who hears them must understand is the people—that is, the people's spirit, that essence that makes it what it is and different from all other peoples. There is no question here of collecting precise historical data, in the fashion of twentieth-century statistical historians, in order to reach abstract rational conclusions and to delineate "factual" causes and effects. "Evidence of dates of battles or exact explanations of places, . . . trustworthy reports," as Gogol puts it (8:91), are all quite beside the point.[11] What one should rather learn are "the elements of character, all the inflections and nuances of feeling, the emotions, the sufferings, the joys of the people being depicted" (8:91). This spirit, this feeling, finally this empathy is what Gogol is after, becoming one with the life of the people, no matter what historical period it may belong to. Gogol tells us, for example, that we must pay attention to these songs because "the songs of Little Russia can be called entirely historical because they are not for a moment divorced from life and are always faithful to the moment of time and to the state of feeling of the time" (8:91). The aim in listening to these songs (and they should be *listened to,* not simply read) is to overcome remoteness and separation or divisiveness, not to engage in musicological analysis. The latter would be like memorizing dates or reconstructing the plans of the old Moscow sewage system, occupations that, to Gogol, were quite irrelevant to history itself (his essays exhibit little of what some of our contemporaries might call "scholarship").

Of course, it is the Russian, rather than anyone else in the modern world, who is peculiarly capable of achieving the empathy that Gogol considered so essential,[12] for the feeling of harmony, the sense of wholeness, is ingrained in him, to such an extent that the form of the Russian state, unlike forms elsewhere in the nineteenth century, is the expression of the Russian people. This is particularly pointed out in the essay "On Estates in the State," written some time between 1831 and 1842 (I have been unable to discover a more precise date of composition). For evidence of the Russian desire for harmony, Gogol goes back to the

Chronicle legend about the invitation to the Varangians to come and rule over Rus. The story is taken as literally true and as an expression of the innate Russian yearning for peace. At a moment of great danger, at a time of internal discord and warfare, the people united, became as one body (they did the same thing when the Romanovs were invited to take the throne), and "thus," says Gogol, "was the legitimacy of the monarch-autocrat determined" (8:490). This foundation was legitimate because of what it expressed, not, as a Westerner might imagine, because of adherence to some legal structure. In this sense of yearning for reconciliation we find the essential Christianity of Russia, even before its conversion historically. Christ the reconciler found His home among that people which was peculiarly disposed to receive Him. Over and over again in "Estates in the State," Gogol stresses legitimate limits and harmonious operation, so that everything in the Russian state— including the *mir,* that favorite organization of the Slavophiles—has its proper place and function, each element always in harmonious relationship with other elements, which results in the formation of a balanced whole that expresses the natural instincts of the people itself. Russia, indeed, is the only one of the modern nations in which this balance has been achieved (as a matter of fact, it might be said that, in Gogol's sense, Russia is the only real nation in the modern world); there each estate and each individual in each estate is in its and his proper place. The implication is that revolution against this most excellent form can only destroy, it cannot construct; it can only do the Antichrist's work. Of course, things may go wrong; of course, abuses may occur; but errors and corruptions, to repeat the point, are only individual, never the fault of the system; they are, indeed, contrary to it. They most assuredly cannot be attributed to the legitimate monarch-autocrat himself, for his office has been legitimately established. If some members of the gentry should fail to fulfill their obligations—that is, should act immorally—"this in no way proves that the sovereigns have been unjust; it only proves that the landowners have themselves degraded their calling" (8:492). In other words, both formal and substantive perfection have been achieved in Russia as a whole, although individual Russians may at times give the impression to a superficial observer, who is applying the wrong criteria, that the nation as such is corrupt. Persons, for various reasons, may step outside the form; but the people or the institutions that embody that form as a whole never do. God's in His Heaven, all's right with Russia, if only all men would see it and live in harmony with it. To deny Russia, to revolt against it, is to advocate chaos and destruction.

In *Selected Passages*, largely the same sentiments are expressed, although Gogol does descend to specifics at times, as in "It is Necessary to Love Russia," "To One Who Occupies an Important Position," and "Rural Justice and Punishment," to name only three instances in addition to those cited previously. He was quite right, in other words, when he said that he had not changed his mind. The results of these attempts to apply general principles to specific cases struck most readers of his time—and continue to strike most contemporary readers—as naïve, if not, in the opinion of many, downright silly. They are so, however, only if the reader persists in regarding Gogol, in his fiction, as a writer who is primarily interested in social affairs—that is, as a portraitist of a "decaying society." Such an attitude could only result in seeing Gogol as a schizoid. If we grant him his vision, however, these essays fall into place (we are not compelled to *agree* with Gogol's opinions, but we are compelled to recognize them as his). He is advocating the unity of theory ("On Estates in the State") and practice (the particular essays of *Selected Passages* we have noted), attempting to awaken his readers to a consciousness of their places within the whole, for it is their task as much as it is Gogol's to actualize reality—it is both their national and Christian duties, a way for every man to become an iconographer and an icon.

Russia was not a subject that was only adverted to by Gogol in specific articles. It also pervades those essays in *Selected Passages* that are overtly devoted to literary subjects. He returns to it, for example, in "*The Odyssey* in Zhukovsky's Translation," which ends with the following paragraph:

> In short, *The Odyssey* will operate on those who suffer and are ill because of their so-called European "perfection." It will remind them of the beauty of their youth now, alas! lost, but which humanity must recover as its legitimate legacy. Many will meditate over many things in it. And, among others, many things about the patriarchal era, with which Russian nature has so much affinity, will invisibly be spread abroad over the face of the Russian land. By the fragrant lips of poetry there will be wafted into the soul something that implies neither law nor power! [*SP*, 40–41]

We note here Gogol's interpretation of *The Odyssey* as a poem pervaded by a certain spirit, a way of life, that is peculiarly close to the Russian, a far different interpretation from the one that the modern Westerner would be likely to accept. It is a claim to both Russian sensibility and Russian stability.

"On the Lyricism of Our Poets," to take another example, makes much of the divine appointment of the house of the Romanovs and of the unity of the Russian people with their tsar, a unity between people and sovereign that exists nowhere else in the world. Gogol dates this essay as having been composed in 1846; we remember what he had written twelve years earlier in "Al-Mamoun." But now Gogol goes further, for when he speaks of Russia, the poet's

> sober, heroic power, which at times is united to an involuntary need to prophesy about Russia, is born of an involuntary contact of thought with that supreme Providence which is so manifestly perceived in the fate of our fatherland. Besides love, a secret awe is also involved at the sight of the events which God has caused to be accomplished in the land appointed to us for a fatherland, a glimpse of a beautiful new edifice which for the moment is not clearly revealed to anyone, and which can only be heard by the all-hearing ear of the poet or by a religious spirit which can discern *the fruit in the seed*. [*SP*, 51]

The last sentence makes no bones about the connections among Russianism, art, and religiosity, as it also envisions that Kingdom of God to be established in the Russian land, that "beautiful new edifice." This is the Chosen People which already occupies the land, whose special characteristic is beauty.

Finally, in "Subjects for the Lyric Poets of the Present Time," Gogol addresses the poet Yazykov in a passage that is reminiscent of the famous troika passage at the end of *Dead Souls,* Part 1:

> In your hymn, celebrate the giant who could issue only from the Russian land, who, suddenly, awakened from his shameful sleep, becomes something other than what he was: in the sight of all spitting on his abominations and infamous vices, he will become the foremost champion of the good [Gofreddo?]. Show how this heroic enterprise is accomplished in a really Russian soul; but show it so that the Russian nature in each cannot help vibrating and so that everyone, even those of the lowest and roughest estates, cries out, "Ah, what a stal-

wart!" feeling that he would be capable of a like deed himself.
[*SP*, 88]

This is a task peculiarly reserved for the lyric poet, despite the epic implications, who sees into his own soul and whose soul is at one with the national soul.

Gogol had just written in the same essay, "O, if you could read . . . what my Plyushkin will say, if I attain to the third volume of *Dead Souls* (*SP*, 87). The implication here is that Gogol planned eventually to rehabilitate those ugly characters, those "monsters" that he had portrayed in his work. Plyushkin would return to the Russian truth after having been purged of the alien influences that had so "uglified" him; that is, his God-given Russian soul would at the end, after purgation, shine forth in its reality, for "Russianness" is a quality that will out, the eventual embodiment of beauty that accomplishes salvation.

Thus, Russia is unique and true, and whatever faults there may be in her have arisen from the introductions of foreign innovations for their own sakes, without regard to Russian nature, blinding this Chosen People much as the Hebrews in the desert were diverted, in their discouragement, by Baal.

None of this is to say that Gogol felt himself to be a political pundit, that he had specific political goals in mind and was advocating them for Russia. Rather, recognition and assertion of spiritual truth were the important things—this was the service to be performed, the service of a prophet of purification, the service performed by the Apostles in the Epistles. The future belongs to this people of ultimate reconciliation and harmony who will save the world through the blessing that has been visited upon it, and Gogol is well convinced that it will all come to pass.

These points are, I think, well illustrated by those digressions of *Dead Souls,* Part 1, that have to do with Russia specifically. As we know, these digressions become increasingly frequent, increasingly lyrical, and increasingly concentrated as the poem advances.[13] Russia is a mysterious land whose glory will eventually be revealed, as Christ's glory was revealed on Mount Tabor. Although the precise future is not predicted by Gogol (he felt that he was a seer, not a fortuneteller), still it will come to pass that "all the virtuous people of other races will seem dead beside them [the Russians], as a book is dead beside the living word! Russian movements will arise . . . and they will see that what only glided through the nature of other peoples has made a profound impression on Russian nature" (6:223). The Russian soul, "the giant who could issue only from the Russian land," will arise as the "champion of the good"; and beauty, to which the Russian is so peculiarly sensitive, will reign forever.

This is no more than Gogol's lyrical expression of faith, his vision of Annunziatia embodied, the Kingdom of God on earth. Certainly, Gogol is not indulging in analysis when he makes statements such as these (and many more examples could be chosen). Nor are these opinions open to discussion, much less controversy, so far as Gogol himself is concerned. As he "knew" of the existence of truth, so he "knew" that Russia was the bearer of truth. He also "knew" that it was his mission to proclaim his knowledge. Once again, Don Quixote and Job came together, but here with a prophetic addition, so that reality could not be explicated (such is not the prophet's task). Explication, in fact, would adulterate the knowledge that Gogol felt he had. Characterizing himself perhaps better than he knew, he wrote to S. T. Aksakov on 22 December 1844: "The Russian mind doesn't like to have a thing explained to it for too long" (P, 152). For him, "the Russian mind" seems to have become identified with his own mind, or rather, with his own feeling, his own conviction.

One might regard this Russia that Gogol believed in as an ideal invention, but I think it would be closer to his attitude to consider it more in terms of a Platonic form, that is, as an existent reality whose truth was not to be doubted, like beauty having its origin in God. It was not arrived at through reason, as Plato arrived at his forms, but through revelation, as the Disciples arrived at Truth on Mount Tabor. Furthermore, the Russia that Gogol had seen with the eyes of his soul was an artistic unity, an ordered and balanced whole, the reconciler of all things; that is, a Christian work of art, a thing of beauty.

11
The Quest That Failed

Gogol spent the last ten years of his life in attempting finally to embody his vision, to bring Annunziata down to earth, so to speak, finally to weld together form and content in a harmonious whole that would make the beauty his soul beheld equally clear to his audience, to paint that final icon.[1] So far as he was concerned, this quest for beauty failed of its object. He might have remembered that even for Plato the form of forms was indescribable, that Dante had settled for less when he ended *Paradiso* with the lines

> All' alta fantasia qui mancò possa;
>   ma già volgeva il mio disiro e il *velle,*
>   sì come rota ch' egualmente è mossa,
> l'amor che move il sole e l' altre stelle,

and that Tasso spent the last nineteen years of his life, the years after the first publication of *Gerusalemme Liberata,* as a psychotic, incessantly trying to justify his work.[2] Gogol's tragedy was that in the long run he aimed too far and that he died in the realization that there was no way to succeed, that the means were lacking, as Dante had discovered long before. Perhaps, if one may be permitted a touch of psychological speculation, he hoped that in death his quest would be fulfilled, that in death he would at last meet the beauty to which his work had so long been devoted. Perhaps, to speculate a little further, here he hoped that art and life would come together, leading to his decision in those last days to fight against the material aid that was pressed upon him. As he wrote in the first lines of the Epilogue to "Hanz Kuechelgarten,"

> In solitude, in wilderness,
> In a brake no one yet knows,
> In my mysterious sacred home,
> Now do the gentle dreams
> Of my soul arise.[3] [1:100]

I submit that these dreams (he is speaking in his own person in the Epilogue) never left Gogol. They were dreams of the same reconciliation that he stressed in his historical articles, in his literary criticism, in his religious statements, and in his fiction. As early as 1 March 1828, he wrote to his mother, "Believe . . . that noble feelings always fill me, that I have never debased myself in my soul, and that I have destined my entire life to Good" (*P*, 27). Some eleven years later, on 30 May 1839, he wrote to M. P. Balabina:

> I swear, incomprehensibly strange is the fate of all that is good among us in Russia! It no sooner manages to manifest itself— and immediately death! Merciless, inexorable death! I don't believe in anything now, and if I come across anything beautiful I immediately shut my eyes and try not to look at it. It wafts the odor of the grave to me. A voice I can hear whispers tonelessly: "It is for a brief instant. It is given only so that the eternal melancholy of regret for it can exist, so that the soul will be deeply and painfully grieved by it." [*P*, 79]

Then, in July or August of 1847, he wrote to V. G. Belinsky: "Man must remember that he is not at all a material brute, but an elevated citizen of an elevated heavenly community. Until he begins to live at least a little bit the life of a citizen of heaven, the earthly community will not come into order" (*P*, 184). One year later, in a letter of 15 June 1848, he said to V. A. Zhukovsky:

> What is it to us whether our words have an influence, whether we are heeded? The point is that we ourselves remained true to the Beautiful to the end of our days, that we were able to love it so as not to be disturbed by anything happening around us and so as to sing it an unceasing song, even at the moment when the earth would be collapsing and everything earthly would be destroyed. To die with singing on the lips—isn't that the irresistible duty of a poet, as a soldier's is to die with his weapon in his hands. [*P*, 195]

Finally, on 2 February 1852, just nineteen days before his death, Gogol again wrote to Zhukovsky: "Pray for me, for my work to be truly conscientious and for me to be even a little worthy of singing a hymn to heavenly beauty" (*P, 208*).

Perhaps in another time and under different circumstances Gogol would have been an allegorist (he did give an allegorical interpretation of *The Inspector General* in 1846 in *The Dénouement of "The Inspector General"*, which makes the piece a kind of later medieval morality play), but this was no more feasible in the first half of the nineteenth century than it is today—if, that is, contemporary settings are to be used. We simply no longer think that this world in which we live, and we ourselves, are allegories. Despite all the influences on him and the varied examples from literatures other than Russian, what he did not have was a definitive form that could be adapted to his vision. He was thus, perforce, an experimentalist and an innovator, compelled to approach his subject in roundabout ways, through the material, which to him was the very negation of the beauty he sought. He was caught, in other words, in a contradiction in terms insofar as embodiment of beauty as he understood it was concerned. Yet Gogol had to pursue that path if he was to retain his integrity as an artist, for the artist was above all a teacher. He was devoted to beauty, but also "art is teaching."[4] In these senses, Gogol made a genuine attempt at an "imitation of Christ" in his art (the "imitation of Christ" in moral life, following Thomas à Kempis's book, which became one of Gogol's favorites, was also Gogol's aim); that is, for a believer of Gogol's persuasion, Christ, the God-man, the God-Who-Became-Flesh, was the ultimately perfect example of artistic creation, the icon of icons; and it was the artist's task, his "service," to follow in His footsteps.

This is not to say that Gogol always felt (in distinction to thought) precisely in these terms. I would contend, however, that the combination of art, religion, and "Russianism" could lead nowhere else, and thus could mean only failure in the long run. It was Gogol's very naïveté, his inability to find a compromise—as his great models had compromised—that defeated him. Only once did he manage a combination that was sufficient to convey his vision, in *The Inspector General*, and even that, he felt, was misunderstood, had failed. When it came to *Dead Souls,* the problem was beyond solution. He told Zhukovsky in his letter of 29 December 1847:

> For a long time I had been occupied by the thought of a *large work* in which all that is good and bad in Russian man would be presented and the *character* of our Russian nature would be revealed before us more visibly. I saw and embraced many parts separately, but I simply could not clarify and define the plan of the whole firmly enough that I could take it up and begin to write. At every step I felt that I was lacking in many things, that I did not know how to put together and unravel events, and that I had to study the structure of the large works of the great masters. [*P*, 190–91]

This indicates that Gogol was himself conscious of where the difficulty lay (he was at the time still deeply involved in the attempt to complete his magnum opus). It might perhaps be argued that he was struggling with his natural genius and his natural method, the ability to see and juxtapose opposites, to put form and content in contrast with each other rather than to make them one. But this attempt was a result of what Gogol regarded as the previous failure of his artistic endeavors, which, while devoted to beauty, were also meant to teach that beauty. The supreme effort was to be made in the succeeding volumes of *Dead Souls*—there, universal harmony and reconciliation were to be revealed concretely (this was, I think, the "secret" of which Gogol spoke). *Selected Passages,* in particular "Easter Sunday," outlines the goal, the object of the quest to which Hanz Kuechelgarten had also in his way been dedicated. Gogol had the word, but how does a mere man make the word flesh? Even Pascal had found it beyond his powers.

On 6 December 1849 Gogol wrote to A. O. Smirnova: "Everything in the world is deception; nothing seems to us what it is in actual fact. In order not to make mistakes about people, it is necessary to see them as Christ orders us to see them" (*P*, 201). This was no change of mind—the same point had been made as far back as the Little Russian tales (and had been repeated in "The Portrait," "Nevsky Prospekt," "The Nose," "The Overcoat," "Diary of a Madman," *The Inspector General,* and *Dead Souls*). He saw, or he believed that he saw; but he found that he could not express what he saw, at least not with the import he wished. The quest for beauty was in this sense a quest for artistic perfection, which, by nature, was thus doomed to failure. Gogol had set himself a task that could never be fulfilled, not because of inadequacy in himself, although he became more and more convinced that this was the reason, but because of inadequacy of means.

Thus Gogol represents the tragedy of the artist who could not be satisfied with what he had done, whose devotion to art was perhaps too great, and who decided that, because his quest had failed, his art had failed. However, although Gogol's vision was never embodied as he wished to embody it, he did make clear in his fiction and in his discursive prose what that vision was, as I have tried to indicate in the preceding pages. It was a vision of the unity and harmony—the beauty—of creation, the Paradise awaiting man, if he would only see it. The question that Gogol could not help worrying about, however, was *why* man did not see it, much as Gogol himself tried to show the proper way. The answers that he reached to this question were over and over again depicted in terms of deception, of lies that obscured the truth. The greatest of these deceptions was the untransfigured material world which men take for the true one, those idols that darken the eyes, stop the ears, and distort the soul, if they do not destroy it. These very idols, these "abominations," which are so well portrayed in his work, plagued Gogol himself:

> In me was a collection of all possible abominations, a little of each, and besides, in such numbers as I have thus far not encountered in any individual. God has given me a many-sided nature. He has also inspired in me, since my birth, some good characteristics; but best of them all, for which I do not know how to thank Him, was *the desire to be better*. I have never loved my bad qualities, and if God's divine love had not commanded that they be revealed to me gradually, a little at a time, instead of being revealed suddenly and immediately before my eyes, at a time when I still had no understanding of His infinite mercy, I would have hanged myself. In proportion to the rate at which they were revealed, the desire to be delivered of them was strengthened in me by a wonderful impulse from on high; by an extraordinary spiritual event, I was driven to transfer them to my heroes. [*SP*, 104]

From this point of view, although not from the Freudian one, Gogol's fiction was intensely autobiographical; it was indeed the baring of a soul, as he might have put it. At the same time he identified others with himself, so that while he was expressing and purging himself, he was also, he believed, expressing and purging others. This is as much as to say that Gogol was on one side a lyric poet, as he sometimes realized, while on the other, he was the missionary impelled to fulfill his duty. In both capacities the Holy Grail of beauty was before him; he may not have embodied it (in this sense his quest failed); but as an artist steadfastly devoted to beauty, whose work refused to let the reader forget this, his was one of the greatest successes in literary history.

There is still, however, one further bit of speculation that may be added: Gogol was a romantic who was agonized by the romantic view. He was caught in a world of absolutes, a modern man who was compelled to make distinctions between the kingdoms of good and evil, when what he wished for was a kingdom of good alone. The unity of the tragic world, in which the choice is between right and right, remained constantly impossible for him, and the romantic absolutism that elevated man to the godhead while ignoring God Himself made it impossible for him to work out the tragedy that he felt and forced him to the comedy that he expressed. Another way of putting it is to say that the ordinary had conquered the heroic. This makes Gogol intensely contemporary, one to whom *Death of a Salesman* would have made sense, but as comedy rather than as pathos. His quest failed because the illumination that is the very purpose and end of tragedy was not possible in the material world that he was faced with. After all, when Freud (if I may be anachronistic) replaces Sophocles, Oedipus can only confess —he cannot go to Colonus, which means that the ego has killed the soul. Romantic self-consciousness had destroyed the demigod, so that Prometheus was no longer a Titan but only a self-discovering, and thus conquering, man. Where is Zeus when it is man who knows the secret, even if man has forgotten it and does not wish to remember? In those Christian terms that Gogol so desperately wished to affirm, Where is God when it is man who forgives? Tragedy, to repeat, turns to comedy.

From Gogol's time to ours, at least, the ancient epic that has been of most interest, indeed, the persistent metaphor, has been *The Odyssey*, not *The Iliad*—the story of a journey, rather than one of achievement (we remember Gogol's admiration of Zhukovsky's translation). *Dead Souls* could not be finished perhaps because Gogol was overwhelmed by the consciousness, or the self-consciousness, of his own limitations—as in Kazantzakis and Wolfe, Ulysses cannot accept Ithaca again. On the other hand, this romantic was unwilling, and unable, to be Faust or Frankenstein, and therein lay another reason for the failure of his quest. Unlike many of the romantics and Dostoevsky, he shrank, despite his vision and because of his faith, from sainting man, for that would mean sainting himself, and his consciousness forbade that. He wrote comedies while wishing for tragedies. But tragedy, understood as the problem of the choice between right and right as well as the lesson of human limitation by comparison with the unlimited, was not possible in a world that was increasingly committed not only to choices between right and wrong but also to the unbounded holiness of man. Absolutes—be they religious, scientific, or secular—provide no home for the golden mean.

Unity and beauty, for Gogol, are ultimately in reconciliation and harmony. But it is precisely that reconciliation that is impossible in the modern romantic world. Thus Chichikov's journey, his "Odyssey," may not end; he may not come home, and Gogol can do no more than die, turning away from a world that he cannot save and that does not wish to be saved, that wishes only that most pitiful of all things— namely, to be, which is the disease of so many of Gogol's central characters, particularly in the Petersburg stories. It is these "be-ers," from Shponka through Nozdryov, who evoke our laughter.

In the long run, then, Gogol's vision could not be attained because the modern world would not allow it—and he came finally, against his will, to realize this. The Renaissance, despite its similarities to nine-teenth-century Russia—and there are many upon which it would be pointless to expound here—and despite its attempt to compromise be-tween the Hellenic and the contemporary (the *romanzo* is an example of this attempted compromise)—simply was inappropriate to the abso-luteness, characteristic of Russia, which had been reinforced by the romantic impact. Once we assume that God and Satan are locked in combat, the mortality rate among men rises. It is to that combat that Gogol's characters—and possibly Gogol himself—fell victim.

Gogol's vision, thus, while it is one of total unity, could not be made real on the purely human level, could not attain to the ultimate resolution that tragedy brings, and thus was self-defeating. Unfortu-nately, to none of Gogol's characters, nor to Gogol himself, would the mermaids sing.

Notes

1: At First

1. For a description of the poem, see Victor Erlich, *Gogol* (New Haven, Conn., and London: Yale University Press, 1969), pp. 21–23.
2. See V. V. Zenkovsky, *N. V. Gogol* (Paris: YMCA Press, 1961), for an extended discussion of Gogol's aestheticism, although Zenkovsky is by no means the only one to have remarked upon the subject. As the reader will discover, my view is quite different, however.
3. Erlich, *Gogol*, p. 23.

2: Little Russia

1. Aside from "Italy" and "Hanz Kuechelgarten," Gogol had published "St. John's Eve," the second tale included in *Evenings on a Farm near Dikanka*, anonymously in March 1830; in December 1830/January 1831 he published, either anonymously or using pseudonyms, a few translations, an article on the teaching of geography (republished in *Arabesques* in 1835), one chapter from the never-completed novel *Hetman*, and two from the never-completed *Terrible Boar*.
2. Robert A. Maguire, ed. and trans., *Gogol from the Twentieth Century* (Princeton, N.J.: Princeton University Press, 1974), p. 3. Maguire's introduction to this volume is just about the best rundown of various interpretations of Gogol's work from Gogol's day to ours.
3. Gogol used the same kind of image in his unfinished *Terrible Boar*. There the teacher is described as an observer of the human ant hill.
4. Whether "Petro" was meant to be a reference to Peter the Great is a matter for conjecture. But this we do know: Gogol was living in St. Petersburg and was thinking of his Petersburg tales when he wrote this story.
5. A good deal of Gogol's work has the episodic—as distinguished from the developmental—character exhibited here.

6. While we cannot be certain that the essays were written in this order, the framework does make artistic sense. And Gogol was an artist.

7. Of these, Fyodor Tyutchev is the first who comes to mind. But the entire notion of wholeness in relation to Russian thought is a large one that would be best explored elsewhere.

8. Gogol does not have in mind here the kind of rational balance that Pope is speaking of in his *Essay on Man*. It is not, that is, a matter of a higher frame of reference; rather, it is the way all things really are, regardless of the point of view. Evil is not just apparent; it is an active lie.

9. One might also note that Gogol alternated the length of the pieces in this volume. *Part 2* does not follow this practice, although it too has a pattern: after an even shorter "Preface" than that of *Part 1*, the stories steadily increase in length.

10. That there was a folkloristic precedent for this story is beside the point of the present discussion.

11. For a summary of other views of *Evenings*, including his own, see Erlich, *Gogol*, pp. 28–45. I do not think there is any incompatibility between the interpretation expressed here and those that Erlich airs.

12. One is struck, in this connection, not only by the resemblance to Dostoevsky, but also by a resemblance to Milton's conception, although no evidence exists that either Gogol or Dostoevsky ever read *Paradise Lost*, which strongly emphasizes both Satan's falsity (in the earlier books) and his ugliness (in the later ones). Goethe's Mephistopheles turns vulgar, we remember, as does Dostoevsky's devil in *The Brothers Karamazov*. Gogol, however, does not make his devil an intellectual.

13. For this reason it is difficult to speak of Gogol in terms of "development." There simply was not that much time involved.

14. For both symbolic and religious reasons, this is the only one of the *Dikanka* stories that takes place in winter.

15. Erlich, *Gogol*, p. 44. I should drop the word "pathetic" from this description, since only a living creature can be the object of pathos, and there are no living creatures—deliberately none—in this story.

16. Zenkovsky, *N .V. Gogol*, p. 13.

17. The resemblance beween this story and some of Chekhov's nostalgic tales is most striking, although quite different motives impelled the two authors. One is also reminded of the work of Goncharov, particularly *Oblomov*, the hero of which is in many ways himself an "Old World Landowner."

18. Possibly, Gogol was still wavering between the Ukraine (noting that all his tales about it concern Cossacks rather than the Ukraine proper) and Great Russia, although he lost little time in making his decision in favor of the latter.

19. A simple perusal of the two works should be sufficient for any interested reader. There is no need to detail the parallels here.

20. Cf. Gogol's remarks in *"The Odyssey* in Zhukovsky's Translation" (*SP*, 32–41).

21. It might be argued that since the lines just quoted were added for the 1842 edition, they indicate a change in Gogol's attitude over the intervening years, that he did not feel in 1835 as he did in 1842. However, the motif of the Orthodox battle against the Roman Catholic Pole and the infidel Jew runs throughout the earlier version, as it does throughout the later. The later version simply made the point more obvious as Gogol continued his struggle against what he considered to be misinterpretations of his work.

22. In his interesting discussion of "Viy," Erlich sees the tale: (1) in terms of psychology, that is, in terms of insights into the sado-masochistic personality; (2) as a Christian story showing the inadequacy of the hero's faith; and (3) as an attack on complacency. Any one of these interpretations can be successfully defended, and Erlich does so, particularly the last (*Gogol,* pp. 62–68). My own interpretation, indeed, may be regarded as a variation of the last. Erlich thinks more of the story as a whole than I do, since he does not see the split that I have emphasized and seems to be more affected by the horror, which I find much less compelling than that in "A Terrible Vengeance." I have also excluded discussion of the impact of language in this story.

23. If the reader detects a resemblance between this and the traditional Roman Catholic view, most poetically expressed by Dante, I quite agree with his suspicion, although despite Gogol's later attachment to Rome as a city, we can be quite certain that he remained always opposed to the Roman faith, at least as expressed in its Church. What we have here is a vision, not a theological statement. The emphasis upon beauty in Orthodoxy—in particular, Russian Orthodoxy—has often been commented upon (see the works of Nicholas Zernov as one example), and it is probable that Gogol's attitude had more in common with the iconographic view than it did with the Roman one (see below, chapter 9).

24. Gogol was to write only one more story that has a split in tone, "Nevsky Prospekt," and only one that maintains a serious attitude throughout, "The Portrait."

25. Again, Gogol anticipates one of the great themes of Dostoevsky.
26. Gogol's anticapitalism, if that's what it is, is a part of his anti-Westernism in general; it does not make him either proliberal or proleftist. He remained a supporter of tsarism, which in his day had little in common with capitalism.
27. Paul Evdokimov discusses this point at great length in his *Gogol et Dostoïevsky; ou, La descente aux enfers* (Paris: Desclée de Brouwer, 1961).
28. The first discussion of Gogol's depiction of this quality is by Gogol himself in "Four Letters to Divers Persons Apropos *Dead Souls*" (*SP*, 96–111). Vladimir Nabokov makes much of it in his book on Gogol (*Nikolai Gogol* [Norfolk, Conn.: New Directions, 1944]). The best discussion, however, is in V. V. Zenkovsky, *N. V. Gogol,* chapter 2.
29. Genesis 1:31 (DV).
30. "Taras Bulba" is one of Gogol's very few attempts at a different fictional approach, as I have tried to suggest.

3: Petersburg

1. It is not my intention to question the various influences on Gogol that have been so ably adduced by the many scholars in the field. They are simply beside the point here.
2. It would be well to keep in mind that through a good part of these years Gogol was also writing and publishing his theatrical pieces and *Dead Souls*. He also, of course, revised "Taras Bulba" for the 1842 edition.
3. *The Collected Tales and Plays of Nikolai Gogol,* ed. Leonard J. Kent (New York: Modern Library, 1969), lists only "Nevsky Prospekt" and "Diary of a Madman" under *Arabesques*. The reason is that the translation of "The Portrait" is from the later 1842 revision (p. 510 n.1), although Kent does point out in his Introduction that the first version of the story was printed in *Arabesques* in 1835 (p. xxxi).
4. Kent in his Introduction (*Collected Tales and Plays*) dismisses "The Portrait" as follows:

> *The Portrait* is Gogol's least representative story, closer but not very close) to *Viy* and *A Terrible Vengeance* than to anything else he ever wrote, especially in the earliest version. It is a German romance which happens to be

written in Russian and, in its final version, suggests that Gogol is the author only because of the unmistakable didacticism infused in it. It is devoid of the grotesque and of Gogol's intense realism. It combines the Gothic, romantic, and didactic, and it is peopled with fleshless allegorical symbols: the hero (Vanity), the mother and daughter (*Poshlost*), the old man in the portratit (Devil), the professor (Reason), the artist who had painted the portrait (Sinner-Expiator). In its final version (1842) its didacticism offers us insight into Gogol's ever-increasing preoccupation with religion, morality, and the horrible wages of sin. [P. xxxi]

As my discussion will show, I do not agree with Kent's assessment. Indeed, I would suggest that Gogol's "least representative story" is probably "Taras Bulba."

5. Such a notion forms the background to the development of Socialist Realism in the Soviet Union. See Jesse Zeldin, "The Place of Socialist Realism in Marxist Communist Ideology," *"South Atlantic Quarterly,* vol. 68, no. 1 (winter 1969).

6. Wordsworth, it will be remembered, held much the same opinion of the difference between the artist and the ordinary man, although he put it in different terms (see his Preface to *Lyrical Ballads*).

7. Gogol may have felt that he was in the same position of having to make a choice when critics and friends ceaselessly importuned him to complete *Dead Souls* not too many years later.

8. Given Gogol's proclivities, one can only be surprised that he did not make the usurer a Westerner.

9. In the first, more mysterious version, the features of the usurer vanish from the painting, and the spectators wonder if it has not all been a dream; in the second version the entire painting is "stolen," although the possibility of a dream is left.

10. As in many things Gogol anticipated Dostoevsky, so here, in his view of art as a reconciling power, he anticipated Tolstoy—at least the Tolstoy who wrote *What Is Art?*

11. See André Meynieux, *Pouchkine homme de lettres et la littérature professionnelle en Russie* (Paris: Librairie des cinq continents, 1966).

12. See Donald Fanger, *Dostoevsky and Romantic Realism* (Cambridge, Mass.: Harvard University Press, 1965), pp. 101–26, for an interesting discussion of Gogol's view of the city as such.

13. V. V. Zenkovsky writes of Gogol's "artistic platonism" (*N. V. Gogol,* pp. 79–93), but he has in mind Gogol's use of the typical,

the "form," not the approach that I am using here, which emphasizes total harmony.

14. See below, p. 148.
15. There is also undoubtedly a personal reference here, since Gogol thought very highly of Schiller and was strongly influenced by Hoffmann.
16. According to the *Primary Chronicle,* Russia chose Orthodoxy rather than Roman Catholicism or Islam because of the beauty of the service as the envoys of Grand Duke Vladimir of Kiev had witnessed it in Constantinople, which was so beautiful, they reported, that they did not know whether they were in Heaven or on earth.
17. In the first part of his book, Evdokimov provides an interesting analysis of the theme of anonymity and evil in Gogol.
18. It has often been said that Gogol's humor is Rabelaisian. I think this is an error. Rabelais, on one level, celebrates physical man; Gogol mocks him. Rabelais's laughter is rooted in a belief in the goodness of physical life and physical man; Gogol's is meant as a metaphysical warning.
19. As Dante puts it in the last lines of *Paradiso:*

> All' alta fantasia qui mancò possa;
>   ma già volgeva il mio disiro e il *velle,*
>   sì come rota ch' egualmente è mossa,
>   l'amor che move il sole e l' altre stelle.

20. It is also notable that the progress is from early fall to winter, an indication of decline and death.
21. "The Nose," one of the two most well known of Gogol's short stories (the other is "The Overcoat"), has been subjected to a great variety of interpretations, ranging from consideration of it as pure nonsense to one that invests it with profound religious significance. It is not my purpose to deny the validity of any of these interpretations, while following my own.
22. I do not find a concentration upon noses so omnipresent in Gogol as Nabokov does, and thus I am very skeptical of the castration-complex theory which recommends itself so easily to those of a Freudian inclination.
23. In the Kent edition the nose declares that it is "an independent individual," (*Collected Tales and Plays,* p. 481) which seems to be overstating the case.
24. Very early in the story we are informed that even Kovalyov's rank is to a certain extent a fraud: "Collegiate assessors who receive that title with the help of academic certificates cannot be compared with

those who are made collegiate assessors in the Caucasus. They are two completely different kinds. Academic collegiate assessors . . . Kovalyov was a Caucasian collegiate assessor" (3:53).

25. Gogol constantly emphasizes the smoothness and blankness of Kovalyov's face without the nose. This reminds one of the story about the emperor's clothes, except that there is no innocent child to point out the emperor's nakedness.

26. This is another of Gogol's themes that Dostoevsky will later take up, although in a very different and more obvious—because argumentative—way.

27. Poprishchin in "The Diary of a Madman" is much distressed at his lack of possessions, which puts him in the same position as Kovalyov.

28. This idea, of course, has a long and honorable history, going back, at least interpretatively, to Plato. I would suggest that Gogol's dislike of material acquisition has this metaphysical root rather than an economic, social, or political one. This does not, I might add, make Gogol a "metaphysician."

29. For Gogol, any purely human "institution," including anarchy, would be subject to equivalent egoistic strains if left on its own level.

30. Gogol was thirty-nine when he began it, and forty when it was finished.

31. Erlich, *Gogol*, p. 143.

32. See Paul Debreczeny, *Nikolay Gogol and His Contemporary Critics* (Philadelphia: American Philosophical Society, 1966), and Robert A. Maguire, *Gogol from the Twentieth Century*, for detailed discussions of the critical receptions of Gogol's works.

33. Much has been made of the resemblance of Akaky Akakyevich's name to the Russian child's expression for defecation. One might point out that the term *"kaka,"* out of which the Russians have constructed the verb *kakat'*, is not peculiarly Russian at all. It is also a common term in French and Italian. Nor is it unusual to name a child after his father (the patronymic would be automatic). It is quite possible, also, that Gogol had the Greek word *akakos*, "innocence," in mind here, as he had the slang for defecation in mind when he used *"kaka"* to refer to the devil in "Christmas Eve."

34. Erlich, *Gogol*, p. 4.

35. This view has also been applied, with greater particularity, to *Dead Souls*. Indeed, I once did so myself (*SP*, xv).

36. Gogol used the same device, although not so obviously, in "The Nose," where we find the following lines: "Russia is such a wonderful country that if you say something about one collegiate as-

sessor, then all collegiate assessors, from Riga to Kamchatka, without fail take it personally. The same goes for all titles and ranks" (3:53).

37. Gogol was not always and necessarily a symbolist (I do not think symbolism is essential to literature), but at least part of his genius did lie in his extraordinary perception of the ways of literature; "The Overcoat" is a case in point. This is one of the reasons that interpretation of Gogol is so difficult. We all know *that* he meant; the question is *what* he meant. One might note, in this connection, that he held the profession of literary criticism in very high esteem (see "A Textbook of Literature for Russian Youth," "Petersburg Notes of 1836," and especially "On *The Contemporary*"), even while insisting that he himself had been grossly misinterpreted, without saying exactly how he *should* have been interpreted.

38. While I do not wish to overdo the etymological, surely the choice of the name Gregory Petrovich is not accidental. It is probable that Gogol is asserting his Orthodoxy and that the devilish reference is to Roman Catholicism: Gregory, son of Peter. The Gregory that Gogol had in mind would be Gregory VII, pope some nineteen years after the final split between the Eastern and Western churches in 1054. Many Orthodox considered Gregory to be the evil genius who, as the power behind the throne, was responsible for destroying the unity of the Church. In Orthodox eyes, he was the founder of the schismatic Church of Rome. It is Roman worldly power and materialism that corrupts the truth and beauty of real Christianity (Orthodoxy). At the same time, the tale takes place in the city of Peter the Great (the tailor is Peter's son also), which Gogol, as we know, regarded as a city foreign to Russia, the embodiment of deception.

39. It needs little imagination to connect these events with the interpretation suggested in note 38: the newness, the opposite direction, the rationality of Akaky Akakyevich's thoughts, the overcoat as a kind of spouse, etc., etc.

40. Erlich, *Gogol,* p. 149.

41. Of course, "overcoat" in Russian is grammatically feminine, and one could enlarge on its enveloping qualities. On the other hand, the Russian word for tower, *bashnya,* as phallic a symbol as one could wish, also happens to be feminine, as is *tour* in French. Surely a little skepticism concerning the Freudian interpretation is justified. (Of course, in Freud's own language, German, *Turm* happens to be masculine.)

42. While doing all, they nothing know,/ While knowing all, they nothing do,/ Chopping changers are the French,/ The more they're weighed, the less you get. (My translation, which is reasonably literal, tries to give the sense that Gogol probably understood.) It would not be amiss to compare Gogol's view of France with that of Dostoevsky in *Winter Notes on Summer Impressions.*
43. In view of the circle that this piece performs, one may legitimately doubt that it is in fact a fragment rather than a finished work.
44. See above, pp. 5–6.
45. *Oeuvres complètes de Nicolas Gogol* (Paris: Gallimard, 1966).

4: The Theater

1. Unless, that is, we consider each part of *Evenings on a Farm near Dikanka, Mirgorod,* and the Petersburg tales as complete and rounded works, as I have tried to indicate that we may. *Dead Souls,* of course, is unfinished.
2. This despite Gogol's expressed disdain for what he called "vaudevilles." See "Petersburg Notes of 1836."
3. The only one to be staged, "The Law Suit," was indifferently received.
4. It is a happy ending that Gogol's contemporaries could not see, used as they were to the conventional denouement in which either boy gets girl, or girl gets boy, depending upon who is doing the chasing.
5. Gogol seems to have been fascinated with card games for money. One plays an important part in "The Morning of a Man-of-Affairs," another is in *The Inspector General,* and one crops up in chapter 10 of *Dead Souls.* There is no evidence, however, that Gogol himself was addicted to such games, unlike Dostoevsky, whose mania for gambling is well known.
6. I am speaking here of Gogol's *revisions,* not his reinterpretation contained in *The Dénouement of "The Inspector General,"* which was written in 1846 and not published until after Gogol's death.
7. One can imagine how Gogol must have spun in his grave when a French translation of the play appeared in 1854, at the height of the Crimean War, under the title *Les Russes peints par eux-mêmes.*
8. Some other changes include the following: the last paragraph of directions preceding the play, which emphasizes the living-statue scene, was added for the 1842 edition; Khlestakov's line in act 3, scene 6, "I was once even taken for the commander in chief," was an 1841 change from the 1836 line, "I was once even taken for the

Turkish ambassador"; the reflections of the Mayor at the beginning of scene 9, act 3, were added in 1841; two-thirds of the Mayor's speech at the end of scene 9, act 3, was added in 1841; the entire first scene of act 4 and the use of Ammos instead of the Postmaster in act 3 were added in 1841 (in 1836 Khlestakov took the initiative in soliciting bribes; in the new version he got the idea from Ammos); all of scene 5, act 4, was added in 1841.

9. This has been noted by many modern commentators. One might add that it is reinforced in the Russian by the extraordinary use of the passive voice (in which the language abounds) in Khlestakov's speeches. Things constantly happen *to* him; he rarely *causes* anything to happen.

10. Perhaps this is why Gogol felt it necessary to add the Mayor's line: "Why are you laughing? You're laughing at yourselves!" The audience had missed the point and, even with this added line, persisted in delusion, so far as Gogol was concerned.

11. One is tempted to ask if this is Gogol's view of original sin. Perhaps, since, for Gogol, man is free.

12. Although the scene was added in 1841 and revised for the edition of 1842, it is really more a rearrangement of the conclusion than it is a change in meaning.

13. One might also wonder if the Policeman, a messenger, is not a parody of the Holy Ghost.

14. The resemblance to Milton's concept in *Paradise Lost* is again striking, even though Lucifer starts out knowing that he is lying; his speciousness, however, is meant to convince the other fallen angels, not the reader (Blake could not have been more wrong when he said that Milton was of Satan's party without knowing it).

15. Hypocrisy, after all, demands a knowledge of the truth; there is a real person behind the mask. This does not apply to Gogol's characters, who are only masks.

16. See Gogol's remarks in "Petersburg Notes of 1836."

17. This could also be translated "a stupid, downright liar." The Garnett-Kent translation, "as stupid as an old grey horse," misses both points (the "gelding" is an obvious reference to Khlestakov's flirtation with the Mayor's wife).

18. This might just as easily be translated "Luka Lukich stinks of himself," since *luka* means "onions" to begin with. Onions, thus, "stink," or are "rotten with," onions. This description is at best redundant, at worst meaningless. Interestingly enough, however, Luka Lukich, upon hearing this statement, replies that he has "never taken an onion in his mouth," thus, by way of a pun, denying

himself. There is a possible double pun here, since Gogol may also have in mind the Latin *lux*, "light" (Luka Lukich is superintendent of schools).

19. The colloquial phrase tyap-lyap (the reverse of Lyapkin-Tyapkin) means "anyhow" or "any old way" in reference to a piece of work that is supposed to be done.

20. The one possible exception is Khlestakov's servant, Osip, who seems to have an awareness of truth. However, he stays out of things so far as he can; his only desire is to escape from falsity rather than to expose it. But Osip, although significant as a chorus who warns the audience, can hardly be regarded as a major character in the play.

21. I would caution against making Gogol a Hegelian on this basis, however.

22. Erlich makes the same point, although in a different context and for different purposes, when he remarks that "verisimilitude was not Gogol's forte, nor was it, most of the time, his avowed goal." He goes on to quote a letter of Gogol's in which Gogol declared: "I never had the desire to reflect reality as it is around us" (*Gogol*, p. 121).

23. An exception seems to be Carl Proffer, who finds "the interpretation somewhat less preposterous than most critics" (*P*, 231).

24. It is often forgotten by those who put *Dead Souls* in the same category as *The Divine Comedy* that the latter is an allegory, and a very precise one at that. Yet allegorical import is denied to *Dead Souls*, as it is to *The Inspector General*.

5: *Dead Souls*, Part 1

1. See above, pp. 65–66.

2. One wonders how much Dostoevsky's *Life of a Great Sinner*, in concept, owes to Gogol.

3. "Rome" was not just a *jeu d'esprit* on Gogol's part; it expressed a life-long attachment going back to his early work.

4. These Italians were well known, either in the original or in translation, to Batyushkov, Kozlov, and Pushkin, as they had been known to the eighteenth-century generation of Kantemir. We might also remember that in a letter to M. P. Balabina written from Rome at the end of April 1838, Gogol, while speaking of the necessity to become better acquainted with modern Italian literature, also said, "The epic literature of the Italians is well known to us, that is, the literature of the XVth and XVIth centuries" (*P*, 74).

5. I do not suggest that this was a conscious rational process on Gogol's part. Rather, it was a process of increasing awareness in the course of his work on Part 1.

6. The total application of an unimportant central character to the *Orlando Furioso* is doubtful, although it is quite possible with *Don Quixote*.

7. Digressions are, of course, common in much eighteenth- and nineteenth-century fiction, both in the West and in Russia. They do not *distinguish* the comic romantic epic, but they are essential to it. Incidentally, it might be arged that the novel, as a form, developed from the *romanzo* to begin with. This seems to me eminently possible. Gogol, however, saw the novel as a distinctive form in its own right.

8. Amusement seems to have extended well beyond the borders of Russia. In 1854, during the Crimean War, an English translation of *Dead Souls* was published under the title *Home Life in Russia*!

9. See my Introduction to *Selected Passages from Correspondence with Friends* for a discussion of the continuation.

10. See Turgenev's *Literary Reminiscences* on this point.

11. Ariosto's task was comparatively easier, since he had a hero who was sane, then went mad, and then had but to recover his writs, which was accomplished by the trick of Astolpho's voyage to the moon. Thus Orlando could remain in character. Not so Chichikov, who starts out mad, from one point of view.

12. Part 1 does have some parallels to the *Inferno,* as will appear below, but I believe that they are not sufficient to indicate that Gogol was following Dante at this stage.

13. Several commentators have taken this line, notably Evdokimov.

14. I recognize how radical such an interpretation may appear, since it presumes Chichikov's innocence rather than his guilt, or at least it presumes a modicum of honesty on his part (nothing he does in Part 1 goes outside anyone's morality). I think the text bears this out, however: deformity and ugliness belong much more to the other characters than they do to him. The only complaint of the man who buys the moneymaking machine is that it doesn't work (and this one does); he can hardly claim that he is a law-abiding citizen. Chichikov may intend eventually to cheat by mortgaging the dead souls, but he does not cheat here, while others do attempt to cheat him.

15. Gogol's personally rather gluttonous eating habits have nothing to do with the case. He was more aware of his own failings, one suspects, than are many of his biographers.

16. Chichikov at least is involved in his scheme for more than simple riches; we will later find out that his prime concern is for his descendants, as well as respectability for himself. In contrast with the lives of most of those he meets, however, his life has been one of material failure.

17. We may here discern a certain similarity to the Dantesque scheme in the *Inferno*.

18. *Dead Souls,* Part 1, remains only tangentially Dantesque, however, for the circles of *Inferno* are ignored, although one could, stretching a point, make this chapter the fifth circle, that of sloth. But Nozdryov will reappear, while, for Dante, reappearance is possible only in *Paradiso*. Furthermore, Gogol seems to be making no attempt to give a scale of sins.

19. Through much of *Dead Souls,* Gogol accomplishes the extraordinary feat of having his central character assume various forms, according to the wishes of his interlocutors, while at the same time remaining separate from them. The only one to whom he becomes a person is the narrator, who starts by describing him as so ordinary as barely to be noticed, and ends with the story of his life, which is far from ordinary. One is tempted to propose the narrator as hero, but the difficulties of such a course are too obvious for it to be pursued.

20. If there is a satanic character in Part 1, I would suggest that it is Nozdryov rather than Chichikov. Interestingly enough, when he tempts Chichikov, he is rejected; but when he later tempts the townspeople, the temptation is accepted. This is indeed to speak well of Chichikov—perhaps he is an Ariosto character after all, and the likeness to the Dantesque scheme therefore lessens.

21. The emphasis on the transparency and on the glowing sun indicates the possibility of a Platonic reference.

22. The word used for "rogue" is *bestiya,* which Garnett, perhaps having the bestiality of Sobakyevich in mind, translates "brute" (*Dead Souls* [New York: Modern Library, 1931], p. 152).

23. Presumably Gogol hoped to accomplish that awakening in Parts 2 and 3.

24. Part 1 does not go beyond intimations and longings on Chichikov's part, however. Gogol hoped that the reader would acknowledge the truth long before Chichikov did and then would watch him do so in succeeding volumes.

25. The second will be the recounting of Chichikov's background. The Plyushkin chapter, incidentally, begins with a digression in which the author recalls his own childhood.

26. Evidently, Gogol intended to accomplish a change in Plyushkin some day, for in his essay "Subjects for the Lyric Poets of the Present Time," written, according to Gogol's date, in 1844, he wrote: "O, if you could read . . . what my Plyushkin will say, if I attain to the third volume of *Dead Souls*" (*SP*, 87).
27. One is also reminded of the first part of "The Portrait."
28. See "The Russian Landowner" (*SP*, 137–46). There is also a reminiscence of "Old World Landowners."
29. Until his rediscovery of proper value, Orlando is also repeatedly taken for a sucker.
30. I admit that this sounds like casuistry, but we might also note that Chichikov does not ask anyone to keep the transaction secret. On the contrary, he insists upon having it all done in proper legal form. In any event, which of the inhabitants of the town of N., or what tax collector, has the right to accuse Chichikov of immorality?
31. The word Gogol uses is *chuzhdyi*, "alien to," "a stranger to," "extraneous to." Garnett unfortunately translates the word as "aloof from" (*Dead Souls*, p. 234), which has quite a different meaning from that intended by Gogol.
32. Interestingly enough, it is just when, in his conversation with the girl, that Chichikov "touched upon the Greek philosopher Diogenes" that Nozdryov turns up (6:171). The Greek who searched for an honest man is put in contrast with the pathological liar!
33. See chapter 6, below, for a discussion of the digressions in *Dead Souls*, Part 1.
34. Gogol was already aware, I suggest, that a formal problem was being posed, although he did not yet realize how serious it was. "Majestic lyrical flow" is not the style of the *romanzo*.
35. The word Gogol uses is *blagopristoinyi* (6:233).
36. See below, chapters 9 and 10.
37. The movement that I am suggesting is even clearer in the digressions.

6: The Digressions of *Dead Souls*, Part 1

1. The fragments of Part 2 that we have are quite different. There the digressions are put in the mouths of various characters, rather than being spoken by the author. This has the effect of making the characters seem to be mere puppets. In this sense, most of Part 2, as we have it, can be considered a digression.

2. Gogol managed a double point here, for he promptly went on to tell his readers that Manilov's peculiarity was his lack of peculiarity (6:24).

3. The reader need not fear: I do not intend to discuss *every* digression in *Dead Souls,* Part 1.

4. The phrase used in the Russian for "of its own accord" is *sama soboyu,* which Garnett unfortunately simply leaves out of her translation. "Another magical current" is turned into "a different and strange mood" (*Dead Souls,* p. 84 of 1931 Modern Library edition).

5. At the end of Part 1 this carriage will turn into the famous troika.

6. See below, chapter 9.

7. There are, of course, others, some written before Gogol's work on *Dead Souls,* which were published in *Arabesques* in 1835; some written after Part 1 had been completed, which were published in *Selected Passages from Correspondence with Friends* in 1847.

8. See below, chapters 9 and 10.

9. See above, pp. 101–2.

10. See below, pp. 120–21.

11. One might also argue that *Dead Souls* is a kind of spiritual biography of Gogol himself, not only in the digressions but in the fiction. See below, chapter 11.

12. The word that Gogol uses here is *pravda,* ultimate truth, rather than *istina,* propositional truth.

13. In the original, of course, this is all accomplished by means of inflections, which the English cannot reproduce: *yesli by pokazali; zabiraitye; nye ostavlyaite; nye podymyetye; nichevo nye prochitayesh'.*

14. *Byeschelovyechnoi starost'.* Gogol uses the word "man" (*chelovyek*) three times in this short passage; the word "human," which is derived from *chelovyek* (*chelovyecheskiye*), once; and the word "inhuman," which is also derived from *chelovyek* (*byeschelovyechnoi*), once, as the penultimate word in the paragraph. That the nature of humanity is of some concern to him seems obvious.

15. See above, pp. 115–16.

16. Chapter 1 introduces Chichikov, the officials of the town, and some of those with whom Chichikov will later have dealings. Chapter 2 is devoted to Manilov; chapter 3 to Korobochka; chapter 4 to Nozdryov; chapter 5 to Sobakyevich; chapter 6 to Plyushkin. Some of these characters appear again, but without the concentration that marked them earlier, without being definitively set off.

17. We will note that Chichikov's downfall in chapter 5 of Part 2 is

brought about in an entirely different way and for entirely different reasons. See below, chapter 7.

18. See above, chapter 4, pp. 105–6.
19. Ibid.
20. Gogol uses the word *narod* here rather than *lyudi,* thus implying a collective rather than individuals.
21. It is out of this, for Gogol, that *poshlost'* arises. *Poshlost'* is an abnormal state, not a normal, natural one.
22. See below, chapter 10.
23. There is a long tradition of such nationalistic pleas in literature, going back at least as far as Dante's *De Vulgaria Eloquentia, La Convito, La Vita Nuova,* and *La Divina Commedia.* The Renaissance also was full of such works. Bellay's *Defence et illustration de la langue françoyse* and Sidney's *Defense of Poesie* are only two examples. The same impulse guided such Russian eighteenth-century theorists as Lomonosov, Tredyakovsky, and Sumarokov.
24. In modern Russian the phrase *mirskaya skhoda* would be enough to mean "peasant meeting," but Gogol prefaces the phrase with *khrest'yanskaya,* or "peasant," thus doubling the emphasis.
25. The Apocalypse has been used by many Russian writers, including Dostoevsky. It seems to have assumed particular importance in the postrevolutionary era: Blok, Olesha, Bulgakov, and Pasternak are only four names that come to mind.
26. One is reminded of Pierre's musings in *War and Peace* when he joins the Masons and just before he decides that he must try to assassinate Napoleon.
27. The words that Gogol uses are *zabluzhdyeniye* (which could also be translated "error") and *iskrivlyeniye.* I would suggest that his choices are quite deliberate; he has more in mind than mere mistakes.
28. Deliberately, Gogol uses a word to evoke a conception of the past, rather than the more modern *Rossiya,* which has more specific "state" connotations.
29. For "distance," Gogol uses only the adjective *dalyokii,* literally "distant, remote," without a modified noun. The translator either supplies what he thinks the noun should be (Garnett gives us "paradise") or he changes *dalyokii* into a noun. I have chosen the latter course as perhaps being closer to Gogol's meaning. He also uses the second person singular when addressing Russia, literally "thee."
30. One is reminded of F. I. Tyutchev's poem, written in 1855:

These villages so poor,
This meager, barren nature:
My native, suffering land,
The Russian people's land!

Proud eyes of foreigners
Will never grasp nor note
The inner light beneath
Your humble nakedness.

Crushed by the cross's burden,
The Heavenly Tsar has traveled
In servile guise across you,
My native land, with blessing.

Poems and Political Letters of F. I. Tyutchev, translated, with introduction and notes, by Jesse Zeldin (Knoxville: University of Tennessee Press, 1974), p. 137. Dostoevsky quoted this same poem in "The Grand Inquisitor" passage of *The Brothers Karamazov.*

31. I would suggest that, while it is correct that the troika was a unique Russian vehicle and thus, in this context, a fitting image to use, the fact that it is drawn by a trinity is also of significance. We remember that, earlier, Chichikov's coachman, Selifan, had a great deal of trouble with these same three horses. Now, however, as Chichikov is rushing over the landscape, the trinity, in harmony with the song, pulls in concord. I would suggest that the religious significance is deliberate on Gogol's part, as is the stress on harmony, which replaces discord.

7: *Dead Souls,* Part 2

1. Of course, a good deal of what we say here can be no more than speculation, since we are not dealing with a completed work, although four of the five chapters do seem to be in sequence.
2. See above, pp. 87–88.
3. This seems to me highly unlikely, given the extraordinary debasement of Chichikov's character that we find in that fragment. I think it was rather a false start, an idea that Gogol tried out and then abandoned as unfit for *any* part of *Dead Souls.* Perhaps it was originally intended for Part 1.
4. Of course, Part 1 also dealt with landowners; from whom else could Chichikov have bought his dead souls? However, in Part 1 he

made trips to various estates, while living in town. In Part 2 he lives in the country, which is perhaps an indication that Gogol was attempting to change his focus.

5. A collegiate secretary was tenth on the Table of Ranks, equivalent to a lieutenant. Chichikov, when he was in the Customs Bureau, had attained the rank of collegiate counselor, sixth on the Table of Ranks and the equivalent of a colonel.

6. Themes later developed by Turgenev in some of his novels, by Goncharov, by Tolstoy, and by Chekhov in some of his short stories, although in very different ways by each of these writers, are already being touched upon by Gogol in these first four fragments of Part 2.

7. Gogol made an additional attempt to answer the question in his essay "The Russian Landowner" (*SP*, 137–45).

8. Gogol gives us one additional detail about Tyentyetnikov, which adds to the general anti-Western and almost Slavophile tone of Part 2: at first he thought that his visitor might be a government official, for when he was younger, Tyentyetnikov had been seduced by a radical movement. "Some philosophers among the Hussars, a semieducated student, and a squandering gambler had organized a philanthropic society under the supreme command of an old rogue, a free mason, a card shark, a drunkard, and a most eloquent man. The society was established with the goal of accomplishing the permanent happiness of all mankind, from the banks of the Thames to Kamchatka. The cash required was enormous; the contributions collected from generous members was incredible. Where it all went only the supreme commander knew. Two friends dragged him into this society; they belonged to the class of disappointed people, good people, who, however, because of frequent toasts in the names of science, enlightenment, and progress, had become confirmed drunkards. Tyentyetnikov soon came to his senses and left this circle. But the society had already succeeded in becoming involved in other activities, not quite fitting to members of the gentry, so that they soon aroused the police. . . . It is therefore no wonder that, although he had left it and broken off all relations with the benefactor of mankind, Tyentyetnikov still could not feel himself at peace. His conscience was not quite comfortable" (7:26–27). Assuming that Part 2 was written sometime between 1840 and 1842, Gogol had already taken a stand against the liberalism that had been invading Russia from Western Europe; it is a stand against the so-called men of the forties who, in Gogol's opinion, had lost touch with their homeland; they were degenerates, as this passage indicates, who seduced the young and destroyed

them. Tyentyetnikov was aware of this ("his conscience was not quite comfortable"), and he, a representative of his generation, should be returned to the right way. This passage constitutes one of Gogol's strongest statements of his nationalistic, quasi-Slavophile convictions.

9. It may be that Gogol was again attempting to adhere to the *romanzo* form and that he planned to complete the tale at some later point.

10. In *Oblomov* also, love comes close to rescuing the hero, although there it definitively fails.

11. It is quite possible, as V. V. Zenkovsky seems to think (*N. V. Gogol*), that Gogol's knowledge of Plato was more than just second-hand; there are too many reminiscences in too many places.

12. There is a lacuna in the manuscript at this point. According to Lyov Arnoldi, Smirnova's half-brother, who had been present at readings of the definitive version, which was later destroyed by Gogol, the following chapter described a day at General Betrishchev's house. The general, conquered by Chichikov after a dinner and an evening spent with him, invited him to come back and bring Tyentyetnikov with him. At this second visit the neighbors were reconciled. At another dinner, Tyentyetnikov declared his feelings for Ulinka, which were returned. He also expressed his patriotic sentiments by evoking the rising of the Russian people in 1812, which gained him the general's sympathy. The latter, giving in to his daughter's entreaties, agreed to the engagement of the young couple. Chichikov, profiting from Tyentyetnikov's gratitude, tried to buy dead souls from him by using the story of his imaginary uncle; but Tyentyetnikov offered to give Chichikov his live souls through a fictitious bill of sale. Chichikov, astounded, cried, "What! Aren't you afraid I'll abuse your confidence?!" But his new friend would not let him finish. Then Chichikov, still thinking of his dead-souls project, offered himself as General Betrishchev's messenger to the general's neighbors and relatives in order to announce Ulinka's engagement. The general gratefully accepted, and that is how Chichikov got hold of a superb coach and four to set off on new visits (Nicolas Gogol, *Oeuvres complètes* [Paris: Gallimard, 1966], pp. 1867–68).

8: The Artist

1. Still one of the best analyses of Gogol's style is Andrey Biely's

(Boris N. Bugaev) *Masterstvo Gogolya*, originally printed in Moscow in 1934 and reprinted by Wilhem Fink Verlag, Munich, in 1969. Biely even supplies a table of Gogol's use of various colors (p. 121), diagrams of the structure of his phrases (pp. 198-99), minute analyses of Gogol's uses of various figures of speech (pp. 196–283), etc., etc.

2. I am aware that this is a matter for debate, since many literary historians contend that the matter of language had been pretty well settled by the time that Gogol appeared on the scene. Insofar as the language was to be Russian rather than some Frenchified or Germanized form, this is undoubtedly true. On the other hand, the questions of the use of colloquialisms, not to say slang, and of inventiveness, not to say coinages, were something else again. Pushkin, after all, still had eight years to live when Gogol came to Petersburg, and Pushkin, a "pure" writer, in prose as well as in verse, still largely dominated the literary world. We might remember that Gogol, despite his admiration for Pushkin and Pushkin's work, did say: "We cannot repeat Pushkin. No, neither Pushkin nor anyone else ought now to be our model: other times have come" (*SP*, 247). It is true that these remarks were published some ten years after Pushkin's death, but they refer to a continuing situation, not just a contemporary one.

3. Stylistically, Gogol bears comparison with Rabelais. Indeed, a study of the two from this point of view might prove to be very rewarding.

4. See Boris Eichenbaum's essay "How Gogol's 'Overcoat' Is Made," in Maguire, *Gogol from the Twentieth Century*, pp. 269–91.

5. See "On Russian Poetry and Its Originality" (*SP*, 199–249) for one example.

6. Perhaps the combination of prose and poetry is best exemplified in *Dead Souls*, if one regards the poetic passages as the digressions and the prose passages as narrative links, thus reversing the notion that the digressions serve as commentaries upon the narrative. This would be somewhat akin to the procedure that Dante followed in *La Vita Nuova*, although the parallel is far from exact.

7. Gogol's greatest influence, from this point of view, is on twentieth-century Russian literature, from Biely to Bulgakov.

8. Gogol's essays on Russian poetry also emphasize sound, as do the essays "Sculpture, Painting, and Music" and "On Little Russian Songs," which stresses the sounds of the songs rather than word meanings or rhythmic patterns. A competent critic might find it profitable to analyze Gogol's dialogue, in both his plays and his stories, from this point of view.

9. It is a pity that, with all his references to music, Gogol did not cite any specific composers. Most of his remarks concern vocal rather than instrumental music. The explanation is, I think, a triple one. First, the Russian Orthodox Church uses no instruments in its services. Second, there is Gogol's conviction that it is in the sounds of the human voice, in the song, that the people's soul is expressed (see "On Little Russian Songs" as one example of this attitude). Hence also, perhaps, Gogol's own language play. How many of his fictional pieces are meant to be "songs"? Third, and this has just been hinted at, he thought that it was in the song, its one means of expression, that the Russian national character was expressed; and Gogol was a Russian nationalist with leanings towards the populism that became so strong among certain groups twenty years after his death.

10. See Zenkovsky's *Aus der Geschichte der ästhetischen Ideen in Russland in 19. und 20. Jahrhunderts,* chap. 1, as well as *N. V. Gogol,* pt. 2.

11. See "Four Letters to Divers Persons Apropos *Dead Souls*" (*SP,* 98–102).

12. One of the most exciting things about Gogol, I think, is his constant attempt to control material, which, both because of the peculiar nature of the Russian situation and because of his own convictions, refused to be controlled. Dostoevsky and Biely, so dissimilar in so many things, faced the same problem. Dostoevsky solved it by *not* solving it, by giving his material free reign; Biely solved it by the imposition of abstract concepts and symbols, making him a highly "intellectual" writer, in contrast to the "existential" Dostoevsky.

13. One might as well acknowledge immediately that Gogol never did solve the formal problem to his own satisfaction, except perhaps in *The Inspector General.* From this point of view, perhaps one of the most attractive things about Gogol, much as it must have tortured him, is his innocence.

14. See above, pp. 20 ff.

15. See Thaïs Lindstrom, *Nikolay Gogol* (New York: Twayne Publishers, 1974), pp. 171 ff., for a discussion of the latter type of contrast.

16. That Gogol felt his hope to be frustrated time after time is beside the point here.

17. We know by the very form of *The Divine Comedy,* for example, what the content will be; we barely even need to read the poem to discover it. Once we have read the poem, however, we find that

the two are indissolubly linked together. Form and content are, so to speak, mirror images of each other.

18. One is reminded of Dirac's remark that, when faced by a number of formulae, any one of which might be correct, he always chose the most "elegant" one. And that "elegant" one always did, in fact, turn out to be the correct one.

19. One might argue that I have simply been describing satire in general. I would reply that the satirical writer, like any other, does cling to unity of form and content, often (as in the cases of *Tartuffe* and *Le Bourgeois gentilhomme*) through balance of forces (there is always at least one character of probity with whom we can empathize, while such characters are rare in Gogol), through denouement, which sets up a new situation (things are seldom solved in Gogol), and often, as in *A Modest Proposal,* through a ridiculousness which invites us immediately to reject the patent nonsense of the *reductio ad absurdum.* This last is also a method used by Dostoevsky, particularly in *The Possessed.*

20. I am excluding *The Inspector General* from this discussion.

21. I am now considering the question from a different point of view from that adopted in chapter 6.

22. See above, p. 99.

23. Cf. Wordsworth's Preface to *Lyrical Ballads.*

24. It is a rare commentator who would disagree with the proposition that Gogol's most effective works are his comic ones. From this point of view, "Taras Bulba," much of "Nevsky Prospekt," all of "The Portrait," and all of "Rome" must be counted among Gogol's lesser efforts.

25. For discussions of these topics, see both Erlich and Maguire.

26. This is not to say that Gogol was incapable of using outright farce for its own sake. This is often an element in some of the Little Russian stories, but it is also of minor importance in such tales as "The Nose," "The Overcoat," "Diary of a Madman," *The Inspector General,* and *Dead Souls.*

27. Ariosto also used comic irony to great effect, although in a somewhat different way. See Rudolf Gottfried, Introduction to Ariosto's *Orlando Furioso,* selections from the translation by Sir John Harrington, edited by Rudolf Gottfried (Bloomington, Ind., and London: Indiana University Press, 1963), for a succinct statement on this subject.

28. In no way does this discussion of "Nevsky Prospekt" contradict that of pp. 38–43 above.

29. Gogol himself was well aware of the connection between comedy and horror. See, for example, "Four Letters Apropos *Dead Souls*" (*SP*, 96–110).
30. One is reminded of the Mayor's remark about the audience's laughter in *The Inspector General*. Is this the kind of warning he meant?
31. Unfortunately, from a logical point of view, Gogol seems to have confused what should be with what is. But he was not thinking in these terms.
32. Many of these remarks could also be applied to *The Inspector General*.
33. It is this method, based upon Gogol's own view of reality, that most clearly distinguishes him from Rabelais, with whom he has so often been compared. More proper comparisons would be, in Russia, Olesha and Bulgakov. Among non-Russian writers, the closest is probably Franz Kafka, as has often been remarked (incidentally, Kafka also encountered difficulty in finishing his longer works).

9: The Christian

1. Zenkovsky, *N. V. Gogol*, p. 110.
2. Almost all of Gogol's fiction would thus have been composed before his religious crisis.
3. See Turgenev's *Literary Reminiscences*.
4. For a discussion of the philosophical and religious climate from which Gogol's feeling and thought arose, see G. Florovsky, *Puti russkago bogosloviya* (Paris: YMCA Press, 1937), chap. 6, pp. 234–42. Florovsky discusses Gogol himself in pp. 260–70.
5. *Medieval Russia's Epics, Chronicles, and Tales*, edited, translated, and with an introduction by Serge A. Zenkovsky (New York: E. P. Dutton, 1963), pp. 67–68. See also, above, p. 43.
6. The subject of German romantic influence has been well explored by V. V. Zenkovsky, Dmitri Chizhevsky, and G. Florovsky, among others. Gogol's religiosity has also been stressed by Mochul'sky, Merezhkovsky, and Evdokimov. Most religious interpretations concentrate upon Gogol's exploration of evil, however (Merezhkovsky's book, for example, is entitled *Gogol and the Devil*, and Evdokimov's, *Gogol et Dostoïevsky; ou, La descente aux enfers*).
7. See Dmitri Merejkowsky, *Gogol et le diable*, translated by Constantin Andronikov (Paris: Gallimard, 1939), pp. 90 ff.

8. The statement that "God is dead" is a contradiction in terms. One can only say that "a god is dead," which is probably what Nietzsche meant.

9. "The Grand Inquisitor" passage in *The Brothers Karamazov* is based on much the same attitude as Gogol's, although Dostoevsky seems clearer in his exposition of it, perhaps because he had Gogol behind him.

10. That there was, and is, valid ground for nonreligious interpretations of Gogol's fiction is beside the point here.

11. See, for example, David Magarshack, *Gogol* (London: Faber & Faber, 1957), pp. 20–21.

12. It might well be argued that the most important biblical texts to Gogol were: *The Gospel According to Saint John;* the *First Epistle of John* (particularly 2:22 and 4:3); the *Second Epistle of John* (particularly 7); and the *Revelation of Saint John the Divine*.

13. The attachment to a *Russian* idea may also be remarked in "Easter Sunday." Gogol's "Russianism" is discussed in chapter 10, below.

14. On this point also, Gogol's religion and art came together.

15. I would suggest that these two passages from *Meditations on the Divine Liturgy,* at a minimum, go far towards clarifying Father Zosima's statement in *The Brothers Karamazov* that this earth is already Paradise, if we would only see it. It is an iconographic statement, of which more below.

16. See Gogol's letters to V. A. Zhukovsky of 29 December 1847 (*P*, 189–93) and of 15 June 1848 (*P*, 195). In a letter to A. O. Smirnova of 6 December 1849, he wrote: "Remember that everything in the world is deception; nothing seems to us what it is in actual fact" (*P*, 201). The concern with "The Beautiful" is manifested as early as 6 April 1827, in a letter to his mother (*P*, 25), and the devotion to God and service is a constant theme in his letters. Art, beauty, service, and God are inextricably mixed together.

17. "Concerning the Holy Icons," in Joseph Myslivec, *The Icon,* translated from the Bohemian by Koloman Lahotsky, edited by Sidney Walls (Charleston, S. C.: Walker, Evans & Cogswell, published under the auspices of the Greek Orthodox Archdiocese of North and South America, 1957), pp. 1–5. On this subject, see also Paul Evdokimov, *L'Art de l'icône: Théologie de la beauté* (Paris: Desclée de Brouwer, 1970).

18. That romantic, Platonic, and medieval influences are also at work here seems too obvious to bear belaboring.

19. In different terminology, it could be said that Chartkov is caught by

Bacon's Idols of the Marketplace, while Piskaryov was deceived by the Idols of the Cave.

20. It is not my purpose here to discuss Gogol's success as an iconographer; it is merely to suggest that, looked at in this way, his work takes on an added dimension.

21. Although this passage belongs to the 1842 revision of "The Portrait" rather than to the 1835 version printed in *Arabesques,* it does not contradict the latter; it is rather an expansion of it. The relevant passage in the 1835 version reads as follows:

> He [the painter] set to work with lofty religious humility: in strict fasting and prayer, in profound meditation and solitude of soul he prepared himself for his task. He spent many nights on his sacred representations, and that is perhaps why you will seldom find productions of even important artists that bear the imprint of such truly Christian feelings and thoughts. There was such a heavenly calm of righteous men in it, such a sincere grief of repentance in it as I have seldom met even in the pictures of well-known artists. Finally, all his thoughts and desires were bent on the depiction of the divine Mother mildly stretching her hands over the praying people. He worked on this production with such self-sacrifice, with such forgetfuless of himself and of all the world, that it seemed a part of the tranquility flowing from his brush into the features of the divine Protectress of the world passed into his own soul. [3:440]

I do not think that the meaning of the first passage has been seriously changed in the second. The only really important difference is the change of emphasis from the Mother to the Child. However, emphasis on the Virgin is precisely what we should expect in 1835.

22. See the discussion of *The Inspector General* on pp. 152–54 above.

23. See above, pp. 173–74.

24. In the Transfiguration, Moses is subordinate to Jesus.

10: The Russian

1. Much of this chapter is based upon a paper that was delivered at the International Slavic Conference in Banff, Alberta, in October 1974.

2. This seems to be a peculiar phenomenon that occurs among political figures in particular, most marked in modern times (I leave aside Alexander the Macedonian), from Henry Tudor the Welshman through the Italian Catherine de Médicis, the Frenchwoman Mary Queen of Scots, Henry of Navarre (as much Spanish as French), the German Catherine the Great of Russia, Napoleon the Corsican (and Bernadotte the Frenchman), the Danish kings of Greece, Queen Victoria (not to mention the Georges who came before her), Hitler the Austrian, Stalin the Georgian, and Khrushchev the Ukrainian. This would make an interesting subject for study (there are many more names that one could mention).

3. This movement attained its greatest success after the revolutions of 1917 when the Ukraine was proclaimed a separate state under German protection. As is well known, it has many adherents today, particularly among emigré groups.

4. See F. I. Tyutchev's political poems and his first three political letters as examples of the latter.

5. Often cited in support of this contention is the letter that Gogol wrote to his mother from St. Petersburg on 2 February 1830: "My entire income consists in occasionally writing or translating some piece for Msrs. the journalists, so don't be angry, my generous mama, if I often bother you with the request to send me information about the Ukraine or something like that" (*P*, 36). The letter goes on to mention some of the kinds of information that Gogol wishes to obtain so that he can write stories about Little Russia.

6. I am discussing Gogol's Little Russian period here in an entirely different context from that of chapter 2 above. I do not believe there is any contradiction involved.

7. The influence we have often mentioned of Platonic doctrine on Gogol has still not been sufficiently studied; V. V. Zenkovsky is one of the very few to have investigated the matter.

8. Gogol was not saying anything here that should have appeared strange to those of his contemporaries of a romantic and/or conservative disposition. F. I. Tyutchev, for example, speaks in much the same terms in both his lyrical poems and in his political poems and letters. In 1880 Dostoevsky was to repeat Gogol's sentiments in his famous speech at the unveiling of the Pushkin memorial in St. Petersburg.

9. K. S. Aksakov, for example, was deeply disturbed by *Selected Passages from Correspondence with Friends*. In May 1848 he wrote to Gogol that Gogol's book was a "lie," because it was, above all, thought Aksakov, "insincere," insincere because Gogol did not

know what he was talking about, because he knew nothing in fact about Russia (S. T. Aksakov, *Istoriya moyego znakomstva s Gogolem* [Moscow: Izdatelstvo akademii nauk SSSR, 1960], pp. 188–89). Interestingly enough, Belinsky, at the time a Westernizer, had said much the same thing in 1847.

10. *The Brothers Karamazov,* translated by Constance Garnett (New York: Illustrated Modern Library, 1943), p. 348.

11. One cannot help but be reminded of Tolstoy's theory of history, as it is expressed in *War and Peace.*

12. Again Gogol anticipated Dostoevsky, particularly the remarks that Dostoevsky made in *The Dairy of a Writer* apropos Pushkin: "What else is the strength of the Russian national spirit than the aspiration . . . for universality and all-embracing humanitarianism?" (translated by Boris Brasol, New York: George Braziller, 1954, pp. 978–79). In *A Raw Youth,* Versilov describes himself as a real Russian because "only to the Russian . . . has been vouchsafed the capacity to become most of all Russian only when he is most European. . . . I am in France a Frenchman, with a German I am a German, with the ancient Greeks I am a Greek, and by that very fact I am a true Russian, . . . bringing out her leading idea. Only Russia lives not for herself, but for an idea" (translated by Constance Garnett, London: William Heinemann, 1950, pp. 464–65).

13. See above, chap. 6.

11: The Quest That Failed

1. We are not speaking here of the validity, much less the correctness, of Gogol's vision. It might well be argued, indeed, that his work is great regardless of his desires rather than because of them, that he was, in other words, a finer artist than he knew. That is immaterial, however, to the present discussion.

2. The subject of Tasso's life has been thoroughly explored by Angelo Solerti, *Vita di Torquato Tasso* (Turin: Loescher, 1895).

3. The "Epilogue" ends with an invocation to Goethe and to the soothing quality of Goethe's poetry.

4. Letter to Zhukovsky of 29 December 1847 (*P*, 192).

Index

Achilles, 140
Acts of the Apostles, 12
Aeneid, The (Vergil), 90
—Aeneas, 130
"Akakos" (Greek word), 55, 58, 207 n.33
Aksakov, K. S., 226 n.9
Aksakov, S. T., 133, 134, 135, 183, 191
Alfieri, Count Vittorio, 60
Alfred, 64
Allegory, 16, 195
"Al-Mamoun," 20, 184, 189; as Russophile statement, 185
Alov, V. *See* Gogol, Nikolai
Ambition: obsession by, 64; world of, 56
Anniversary Poems (Donne), 139
Annunziata, 59, 60
—Annunziata, 60, 61, 74, 130, 138, 139, 171, 175, 191, 193; as vision of loveliness, 59
Anonymity, 21, 31
Antichrist, 126, 187
Apocalypse, 126, 169
Appearance, 50, 105, 111; available to outer eye, 139; concrete, 39; material, 47; and reality, 107, 122
Aquinas, Saint Thomas, 132
Arabesques, 15, 20, 23, 33, 61, 87, 127, 149, 165, 201 n.1 (chap. 2), 204 n.3
Ariosto, Ludovico, 89, 90, 91, 112, 132, 134, 179, 212 n.11
Art: attitude towards 38; classical view of, 148; content of, 35; essence of Gogol's, 163; Gogol's theory of, 37; lands of, 1; literary, 83; lofty cre-

ations of, 37; man as work of, 177; object of, 35; point of view of, 175; production of, 34; reconciling power of, 205 n.10; Russia as Christian work of, 191; symbol of pure, 139; work of, 36; world of, 42
Artists: aspiration of, 122; devoted to God, 170; feelings of, 37; genuine, 143; goals of, 148; Gogol on nature of, 34; job of, 40, 195; and morality, 35; as prophets, 35; as teachers, 35
Astraea, 139
Audiences: comprehension of, 113; danger of deceiving, 35; Gogol's, 70–71; imagination of, 71; Russian, 154; trap laid for, 68; world of, 51
Augustine, Saint, 132, 167
"Author's Confession, An," 168, 169
"Awakening, The," 10

Baal, 190
Babel, Isaac, 151
Bacon, Sir Francis, 224 n.19
Balabina, M. P., 194
Beatrice (Dante's), 139, 140
Beauty: absence of, 32; actualization of, 23, 128, 134; attachment to, 43; Chartkov's assault on, 35; denial of, 27, 28; devotee of, 36; devotion to, 35; divine, 5; embodiment of, 2, 113, 190, 195, in Italy and Greece, 1; emptiness as opposite of, 18; eternal, 85; "given," 3; as goal, 3; God-created, 7; Gogol's attraction to, 156; Gogol's concern with, 172; Gogol's treatment of, in "Viy," 26; guise of,

229

209 nn.1 and 5, 220 n.2; as artistic problem, 113; as balanced poem, 143; completion of, 35, 135; digressions in, 154, 190; disunity of, 143; formal failure of, 149; as negative achievement, 92; sequel to, 133
Dead Souls, Part 1, 53, 87–132 passim, 138, 143, 156, 168, 176, 189, 195, 196; Apocalyptic terms in, 126; and censor, 95; as Dantesque, 213 n.18; digressions in, as rhetorical exercise, 121; fictional content of, 123, and digressions in, 119; form of, 91; formal shift in, 122; and negation, 163; revisions of, 133; style and tone of, 143
—General Betrishchev, 142
—Chichikov, 91–144 passim, 156, 163, 164, 168, 171, 175, 176, 178; "adventures" of, 95, 101; anonymity of, 92; appearance of, 92; awakening of, 101; background of, 34; biography of, 112, 113, 127, 130, 132; as central focus, 112; changes in, 91, 95, 116; character and origins of, 110; chooses alien means, 130; compliment to, 106; contrasts with surroundings, 143; description of, 162; desires respectability, 104; development of, 121; difficulty of, 181–82; escapes from death, 109; as exception, 103; fault of, 93; flees from N., 106; growth in, 113; as innocent, 103, 212 n.14; his intimations of truth, 157; life of, 91; as mirror image, 97; and moral question, 107; personality of, 95; as a poet, 106; possibility of his life, 94; and proper, inward path, 111, 131; quest of, 140; reform of his character, 92, 141; regeneration of, 35, 143; responses of, 163; rest for, 140; as satanic figure, 93; schemes of, 111; his spiritual reawakening, 92; symbolic character of, 131; transformation of, 127; as uncalculating, 96;

uncertainty in his character, 141; value as a symbol of, 113; vision of, 142; his vision of beauty, 98; yearning within, 111
—Governor's daughter, 94, 107, 157, 164, 171
—Captain Kopeikin, 87, 88, 108
—Korobochka, 93, 96, 97, 100, 104, 117, 163
—Manilov, 93, 95–96, 97, 104, 163
—Mizhuev, 96
—Nozdryov, 93–98 passim, 104–8 passim, 118, 126, 199, 213 n.20, 214 n.32
—Plyushkin, 94, 101–4 passim, 119, 120, 121, 136, 190; acquisitiveness of, 97; alien influences on, 190; deterioration of, 102
—Selifan, 163
—Sobakyevich, 94, 96, 99–101, 104, 163; reality of, 97; his souls, 100
Dead Souls, Part 2, 110, 133–44 passim, 171, 176, 214 n.1; merit of, 136
—Andrei Ivanovich Tyentyetnikov, 136–42 passim, 171, 218 n.8
—Lyenitsyn, 142
—Platon Platonovich Platonov, 140, 141, 143, 171; and spiritual lethargy, 142
—Skudronzhoglo, 141, 142
—Ulinka, 138–42 passim
—Vasily (Platon's brother), 142
Dead Souls, Part 3, 171, 219 n.12
Death: change from life to, 28; "Old World Landowners" pervaded by, 23; physical, 21, 22; real, 27; reward in, 27; ugliness of, 74
Death of a Salesman (Miller), 198
Deception, 7, 65, 66; degree of, 70; domination by, 67; embodiment of, 208 n.38; for evil, 19; kinds of, 11; material, 59; in "Old World Landowners," 21; possession by, 68; power of, 124; ugliness, falsity, and, 12; victory of, 21
Delusion, persistence of, in *Dead Souls,* 96

—Rudy Panko, 6, 12, 19, 151

Evenings on a Farm near Dikanka, Part 2, 13, 14, 150, 183; air of unreality in, 17, 18

—Danilo, 16

Everyman, 55, 56

Evil: agreement with, 9; deceptive, 7; defeat of, 11; discord as, 168; face of, 9; imagined or real, 7; mark of, 10; nature of, 54; powers of, 54; sinister, 9; ugly, 7, 8, 9

Evocations, lyrical, 137, 152

Exaggeration, Gogol's use of, 84, 157

Existence, independent, 21

Exorcist practices, 6

Experiment, failure of Kovalyov's, 51

Expression: artistic, 10; necessity for positive, 112

Faerie Queene, The (Spenser), 139

—Gloriana, 139

Failure: Gogol's artistic, 84, 143; formal, of *Dead Souls,* 149

"Fair at Sorochintsy, The" 6, 8, 9, 14, 155; Gogol's cinematic technique in, 7

Faith: Christian, 13; Orthodox Russian, 24; possibility of, 9; Roman Catholic Polish oppression of true, 24

Fakery, relief from, 123

Fall, man's, 56

False, the: acceptance of, 27; connected with the rational, 51; exposure of, 47; portrayal of, 32

Falsity, 77; acceptance of, 105; agreement with, 26; and boisterousness, 19; cacophonous, 73; depiction of, 36; and evil, 16; introduction of, 8; overt, 123; Petersburg as symbol of, 162; realization of, 75; recognition of, 9; unmasking of, 26; world of devils, witches, and sorcerers of, 6

Fanaticism, Gogol's religious, 35

Fantasies, preconceived, 74

Farce, Gogol's use of, 222 n.26

Faust (in Goethe's *Faust*), 198

Feeling: artistic, 180; nationalistic, 145

"Few Words on Pushkin, A," 13, 34, 183

Ficino, Marsilio, 138

Fiction: Gogol's, 104, 167; Gogol's historical, 23; prose, 145; sequence of Gogol's, 124; and truth, 79

Fielding, Henry, 89

Flaubert, Gustav, 88

Flesh: abdication in favor of, 94; mortification of, 36

Florovsky, Father Georges, 166, 173

"Flunkeys, The," 63

Foreign ways, adoption of, 124

Form: artistic, 113; beautiful, 148; change of, 143; Christian, 128; and content, 65; Dantesque, 89; Gogol's yearning for, 148; harmonic, 176; harmony and beauty of, 84; lack of, 101; outer, 49, 50; parodic, 73; perfection of, 84; Platonic, 191; plotted, 88; Russian, 181; shift in, 135

Formula, mathematical, 153

"Four Letters to Divers Persons Apropos *Dead Souls,*" 163, 181

"Fragment, A," 59, 63

France, 60, 61, 87, 138, 209 n.42

Frankenstein, 198

Fraud: attempts at, 67; material, 59

Freedom, exercise of, 124

Free Will, doctrine of, 36

French (language), 124

Freud, Sigmund, 198

Gadyach, 17

Galician land, 16

Gamblers, The, 64, 67–68, 77; theatrical technique in, 68

—Ikharev, 67, 68, 157

"Ganna," 10

Geography: cosmic, 132; universal, 20

Germans, 42

Germany, 87

Gerusalemme Liberata (Tasso), 90, 113, 132, 193; as Gogol's Italian model, 90

—Gofreddo, 132, 134, 143

Gippius, Zinaida, 165